Praise for *The Rebel's Guide to Email Marketing*

"After reading this book, the debate over email marketing being dead is without a doubt over. DJ and Jason talk about email coming alive and letting it work for your organization in many ways that you have heard don't work. Whether you are newbie or a seasoned veteran, this book will get you screaming at the top of your lungs that EMAIL IS THRIVING!"

—**Andrew Kordek**, cofounder and chief strategist of Trendline Interactive, a strategic email marketing agency

"Social media gets more attention, but email is still the spine of effective digital marketing. In this practical book that you'll refer to constantly, Waldow and Falls shed much-needed light on how to build, operate, and optimize a knock-out email program. It's a useful book, perfectly executed."

—**Jay Baer**, coauthor of *The NOW Revolution: 7 Shifts to Make Your Business Faster, Smarter, and More Social*

"I would take 1,000 opt-in email addresses above 1,000 followers or Likes any day of the week. This from one of the biggest social media fans alive. Email is not dead; it's stronger than ever for the ones who use it right. DJ and Jason are the guys to show you how with this masterpiece."

—**Scott Stratten**, best-selling author of *UnMarketing*

"At a time when all the buzz is about social, DJ and Jason's fun, insightful, and down-to-earth style will give any marketer a renewed excitement for email."

—**Halley Silver**, director of online services, The King Arthur Flour Co.

"Non-practitioner pundits have been declaring email marketing dead for years. They're still wrong. Email marketing remains the best way to get people to take action, so read this book if you want your business to grow."

—**Brian Clark**, CEO of Copyblogger Media

"You might call email the glue that holds so much of business marketing efforts together. You might call it the backbone, or the connective tissue, or the linchpin. But whatever you call it, you need it. And this is the book that shows you not just why you need it, but how to use it to grow your business.

"*Rebel's Guide* is the book I've been waiting for, because this is the book that talks (in real, relevant, updated terms) about how email is that critical thing businesses need to market in a digital age."

—**Ann Handley**, chief content officer of MarketingProfs and coauthor of *Content Rules: How to Create Killer Blogs, Podcasts, Videos, Ebooks, Webinars (and More) That Engage Customers and Ignite Your Business* (Wiley, updated 2012)

DJ WALDOW · JASON FALLS

THE REBEL'S GUIDE TO EMAIL MARKETING

Grow Your List, Break the Rules, and Win

 800 East 96th Street,
Indianapolis, Indiana 46240 USA

The Rebel's Guide to Email Marketing

ISBN-13: 978-0-7897-4969-7
ISBN-10: 0-7897-4969-6

Library of Congress Cataloging-in-Publication Data is on file.

Printed in the United States of America

First Printing: August 2012

Trademarks

Warning and Disclaimer

Bulk Sales

Que Publishing offers excellent discounts on this book when ordered in quantity for bulk purchases or special sales. For more information, please contact

U.S. Corporate and Government Sales
1-800-382-3419
corpsales@pearsontechgroup.com

For sales outside of the U.S., please contact

International Sales
international@pearsoned.com

Editor-in-Chief
Greg Wiegand

Senior Acquisitions Editor
Katherine Bull

Development Editor
Leslie T. O'Neill

Managing Editor
Kristy Hart

Project Editor
Betsy Harris

Copy Editor
Paula Lowell

Senior Indexer
Cheryl Lenser

Proofreader
Kathy Ruiz

Technical Editor
Bill McCloskey

Editorial Assistants
Romny French
Cindy Teeters

Interior Designer
Anne Jones

Cover Designer
Alan Clements

Compositor
Nonie Ratcliff

Que Biz-Tech Editorial Board
Michael Brito
Jason Falls
Rebecca Lieb
Simon Salt
Peter Shankman

CONTENTS AT A GLANCE

TABLE OF CONTENTS

II THE ANATOMY OF AN EMAIL

4 Examining an Email's Body Parts   57

5 The First Impression   67

6 The Meat and Potatoes   81

7 The Finishing Touches   97

III   BREAKING THE RULES

8   Are Best Practices Really "Best"?   107

9   My Word! You Must Read This Now!   113

10   The Perfect-Looking Email   133

About the Author

DJ Waldow is an email marketing consultant, writer, blogger, speaker, and (now) author. He is the founder and CEO of Waldow Social, a company that helps clients take email marketing to the next level. DJ has spent nearly 7 years in the email, social, and community-building world, advising clients on how to optimize their email marketing campaigns and, on occasion, break some of the "best practice" rules. DJ can be found on most social networks under the handle "djwaldow" or by searching "DJ Waldow."

Jason Falls is an author, speaker, and CEO, the latter of Social Media Explorer, a digital marketing agency and information products company. From client strategies to industry research reports to conference-style events, Falls spearheads efforts to bridge the gap between professional communicators and business owners and the strategic use of digital marketing and technology. An award-winning social media strategist and widely read industry pundit, Falls has been noted as a top influencer in the social technology and marketing space by *Forbes, Entrepreneur, Advertising Age*, and others. He is the coauthor of two books, this one and *No Bullshit Social Media: The All-Business, No-Hype Guide to Social Media Marketing* (Que 2011).

Dedication

To K-Dawg, Eva Claire, and Cal Viking—I love you all, always and forever.
—DJ

To my mother, for all those things mothers do, then all the extra she did
to get me where I am. I love you, Mom.
—Jason

Acknowledgments

When Jason first suggested we write a book together, I remember having this feeling of excitement mixed with terror. I've been writing in some form since as early as I can recall, but a book? Holy cats! Well, nine months later I can honestly say it's all excitement now. We did it!

However, we did not do it alone.

This book would not have been possible without the people at Pearson Education and Que Publishing. To Katherine Bull, our editor: Thanks for believing in me and answering every single (sometimes silly) question I had. To our editorial team, Leslie O'Neill, Betsy Harris, and Paula Lowell: Thanks for teaching me when to use *then* versus *than* and *their* versus *its*, as well as how to cut unnecessary/repetitive sentences and paragraphs. Thanks to Alan Clements for designing the kick-ass cover. To Dan Powell, Lisa Jacobson-Brown, Romny French, and the rest of the Pearson crew: We appreciate everything you've done!

Thanks to Bill McCloskey for agreeing to be our technical editor. We chose Bill, the Godfather of email marketing, to keep us honest. Thanks, Bill, for doing that and then some!

Thank you to everyone who contributed to this book with your quotes and case studies. Your endless patience in not only sharing your stories but ensuring that we told them correctly was essential to this book.

To Chris Penn, who not only contributed to the book but has also been a good friend, colleague, and mentor for many years now. I can always count on you for honest, valuable, direct feedback. Thanks, CP!

To you (yeah, YOU)! Thanks for reading this book. It means a ton.

To Sal Tripi, who over several cocktails in Miami a few years ago convinced me that ugly emails can work. Thanks for being an inspiration for this book.

To Ann Handley, who pointed me to her blog post on the "14 Stages of Writing a Book" at the exact time I needed it. Thanks, Ann—LOL.

To my family—my mother Sharon, my father Warren, and my sister Jennifer— thank you for believing in and supporting me over these last nine months, and for always being there—always—over the past 36+ years.

To Joe Colopy and Chaz Felix, the cofounders of Bronto: When I walked into the world's smallest conference room for my Bronto interview in 2005, with zero experience in email marketing, you guys took a chance on me. Without the opportunities Bronto gave me in four years, this book would never have happened. Thanks!

To Eugenie Jaffe, the first non-family member whom I told about the book. When I was contemplating the decision to write this book, I asked you what I should do. You didn't hesitate. Thanks for giving me the nudge I needed.

To Jason Falls, my coauthor, colleague, and dear friend. Jason, I've always looked up to you for your "no bullshit" approach to business and life. You tell it how you see it and have an amazing ability to take the complex and make it easy to understand. Thank you for asking me to join you on this book-writing journey. I'm honored to call you my coauthor and friend.

To my amazingly patient wife, Kristina: Thank you for being my biggest supporter and fan. I know the phrase "I need to do some writing tonight" quickly became the seven words you dreaded to hear, but you stuck with me. You believed in me. I love you—always and forever.

And finally, to @babywaldow Eva, whose curiosity and "Daddy, whatcha doing, Daddy?" question always brings a smile to my face. I love you, baby girl.

—DJ

Writing a book is a process and we could not have done it without the wonderful folks at Pearson Education and Que Publishing. To Katherine Bull, our editor, and the leadership team led by Greg Wiegand and others: Thank you for your faith and patience. To Leslie O'Neill, Betsy Harris, Paula Lowell, and Bill McCloskey: You make us sound like we know what we're doing. Many thanks for that! We sure needed the help! To Dan Powell, Lisa Jacobson-Brown, Romny French, and the rest of the Pearson/Que team: We couldn't have done it without you! Thanks a ton!

Now for the selfish part. I would like to thank DJ for his infectious enthusiasm and friendship, for agreeing to tackle this project together and for teaching me far more about email marketing over the years than I expected to learn. There are also several other industry colleagues who keep me thinking and sharp, and help me stay on top of my own game, whether they know it or not. In no particular order and including, but not limited to, I would like to offer heartfelt tips of the cap to Tom Webster, Tamsen McMahon, Mike Schneider, Jay Baer, Amber Naslund, Matt Ridings, Chris Penn, Tim Hayden, Zena Weist, Scott Stratten, David Meerman Scott, Paul Gillin, Bob Hoffman, Todd Defren, Jeremiah Owyang, Chris Brogan, Mark Schaefer, Aaron Perlut, Valeria Maltoni, and Emily Kirkpatrick. To my clients, sponsors, and partners over the years: Thank you so much. It has been and will be an honor, always.

To my team at Social Media Explorer—Aaron Marshall, Nichole Marshall, Nichole Kelly, Tom Heseltine, et. al.—I wouldn't want to go to bat with anyone else. You guys rock! And to my readers, followers, believers, and tribe: The fact that I can think, write, and say stuff and there's someone there to listen continues to be one of the most humbling notions that passes my brain. I'm honored by you daily. Thank you.

Finally, thank you, thank you, forever thank you to Nancy, Grant, and Katie for the three best reasons to get up and do what I do everyday.

—Jason

We Want to Hear from You!

As the reader of this book, *you* are our most important critic and commentator. We value your opinion and want to know what we're doing right, what we could do better, what areas you'd like to see us publish in, and any other words of wisdom you're willing to pass our way.

We welcome your comments. You can email or write to let us know what you did or didn't like about this book—as well as what we can do to make our books better.

Please note that we cannot help you with technical problems related to the topic of this book.

When you write, please be sure to include this book's title and author as well as your name and email address. We will carefully review your comments and share them with the author and editors who worked on the book.

Email: feedback@quepublishing.com

Mail: Que Publishing
ATTN: Reader Feedback
800 East 96th Street
Indianapolis, IN 46240 USA

Reader Services

Visit our website and register this book at quepublishing.com/register for convenient access to any updates, downloads, or errata that might be available for this book.

Email Marketing Is (Not) Dead

It's not every day that one gets to pick on the Wall Street Journal. *It still stands, after all, as one of the most respected and formidable news outlets in the world. Sometimes, however, even the* Journal *can't get out of its own way. Such was the case on October 12, 2009, when it published a story by senior tech reporter Jessica Vascellaro.*

The piece, entitled, "Why Email No Longer Rules," declared that electronic mail communications had a good run as king, but that its reign was over. The irony was that when you visited the Wall Street Journal's *website that day and read the article, you were likely to email it to a friend. In fact, Vascellaro's piece sat right at the top of the* Journal's *automatic listing of the most emailed articles of the day.*

"Email is dead" is a phrase you hear now and then, sometimes from respected media members and sometimes from aggressive Internet consultants bent on selling you some social media or mobile marketing doomaflitchit—that is, of course, in between spastic glances at their iPhones to see whether they've received...new email.

Think for a moment about your typical day. How many times do you check your email? How long can you go without checking it before curiosity gets the best of you and you simply cannot resist the urge any longer?

Emily is a typical 30-something professional. She first looks at her iPhone sometime between getting out of bed and her first cup of coffee. She glances at it after her shower but before getting dressed and then again after brushing her teeth. She stops to reply to a message before leaving for the commute to work, and then responds to messages for a few minutes on the bus.

When Emily arrives at the office, she fires up her laptop and plows through a few emails before the 9 a.m. staff meeting. During the meeting she glances down at her phone a few times (any email?). Before 10:30, she sneaks a peek at least once, if not twice, at her iPhone to see whether something urgent has come in. She does another quick check between phone calls, takes a few minutes to reply to the morning meeting notes that were sent around the office, and she's off to lunch.

The workday is not yet five hours old and Emily has been in her inbox more than a dozen times.

Emily is not an unusual case study in today's on-the-go but in-the-know business world. She depends on her email for the news of the day, her vital work documents and meeting notices, notifications that friends have posted new information on their social networking profiles, ads and coupons from retailers, as well as information from online daily deal sites, notifications from the local arts center of new dramatic productions, and the occasional message from mom.

Try telling Emily email is dead.

Is it really? Well, take a moment to think about how you start your day. How often in your routine do you pick up your smart phone or tablet, or walk by your computer only to wiggle the mouse and see how many notifications your inbox shows? Do you check your email from bed? While combing your hair? While eating breakfast? Is it hard for you not to check messages while having dinner with your friends or family?

Now think about the totality of your day—work or otherwise. When you're using a device connected to the Internet, we're willing to bet checking email is one of your top three tasks, if not the number one thing you do. You might also read blog posts, update social networking sites, and search for products or information and the like, but you probably always come back to your inbox.

In fact, we're pretty sure you've checked your email today. Some of you may have even paused a moment ago, put down the book and glanced at your inbox. (It's okay. DJ stopped after the Emily part and checked his.) Email has become what we do online. It's ubiquitous and a huge part of our daily routine. For many of us, it's the first thing we do in the morning. (Jason is guilty of that one.) For some, it's the last thing we do before closing our eyes at night. We are a world addicted to email.

Email Is Dead?

If you type "email is dead" into Google to see how many references are online that include that phrase (use quotation marks to get an exact phrase match), you'll find more than one million results. Lots of people are saying email is dead. To put it into perspective, similar searches return just 12,000 results for "LinkedIn is dead," 46,000 for "Google+ is dead," and 309,000 for "social media is dead." If you believe what people are saying online, it would appear most major communications mediums are dying.

"Email is not dead. But email IS changing," declares Mark Brownlow's counter-point website EmailIsNotDead.com.[1] Brownlow is the journalist, blogger, and independent publisher behind the notable industry resource Email Marketing Reports.[2] When asked why he created EmailIsNotDead.com, Brownlow told us that "it was just a spur of the moment, half-serious, half-a-laugh decision when the media was full of 'email is dead' headlines. Got fed up of these absolute black and white statements about one channel or the other: I prefer to live in the gray areas."

The Email Is Not Dead site is chock-full of statistics and research Brownlow has collected to thwart any naysayers. A tour through the major ones paints a convincing picture.

94%

Ninety-four percent of people send or read email! That's more than 9 in every 10 human beings. That's according to Pew Internet and American Life Project's Generations 2010 report.[3] Frankly, we're a little worried about the 6 percent. Don't they know what they're missing? Ninety-four percent!

Email is dead?

The 94 percent figure is for all online adults. Certainly the numbers change by age bracket, right? Not really—teens (ages 12 to 17) come in at 73 percent, presumably because the younger members of that age group might not yet have a use for or be allowed to use emails. Millennials (ages 18 to 33) stand at 96 percent. The use of daily email by Generation X (ages 33 to 45) is 94 percent, and 91 percent of young Boomers (ages 46 to 55) use email. The drop-off beyond isn't significant. Older Boomers (56 to 64), the Silent Generation (65 to 73), and the G.I. Generation (74 and up) register email usage at 93, 90, and 88 percent, respectively.

The Pew Internet and American Life Project's Generations 2010 report states that email is the number-one online activity, ahead of generic search (87 percent of all U.S. adults), looking for health information (83 percent), and getting news (75 percent).

Email is dead?

To put a different spin on the sheer volume of the American consumer's email addiction, in 2009, David Daniels (then of Forrester Research) predicted the number of online adults who regularly use email would grow to 153 million by 2014.[4] A more recent study by the Radicati Group, Inc. stated in 2011 that "the number of worldwide email accounts is expected to increase from an installed base [active accounts, which have been accessed at least once within the last three months] of 3.1 billion in 2011 to nearly 4.1 billion by year-end 2015. This represents an average annual growth rate of 7 percent over the next four years."[5]

Email is dead?

Email is so ingrained in most people's daily routines and habits that one email account isn't enough. We'd be willing to bet you maintain at least two email accounts—one for work, another for personal communications. If you are in school, have recently graduated, or are an active alumnus, it's quite possible you have a third. You may even have a fourth as a catch-all email account for email marketing or social network notifications and updates. Name another product or service that you can't get by with just one of that is dying as an industry.

"But social media is killing email. So is mobile!"

We've heard that from naysayers, too. If you can reach out to people on Facebook or Twitter, why on earth would you clutter their inbox? That's been the stance of many a social media pundit in the last decade. They claim that social media has (or will) kill email. These folks just aren't doing their homework. If anything, social media is increasing the use of email. According to a well-done whitepaper called "View from the Digital Inbox 2011," from Merckle, a customer relationship management agency, people who use social networks are more likely to be what it terms "hyper email checkers," meaning someone who checks email four or more times each day.[6]

Merckle's report also suggests that mobile email users tend to fall into the same category. Forty-three percent of mobile email users check their email four or more times per day, compared to 29 percent of those who do not use email on a mobile device.

"But people check for personal emails, not commercial ones."

Wrong.

Merckle's data shows that in regard to the amount of time people spend on email (meaning reading and responding to it) by type (categorized as friends and family, commercial, work, and other), email marketing—that which is classified as "commercial"—has risen steadily from 23 percent in 2007 to 30 percent in 2010. During that same time period, emails to friends and family have fallen from 43 percent to 37 percent. Work and other types of email have remained fairly steady as a percentage of overall email.

This data can be interpreted a couple different ways:

- As the volume of commercial email has risen, so has the amount of time people spend reading and interacting with it (clicking, sharing, and so on).

- Marketers might be getting smarter about sending timely, relevant, valuable content to their subscribers; thus, people are spending more time engaging with those email marketing messages.

What is not clear from the Merckle study is how click-throughs and conversions (sales, webinar sign-ups, and so on) are being impacted by the rise in time spent interacting with commercial email. In the long run, these metrics might be more important for marketers.

Either way, what is apparent is that consumers are shifting their email consumption time in favor of commercial emails.

Finally, regardless of the user's age, email is the preferred method of communication for commercial messages—by far. Merckle reports that 74 percent of all online adults say so. Compared to direct mail, email is preferred at a rate of five to one.

2.9 Billion

There are 2.9 billion email accounts in the world. 2.9 BILLION! To put that number in perspective, the world population is around 7 billion.[7] People send 56 million non-spam email messages per day. At least, they did in 2010 according to the Radicati Group.[8] Comparing that figure to the total accounts and daily activity of Facebook, Twitter, Google+, and websites, you can start to see how alive email really is (see Figure IN.1).

As you can see, a vast difference exists in both the number of accounts and the activity in the channel.

Email is dead?

To clarify, the 188 million emails sent per day in 2010 does not include spam emails. Unfortunately, spam exists. It can be defined in a few ways:

- From a consumer perspective, spam is any unwanted email.

- From the legal perspective, spam is email that does not comply with the requirements of the CAN-SPAM Act—a bill signed into law in the

United States in 2003 (and updated in 2008) that outlines rules and requirements for sending commercial email.[9]

- From an Internet Service Provider (ISP) perspective, spam is a message that contains viruses or malicious content.

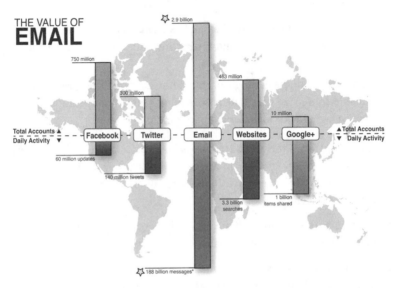

Figure IN.1 *A comparison of the total accounts and daily activity of Facebook, Twitter, Google+, and websites along with email show a distinct advantage of using the true inbox as a source for Internet users' information.*[10, 11, 12, 13] *(Figure source: http://smartertools.files.wordpress.com/2011/08/infographic_abs_final.png)*

As it stands, the worldwide email spam rate is at 70.5 percent.[14] That's right—nearly three out of every four emails sent around the world is spam. What that means is that the true total of all emails sent per day in 2010 was somewhere north of 550 million! If email truly were dead, do you think those spammers would waste their time?

If you look beyond the spam, you can see that permission-based, commercial emails reach the inbox. That is to say, emails that the person has subscribed to voluntarily, opted into purposefully, but that are also commercial in nature, arrive intact. In fact, 76.5 percent of all permission-based, opt-in emails make it to inboxes around the world.[15] The other 23.5 percent either get lost (15.1 percent) or land in the spam or junk folder (8.4 percent).

Yes, people do welcome companies to their inboxes. Although 50 percent of all email in the average user's inbox is newsletters and deals, they are typically email marketing efforts the user opted in to receive.[16]

Email versus Email Marketing

All the statistics in the world fail to tell the true story of email. Although we try to give you a holistic look of email marketing in this book, drawing some distinctions and bringing some clarity to the world of electronic mail communications is also probably good. This allows us to level set what we'll cover and what we might not.

Knowing the difference between email and email marketing is important. Email consists of messages between friends, families, co-workers, and colleagues. It is generally one message sent to one person, or one message sent to a small group of people. Email is usually meant as a way to communicate ideas, ask questions, request information, and so on.

Email marketing, on the other hand, is a marketing channel that allows individuals and companies to communicate en masse with their customers, prospects, fans, and subscribers. For many businesses, email marketing is the channel to alert people to upcoming events, new business developments, and new product and service announcements. From a business-to-consumer (B2C) perspective, email marketing is often a key driver of sales. It is also powerful for business-to-business (B2B) communications.

We are focused on the latter of those two: email marketing. It can be, and often is, the glue that holds a company's marketing together. You can focus on customer acquisition, which can start with giving prospects a compelling reason to subscribe to an electronic communication from you. Your email marketing can then guide them through the consideration and trial stages all the way to purchase, repeat purchase, loyalty, and even advocacy. Why? Because you have their email addresses and they've identified themselves as at least minimally interested in you or your product. If you then segment, or divide your audience into subgroups, and communicate with them appropriately, you can nurse them along every step through your marketing funnel.

You can focus on customer retention, delivering timely, relevant messages to existing customers that drive top-of-mind awareness, increased involvement, increased purchase, and even recommendations and referrals. Why? Because you have their email addresses. They don't mind the occasional outreach. By communicating with them appropriately, you can lead them through a repeat buying cycle or build them into loyal advocates for your brand.

You can focus on demand generation, teasing customers about new products or opportunities to enhance or enrich their experiences with or around your product. Why? Because you have their email addresses. They've raised their hand and said, "Yeah. I want to hear from this company." By designing communications that deliver the appropriate messages at the appropriate times, you can work them into a frenzy, demanding you let them pay you more money for more stuff.

And the list goes on.

Email marketing is not only not dead, but it is the cornerstone of many a successful digital marketing campaign. Why? Because it is effective, and when we say effective, we have to talk about the all-important business metric behind any marketing effort: ROI.

The ROI of Email Marketing

Honestly, the first 40 or so years of email's existence have been bumpy. While this new, fast, and convenient channel has revolutionized the speed and efficiency of business in some ways, it has also turned consumers off in others. Remember the 550 million spam messages sent each day?

It's a wonder email has lasted this long, right? But where there's a survivor, there's a reason, and the main reason email marketing has been able to weather government intervention and regulation, business experimentation—including both successes and failures, and consumer frustrations is wrapped up in three letters: *ROI*.

If you haven't heard the acronym, short for *return on investment*, you've not been around smart business people much. Nothing happens in successful business without someone scrutinizing the return on investment of various campaigns, programs, efforts, and processes. Nearly every CEO and most CMOs (chief marketing officers) ask, "What's our ROI there?" daily.

Understanding ROI is surprisingly simple, even for the math averse. It is a mathematical formula where you subtract the amount of money you invest in something from the amount of money you made, and then divide by the amount of money you invested (see Figure IN.2).

$$ROI = \frac{(\text{Gain from investment} - \text{cost of investment})}{\text{Cost of investment}}$$

Figure IN.2   *You calculate return on investment by subtracting the amount of money spent on a project from the amount of money made on a project, then dividing that number by the amount of money spent on the project. If the result is a percentage more than 100 percent, you have positive ROI.*

The result is a decimal number that can be translated into a percentage. If your percentage is above 100, you have a positive ROI. Your revenue exceeded your expense. Depending on your business, the amount of money you charge for your product or service, and the breadth or depth of your prospective audience, among other factors, a good ROI could be 105 percent, 150 percent, or 1000 percent. The higher, the better because that means more return for the effort (investment).

ROI can also be translated into dollars using that same equation. An ROI of 1.00 means you got one dollar back for every one dollar spent, so you can say your ROI rate is $1.00. A 200 percent ROI then translates to a $2.00 dollar return rate. It's just a different way of expressing the value you're getting back. For every dollar you put into the effort you get X or Y dollars in return.

For the past few years, the Direct Marketing Association (DMA) has calculated and reported the overall industry return on investment rate of email marketing. Its findings might surprise you.

Email marketing brought in $40.56 for every dollar spent on the efforts in 2011, the DMA reported.[17] That's an ROI of more than 4000 percent! Compare that to the other communications mechanisms the DMA also reports and you start to see why businesses would (or should) bother and why two guys like us might think writing a book about email marketing is a good idea.

Is a catalog an effective way to market? The catalog industry drove a dollar-return rate of $7.30 in 2011. Search engine marketing, often described as the one area of digital marketing that has proven its worth, comes in at $22.24 for every dollar spent. That's good, but it's not $40.56. Internet display advertising, which is a smoke-and-mirrors way of saying banner ads, came in at $19.72. Social networking spend turned around a rate of $12.71. Mobile marketing in 2011 drove a dollar return rate of $10.51. Although we assume both social networking and mobile marketing rates have nowhere to go but up, they have a while to go before they get to the efficiency level of email marketing.

What to Expect from This Book

For the foreseeable future for your company, no other Internet marketing medium can match the numbers of email marketing. For this and all the reasons baked into statistics we've shared in the preceding pages, we want to take you on a helpful journey throughout the world of email marketing. Our hope is that by book's end, you'll be prepared to not only select an email service provider and start crafting that first email, but also build and continually grow your list, implement email marketing campaigns and strategies, and get your piece of that $40.56.

Here's how we'll get you there:

- **Part I, "The Secret to Email Marketing: List Growth":** When we say it's the secret, we mean it's *the* secret. Through this section, you'll learn why growing your list is the secret to email marketing; how to make it easy and obvious for your customers and prospects to join; and how to grow your list using technology, social media, and offline channels. These chapters explain the intricacies of the sign-up process, walk you through important setup decisions, and help you complete the process of signing folks up by sending a killer welcome email.

- **Part II, "The Anatomy of an Email":** In this part, you'll learn what makes an outstanding email marketing message. We'll dive into details such as subject lines, From names, preheaders, and headers. We'll show you the importance of having a table of contents, main calls to action, and secondary and even tertiary calls to action to make that email deliver results for your business. We'll talk about buttons, links, images, social sharing...even how to craft an effective page footer. We then discuss the all-important unsubscribe links and process, which can help you maintain compliance with email marketing legislation and keep your customers happy, even when they want to opt out.

- **Part III, "Breaking the Rules":** This part is where we throw out convention and start going through all the "rules" and "best practices" of email marketing you might have heard over the years. It's not that we think they're all bunk, but within each one we can illustrate examples of being successful while breaking those rules. We'll discuss the practice of sending one big image in your emails. We'll slice and dice the nit-picky orders you might have heard about subject lines, ALL CAPS, the word *free*, pop-up collection forms, text versus HTML formatting, and "rules" about opting in and opting out. We'll also address the issue of buying lists, having good graphic design, and even some misconceptions about your ability to send unsolicited (non-permission) emails to people. By the end of this section of the book, we hope to give you the confidence to establish a set of rules and best practices that work for you.

- **Part IV, "Batman (Email Marketing) and Robin (Social Media)":** Email marketing alone is pretty powerful, but combine its forces with the mass appeal and power of social media and social networking and you have yourself a marketing juggernaut, much like the crime-fighting one of Batman and Robin. This part shows you how social sharing and connectivity can drastically ramp up your email marketing and how email marketing can, in turn, ramp up your social media efforts. We'll discuss the commonalities in approaching content creation for social media and email marketing and give you some great ideas and direction to light a fire under your customer engagement and conversion.

- **Part V, "The Future of Email Marketing":** In the final section, we attempt to look into the coming years to see what email marketing will look like in the short-term and long-term. Although it is true that Internet and digital technologies change in the amount of time it takes to publish most books, we want you to feel confident and assured that you can apply your newfound email marketing wisdom both now and down the road. Your business's future might well depend on email marketing. So we want you to have one eye on that future while the other is kicking ass and taking names in the present.

By the time you finish this book, you will have the knowledge you need to tackle email marketing with gusto. You'll be ready to grow your list, develop your email marketing content, and drive business with your Send button.

But first things are always first: You have to grow your list.

Endnotes

1. Brownlow, Mark, "Email Is Not Dead," www.emailisnotdead.com

2. Brownlow, Mark, "Email Marketing Reports," www.email-marketing-reports.com

3. "Generations 2010," *Pew Internet & American Life Project*, http://www.pewinternet.org

4. "Email Marketing Forecast," *Forrester Research*, http://www.forrester.com/rb/Research/us_email_marketing_forecast%2C_2009_to_2014/q/id/53620/t/2

5. "Email Statistics report 2011-2015," *Radicati Group, Inc.,* http://www.radicati.com/wp/wp-content/uploads/2011/05/Email-Statistics-Report-2011-2015-Executive-Summary.pdf

6. "View from the Digital Inbox 2011," *Merckle*, http://www.merkleinc.com/sites/default/files/whitepapers/WP-DigitalInbox_11Jul_0.pdf

7. "World POPClock Projection," http://www.census.gov/population/popclockworld.html

8. "Email Statistics Report, 2009–2013," *Radicati Group, Inc.* http://www.radicati.com/wp/wp-content/uploads/2009/05/email-stats-report-exec-summary.pdf

9. "The CAN-SPAM Act: A Compliance Guide for Business," http://business.ftc.gov/documents/bus61-can-spam-act-compliance-guide-business

10. "Email & Website Statistics, Email Marketing Reports," http://www.email-marketing-reports.com/metrics/email-statistics.htm

11. Axon, Samuel, "Twitter Now Getting More Traffic Than MySpace," September 28, 2010. http://mashable.com/2010/09/28/twitter-now-getting-more-traffic-than-myspace/

12. Kincaid, Jason, "Facebook Now Has 750 Million Users," June 23, 2011. http://techcrunch.com/2011/06/23/facebook-750-million-users/

13. MaGee, Matt, "By the Numbers: Twitter vs. Facebook vs. Google Buzz," *Search Engine Land* February 23, 2010. http://searchengineland.com/by-the-numbers-twitter-vs-facebook-vs-google-buzz-36709

14. "Symantec Intelligence Report: November 2011," *Symantec*, http://www.symanteccloud.com/mlireport/SYMCINT_2011_11_November_FINAL-en.pdf

15. "The Global Email Deliverability Benchmark Report, 2H 2011" *Return Path*, http://www.returnpath.net/downloads/reports/returnpath_globaldeliverability2h11.pdf

16. Craddock, Dick, "Hotmail Declares War on Graymail," *Windows Live*, October 3, 2011. http://windowsteamblog.com/windows_live/b/windowslive/archive/2011/10/03/hotmail-declares-war-on-graymail.aspx

17. "Email Remains ROI King," *The Magill Report*, http://www.magillreport.com/Email-Remains-ROI-King-Net-Marketing-Set-to-Overtake-DM/

Why List Growth Matters

If you haven't read the Introduction, read it now! We're not kidding. The Introduction sets the stage for the rest of the book. If you have and still aren't convinced that email is far from dead, you might want to put this book down now. Seriously. It's okay. We know that you have other, more important things to do—like check your email. (Busted!)

For those who are sticking around, it's time for us to share with you the secret to email marketing.

Imagine for a moment that you are in charge of email marketing at your company, which sells a product that everyone in the world needs: clean air. Yes, your company sells air. Literally everyone needs it. You have built the best, most helpful, 24 hours per day, seven days per week, 365 days per year customer support team for folks who have questions about air. You have incredible pricing (nearly free). Customers are knocking down your virtual doors to get some of your air. You work at the most perfect company in the entire universe.

You've just read the Introduction to the book you are holding now and are certain that email marketing is not only not dead, it's alive and well. Email is going to be the number-one channel for you to sell your air to those on planet Earth.

You skip ahead in this book to Part II, "The Anatomy of an Email," and educate yourself all about the structure of an email. You now know about preheaders and the importance of the From name and Subject line. You understand what a call to action is (BUY AIR!) and know how to include social media sharing options in every email. Armed with that knowledge, you craft a killer email, one that uses everything you've learned. You're excited. This single email will forever transform your business, your career.

You click the Send button and wait for the sales to flow in.

And nothing happens.

You wait. And wait. And wait. And wait.

Something must be wrong with the Internet! How can this be? Nothing is happening! What could have gone wrong? You check to be sure that your computer is on. You wiggle a few cables to ensure you have a connection to the Internet. You spin around in your chair three times. You take a lap around your office. All seems normal.

You then check your sent email folder and immediately notice the problem: You didn't send the email to anyone. It's not that you meant to send the email to nobody. In fact, you did everything "right" except for one thing: You forgot the secret to email marketing—growing your list.

Clearly that imaginary story was a bit overly dramatic. However, we share it with you merely as an example—one that's not all that far from reality for many marketers. Too often we see companies that have an amazing product, offered at the right price, with great customer service, who send incredibly compelling emails. Yet, they forget to start with the foundation—growing their email lists.

We are not suggesting that you need an email list size in the millions or even the hundreds of thousands of subscribers, but one thing is certain. Without a list of email addresses in your database, you cannot do any email marketing.

In this chapter, if we haven't already, our goal is to convince you that email marketing starts with an email list.

List Churn and List Fatigue

Just having a list of people to send your emails to is not enough. In farming, if you are not both sowing and reaping, eventually you will not produce a crop. In sales, if you are not continuing to fill your lead pipeline with potential customers, you will eventually not have any prospects to call on. The same thing holds true with email list building. It's not a one-time event. Constantly adding email addresses to your list is important.

30%

If you've ever deployed an email marketing campaign, you know that with each and every send, your list shrinks. In fact this "churn rate" (also called shrinkage or attrition rate) is about 30 percent[1] per year for the average email marketing list.

What is *churn rate*? Simply put, an email churn rate is the percent of subscribers who are no longer receiving email from you divided by the total email addresses in your file (see Figure 1.1).

$$\text{Churn rate} = \frac{\text{\# of subscribers no longer receiving your emails}}{\text{Total \# of email addresses on your list}}$$

Figure 1.1   *The formula to determine your list's churn rate is found by taking the number of subscribers no longer receiving your email and dividing that by the total number of email addresses on your list.*

For example, you start the year with 1,000 email addresses. Throughout the year, you lose 300 subscribers—some from unsubscribing, others from bouncing due to an invalid email address, and still others from marking your emails as spam. Your churn rate equals 30 percent.

If you want to grow your email list year over year (something all marketers should strive toward), you first have to account for the total number of emails that you are expected to lose. If your churn is similar to the industry average (30 percent, discussed earlier), you would have to add 300 email addresses just to maintain your list size. This is before you put any time or effort into growing your email list.

Now take that 30 percent annual churn rate and toss in *list fatigue*—the group of email subscribers on your list who have not taken an action, such as opening an email, clicking an email, or converting (purchasing, registering for a webinar, and so on), over a specified period of time. They are dormant, inactive, not engaging with your emails in any way, shape, or form. However, they are not unsubscribing. They are not marking your emails as spam. They are simply deleting, archiving, or using some filtering mechanism so your emails are never opened or read.

Although it's possible to reduce list fatigue by sending timely, targeted, relevant emails to subscribers who have opted in, it's nearly impossible to eliminate it entirely.

Think about list fatigue from a consumer point of view. Everyone receives emails that cause fatigue—those emails that you delete every single time they land in your inbox. If you use email services such as Gmail or Outlook, you might have even gone through the effort of creating a rule or filter for these types of emails so they never appear in your inbox. Again, you don't unsubscribe for whatever reason— too much work, thinking that "some day" you'll open their email, whatever the reason might be. The reality is that you don't. We don't. We just keep deleting the email, over and over. We are the inactives.

However, having inactives on your list doesn't necessarily mean you should remove those email addresses from your database. The possibility exists that some people interact with email marketing messages months after they've been delivered. They either save email newsletters to read at a later date or file away that email with a nonexpiring coupon to use when they are ready to purchase. We are not advocating you delete your inactive email addresses; simply be aware they exist.

From the perspective of an email marketer, inactives can represent a significant chunk of his email list. Many email marketing specialists have attempted to estimate this figure. Clearly, it's going to be different for every person, every company, and every list or segment of a list. However, make no mistake—your list includes inactive email addresses.

Some email experts such as Dela Quist of Alchemy Worx don't have a problem with inactive email addresses. In fact, Quist thinks most marketers are too quick to purge them from their lists.

"Inactivity is normal activity," said Quist in an interview with the Magill Report.[2] "Highly engaged people are outliers." According to Quist, "Half of a typical list will always be inactive for a year or more, but which half is a shifting target."

Whether or not you agree with Quist's assertion, being aware of those email addresses on your list who are not actively engaging—and having a strategy to communicate with them—is important.

Now, combine list churn of 30 percent per year with a chunk of your database not engaging with your emails (the "inactives"), and you have a lot of work to do to continuously grow your email list. That's why we've dedicated all of Part I, "The Secret to Email Marketing: List Growth," to growing your email list.

 Note

Remember: If you do not have email addresses to send to, nothing else in this book matters. Seriously. Think about it.

A Few Words about Effective Tactics

If you don't have an email list, the anatomy of an email is pointless. Who cares about the various components of an email—the subject line, the preheader, the call to action, the footer, the social sharing components—if you have an email list size of zero?

If you don't have an email list, breaking the rules of email marketing (being a rebel!) is silly. Unsubscribe at the top or the bottom? It doesn't matter. Send one big image or an all-text email? If nobody sees your email—because you have a list of zero—it's all for naught.

If you don't have an email list, who cares about email and social interacting? Integrating these two channels is pointless without email addresses to send to. Sure, you can include links to your Twitter and Facebook profiles, but if you don't have anybody on your email list, getting anyone to see those links is going to be tough!

If you don't have an email list, email really is dead (for you).

 Note

We talk a bit more about buying lists in Chapter 11, "The Best Ways to Grow Your List"; however, even if you choose alternative methods to grow your list, considering ways to organically grow your list is still important.

All too often, in email marketing—and the business world—we want to run (or even sprint) before we walk (or crawl). We get frustrated when something doesn't work as advertised. We can't figure out why we are not getting that $40.56 return on investment that everyone promised, and we just give up.

Giving up too soon is not a problem limited to just email marketing. Many business people are looking for the Easy Button. (Thanks for ingraining that image in our heads, Staples!) Admit it. Everyone does it. You try something for a few months and when it doesn't work, you move on to the next shiny object. With the amount of new technology that is being developed every day and the bombardment of information people face, it's no wonder. Every advertisement we see online, on TV, and on billboards all promise faster, cheaper, better results. They all guarantee the "quick win." However, as we all know, not much in life or business comes that easy.

It's the same with email marketing. Building a list takes work and time. Very few companies out there have grown their email lists without putting a ton of time and effort into it. The Groupons of the world are the exceptions, not the rules. Far from it.

That's why we feel so strongly about growing your email list first. Your list is your foundation, your database, and where the money is.

You can grow your list in many ways, and this book covers many of them. But let's ground your thinking first with a little data on what tends to be the most effective ways. In MarketingSherpa's 2012 Email Benchmarking Report, email marketers were asked to indicate the level of effectiveness of a number of popular list growth tactics. The hands-down winner was registering people for an email newsletter when they purchase an item from your online store.[3] Some 61 percent of email marketers indicate that it was a highly effective way to grow their lists.

Note that some of the list-building tactics work better for business-to-consumer (B2C) companies whereas others are more effective for business-to-business (B2B). If you are in the B2B space, the item-for-purchase incentive might be an eBook or whitepaper. However, if your company doesn't sell anything, another way to grow your list is to ask for an email opt-in during some type of registration process.

As shown in Figure 1.2, the report pointed out other ways email marketers found to effectively grow their list, such as capturing opt-ins during online events such as webinars that customers would register for (B2B); a registration page on your company website (B2B or B2C); paid search advertisements inviting people to sign up for your list (B2B or B2C); and offline events such as in-store promotions and calls to action (B2C).

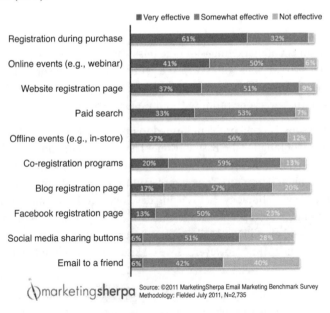

Figure 1.2   *MarketingSherpa Effectiveness chart[4] showing which email list growth tactics are the most effective.*

As you can tell, a number of tactics are considered at least somewhat effective for driving list growth. Some will work better for you than others. In fact, the top one in MarketingSherpa's list—registration during purchase—might not even apply to you and your company. The key is finding what method(s) work for you and your audience and maximizing their use.

List growth is of vital importance. The next two chapters walk through several ways to grow your email list, show you examples of people doing so effectively, and illustrate both why and how building your list is not a "get-as-many-new-subscribers-as-I-can-and-then-stop" approach. Rather, we'll focus on list growth tactics that are sustainable over time.

Some of the tips in the following chapters are going to seem quite obvious, whereas others will have you thinking, "Hmmm. I never thought of that." The majority of the suggestions are actionable—things that you can start implementing immediately. A few take a bit more work, but remember—we never said growing your list was easy, only that it was the secret to email marketing.

Endnotes

1. Daniels, David, "The Social Inbox: The Impact of Facebook Messages on Email Marketing," *The Relevancy Group*. http://relevancygroup.com/TheSocialInbox.htm

2. Magill, Ken, "Inactive Schminactive: Keep the Names, Says Quist," February 28, 2012. http://www.magillreport.com/Inactive-Schminactive-Keep-the-Names-Says-Quist/

3. "MarketingSherpa 2012 Email Benchmarking Report," http://www.meclabs.com/training/publications/benchmark-report/2012-email-marketing

4. "MarketingSherpa 2012 Email Benchmarking Report," http://www.meclabs.com/training/publications/benchmark-report/2012-email-marketing

How to Grow Your List

Quick. On the next page, we've inserted a worksheet. Either use that, or grab a scrap piece of paper and a writing utensil—pen, pencil, chalk, crayon, lipstick—whatever. Next, locate some type of timekeeping device like a watch, stopwatch, or clock. Finally, fire up your computer and open a browser such as Google, Yahoo!, or Bing.

Ready? Now follow these steps:

1. *Off the top of your head, write down the first three companies that come to mind that are not named Google, Yahoo!, or Microsoft. Write them down on your paper under "Company Name."*

2. *Search online for the website of the first company on your list. After you get there, start the timer. Locate the place on that website (likely some type of form) where you can enter your email address to opt-in for that company's emails. If you don't see it immediately on the main site, you might have to go to other pages. After you find it, stop the timer and record how long it took under "Time #1."*

Company Name	Time #1	Time #2

3. Start the timer again and fill out the email sign-up form. Be sure to complete all the required fields (often denoted by an asterisk). You can enter fake information if you want, but please be sure to enter a valid email address (more on that later). Click Enter/Submit/Go or whatever button you need to click to complete the signup. Stop the timer and record the number under "Time #2."

4. Repeat steps 2 and 3 for the other two companies on your list.

5. Finally, repeat steps 2 and 3 one more time for your own company's website.

 Note

Important: If you receive an email from one of the companies you visited, please do not delete it or unsubscribe. Not yet, at least. In fact, please save them in their own, special folder; maybe even call it, "Rebel's Guide." We will be revisiting those emails throughout this book.

If you've followed instructions correctly, you should have opted-in to receive emails from three companies (plus your own) and you have eight different times written down on your paper—two per company. This is the exact exercise that DJ performed while teaching a University of Utah Business School MBA class in 2010. We're going to guess that the experience you had is similar to the results DJ found that evening:

- For one thing, we're willing to bet it took more than 30 seconds to find the email opt-in form for at least one of the four companies on your list. Quite possibly it took even longer. A chance exists that you didn't ever find an email sign-up form and just gave up. In some cases, you might have had to create an account first and then opt-in to the email program.

- We're also confident it took you several minutes to fill out the email sign-up form for at least one of the four companies on your list. You might have had to enter your email address twice for one form. You might have had to enter in your mailing address, city, state, and ZIP code.

- For at least one of the four companies on your list, we bet you were a bit frustrated. Maybe finding the email opt-in form took a long time. Maybe after you found it, you had to type in a bunch of letters that were hard to read to confirm that you were a human.

- You might also have just sent an email to someone on your team asking him why no email opt-in form is on your site or, if it's there, why it took you 4 minutes and 37 seconds to fill it out.

This chapter is all about growing your email list. We'll cover some effective tactics for adding email addresses to your database, including ensuring your opt-in form is obvious to find on your website and easy to complete—quite the opposite of the exercise you just went through. We'll also suggest a few techniques to grow your email list that you might not have thought about, such as using QR codes, smartphone apps, and social media. Finally, although this chapter does not discuss every single possible way to grow your list, we hope it provides a few things to think about and gets you on the right track.

Making the Opt-In Process Obvious and Easy

In case it is not clear by this point, we took you through the preceding exercise to experience first-hand what your prospects, customers, and fans experience when they want to opt-in to get emails from you. These are people who are actively seeking to add themselves to your email list. Simply put: If you don't have an obvious and easy-to-complete email sign-up form prominently placed on your website, you are going to have a tough time growing your list.

Sure, if yours is a business-to-consumer (B2C) company, you can collect email addresses during the checkout process. And yes, if yours is a business-to-business (B2B) company, you can invite your current customers to subscribe to your email list. However, you are leaving out a huge group of people who might want to hear from you through email. Do you recall that statistic from the Merckle report we discussed in the Introduction? If not, here it is again:

"Finally, regardless of the user's age, email is the preferred method of communication for commercial messages—by far. Merckle reports that 74 percent of all online adults say so. Compared to direct mail, email is preferred at a rate of five to one."[1]

People prefer that you communicate with them through email, and yet many companies are failing to connect customers to their email offerings at an opportune moment.

We know a few individuals and organizations who have found a tremendous amount of success making their email sign-up process painfully obvious and super-easy. Laura Roeder is the founder of LKR, a company that provides technology-focused training resources for small business clients. LKR sends a free weekly marketing to-do email every Wednesday called "The Dash." With more than 30,000 subscribers—cultivated over a two-and-a-half-year period—this weekly newsletter is a huge part of the company's business. Roeder and her team have been doing email marketing since 2007, the year she founded LKR.

If you visit the LKR website—lauraroeder.com—one thing jumps out immediately. As Figure 2.1 shows, the majority of the real estate on that page is a big email sign-up form. How's that for obvious?

Figure 2.1 *LKR's email sign-up form is front and center on lauraroeder.com.*

Clearly, Roeder and her team feel that growing their email list is critical to their business. This is not something new for LKR. According to Roeder, it's been that way from day one, in some shape or form.

"Email sign-up should always be the most prominent call-to-action on your website," Roeder told us, "because it's extremely rare that someone makes a purchase the first time they ever hear of you. Even small purchases we usually research, revisit and consider, instead of buying the first time we hear of something.

"If you don't collect email, you're putting the onus on the prospect to remember to revisit your website," she continued. "If you collect email now, you can take the lead on guiding your prospect to a sale."

We could not agree more.

How many times have you searched for something online, found a website you were interested in, but didn't find exactly what you were looking for? How long do you stay? We know the answer: not very long. However, if the site had an obvious email sign-up form—like the one on LKR—wouldn't you be more likely to opt-in, especially if there is some incentive to subscribe? Putting the email sign-up form front and center provides a way for people to stay in touch with you. From your perspective, you now have permission to begin marketing to them through email.

We also asked Roeder about the data she collects on her email form. She only asks for subscribers to complete two fields—first name and email address. That's it! Think about how many email forms you've completed in your life that ask for a lot more than that. We've both filled out forms that ask for our street address, state, ZIP code, and sometimes phone number. As Roeder said, "The fewer the fields, the lower the barriers to filling out the form." She even told us that they have some forms that only ask for email address. We like it. However, what Roeder does is just one method.

Another approach many email marketers take is to collect more data from subscribers (not just name and email address). This allows them to segment their list to send more targeted emails. One segmentation tactic we see often is collecting birthday information so they can send "Happy Birthday" emails to subscribers. Additionally, online retailers often ask for product category interests such as men's versus women's versus children's clothing. This enables them to segment their list and offer more relevant content to their subscribers.

If you view the LKR website online, notice how the two sign-up fields are highlighted in yellow. Pretty hard to miss, right? Your eyes are almost naturally drawn there. This is one aspect of the opt-in form that Roeder's team has added recently. When asked why they made the two fields stand out so much, Roeder responded, "[We] wanted a visual aid to immediately direct the eye to the list signup when someone looks at the homepage." The best part? It works. Roeder told us that since adding the yellow highlight, conversions have gone up quite a bit.

Go back to your own website. How obvious is your email opt-in form? Does it stand out or does the customer have to hunt for it? Do you make signing up easy for your potential subscribers or do you make them work for it?

To be clear, we are not suggesting that you need to dedicate the entire home page to the email opt-in form like Roeder has done. However, if you are trying to grow your list, ensuring that the form is prominently placed and easy to fill out is critical.

You next need to invite subscribers to fill in that form.

Asking Website Visitors to Subscribe

Remember when we told you in Chapter 1, "Why List Growth Matters," that some of these tips are going to seem quite obvious? Well, asking visitors to sign up is one of those instances. However, just like making your email sign-up form obvious and easy, we have found that many companies simply forget to ask. Just like in sales, if you don't ask for your audience to opt-in, it's a lot less likely they will.

Tasting Table is "a free daily email publication that delivers the best of food and drink culture to adventurous eaters across the country."[2] This company sends its membership database of nearly one million email subscribers[3] an email each weekday that includes recommendations for dining out or cooking at home as well as different wines, cocktails, and chefs to know.

Did we mention that its email database has grown to nearly one million subscribers in just over three years? Not too shabby.

How did Tasting Table do it? Simple. It asked.

If you go to tastingtable.com, missing the email opt-in form is hard because it's front and center, as shown in Figure 2.2. In fact, even if you scroll (try it), the sign-up form remains in the middle of the home page.

Figure 2.2   *The email opt-in form on tastingtable.com doesn't beat around the bush. It just asks people to sign up for the list to get daily emails.*

Do you notice what Tasting Table does that is different from most websites—probably different from your company's website? Most companies include an email opt-in form as an afterthought. They bury it somewhere in the top of the site or off to the right where you have to search to actually find it. Tasting Table not only has its email sign-up form as the main call to action on the home page, it actually asks you to subscribe. Notice the language: "Tasting Table is the free daily email for adventurous eaters everywhere. *Hungry? Sign up*."

We're not sure about you, but just reading this blurb made DJ hungry. Sure, it was 11 a.m. when he wrote that last paragraph, but still, the language is enticing and it works—to the tune of one million email subscribers!

To make the offer to sign up even more appealing and easier, the folks from Tasting Table include a big, red button that reads, "JOIN FREE." They are inviting you to opt-in to their daily email list.

Another company that does a nice job with asking for an email address is Digitwirl. Founder Carley Knobloch and her team describe Digitwirl as "a weekly web show that helps you discover the very best technology that will save you time, money, and a few gray hairs."[4]

Knobloch sends out a weekly email to her list of 6,500 subscribers, a list she's been growing organically since Digitwirl launched in early 2011. She told us that it's the main vehicle for her to communicate regularly with her community. The email is short, simple, and most importantly, it yields positive results!

"The email has been a prompt to watch the video," said Knobloch. "We see a huge surge every Tuesday in our video views because that's when we send the email out."

When asked, "Why email marketing?" Knobloch told us that, "Building an audience with video is a whole separate animal. I knew I wanted to have a list to share content with people regularly. I preach this to other entrepreneurs all the time," she continued. "It's all about having a list. Once you have 'em you don't need to worry about acquiring."

Knobloch credits this incredible list growth to one thing. Any guesses? Take a look at Figure 2.3. This is a screenshot of the top, above-the-fold section of Digitwirl. com.

Does anything jump out at you (besides the video of Carley Knobloch, relaxing in her chair with a bowl of Granny Smith apples on the table and a cool piano in the background)? How about that big blue box that clearly explains what you will get if you choose to opt-in for the Digitwirl emails? Again, although asking for someone's email address might seem obvious, Knobloch and the Digitwirl team actually ask their audience to subscribe to their emails. Asking for an email address is not

Figure 2.3   *Digitwirl.com uses the majority of the "above-the-fold" section of its website to funnel people to subscribe to its email marketing list.*

rocket science, but far too often we see companies and individuals who simply do not ask.

We could not resist commenting on how Digitwirl does an excellent job of asking visitors to sign up. In Figure 2.3, notice the section just to the left of the big opt-in form called "Why sign up?" It uses persuasive phrases such as "get first look" and "exclusive deep discounts, deals, and gadgety giveaways."

As Knobloch said, "I don't take it lightly that people are giving me their email address. It's no longer a given. We have to remember as business owners to think like a consumer. Tell me what I'm going to get. Why should I sign up?"

Knobloch chose to dedicate so much real estate on the home page to asking for someone to opt-in to the email list because she understands typical user behavior online. Web traffic comes and goes. People pop on to the site on a mobile phone, then pop off. They browse, they jump. If you hit them at the first point of entry with a call to action (CTA), you've given them a little task to perform. Many of them will perform that task and fill out the subscription form.

Offering a clear invitation to your audience, regardless of whether it's on your website, Facebook page, or any other medium of communication, isn't just a smart way to build your list. It's also the smart way to achieve anything in digital marketing. The call to action is the most important feature on any web page. Yes, you can have several of them. However, the fewer there are and the easier they are to find and execute, the better marketing results you'll get from the website.

When smart marketers and companies want to track their website's performance, they typically start with a simple conversion point: an email newsletter subscription form. They ask their customers to sign up for their lists. The conversion happens when a site visitor "converts" to a subscriber by inputting their email address.

Most of the time, ensuring that your sign-up form is obvious to find and super-easy to fill out, as well as remembering to extend a subscription invitation to visitors, will increase your email opt-in list. Sometimes, however, you need to stand out from the crowd a bit and do something unique.

Using Humor and Creativity to Increase Opt-Ins

In today's Information Age, everyone is bombarded with marketing messages. It seems like no matter where you are, whatever you are doing, multiple marketing sources are vying for your attention. They are asking you to do something.

In fact, we believe mass marketing is to the point that most consumers just tune stuff out. Television commercials? Nope. That's what a DVR is for. Billboards? What billboards? People are usually busy texting while they're driving. (*Disclaimer: It's dangerous—and in some states illegal—to text while driving. We in no way endorse it, just in case you were curious.*)

However, most people ignore most marketing messages not simply because of tuning them out. The truth is, most marketing looks the same. It simply does not stand out from the crowd. No matter what the intention, most marketing messages fail to grab people's attention and get them to take action.

As Jason said in a blog post in December 2011,[5] you have to craft a compelling message.

"It doesn't matter if you're 'human' as a company. It doesn't matter if you 'join the conversation'...If you can't offer up a message to your audience that makes them pull back, double take and say, 'Holy [cow]! That's cool!' You're just going to be another hack trying to 'engage.'"

We believe this same concept applies to email opt-in forms. For the most part, they all look the same. They have a form with a field to fill in your email address and some basic copy that reads, "Subscribe" or "Sign Up." That's it.

Boring.

That's why we love what the Funny or Die crew has done with its email subscription form (see Figure 2.4). If you are not familiar with Funny or Die, it is a comedy video site that mixes original content from the site's creators, including funnyman Will Ferrell, with user-generated humorous videos. It was created several years ago by Ferrell and actors/comedians/writers Adam McKay and Chris Henchy as well as some folks from Silicon Valley. Their content often falls into the "not safe for work" (NSFW) category, but is usually good for a few laughs.

Figure 2.4   *Funny or Die uses humor in its email opt-in form.*

"The #1 goal of marketing is to drive more traffic back to site," Patrick Starzan, Funny or Die's VP of Marketing & Distribution, told us. Email is one of the major ways the company accomplishes this goal.

Neither of us was surprised when we looked at its email opt-in form, which was a pop-up form on its website. (We discuss pop-ups more in Part III, "Breaking the Rules.")

As you can see from Figure 2.4, the Funny or Die team makes joining its list easy for new subscribers—just type in your email address and click the Submit button, a method consistent with the earlier examples in this chapter. However, what this team does that is unique—the thing that makes its email opt-in form stand out from the crowd and makes you say, "Holy cow! That's cool...and pretty funny!"— is the text under the opt-in:

"We will not use your email for anything sneaky."

But that's not all Funny or Die does to add some levity to its opt-in form. If you land on this form and change your mind, you have two options. You could close the form by clicking the gray "X" in the upper right, or you could click the second button on that form, where Funny or Die drops in a bit more humor by labeling it, "No Thanks, I Can't Read." Starzan explained that this text is a way for users to say they didn't want the emails, but in a funny manner, sticking with the tone of the site and brand.

In just over five years, the team at Funny or Die has grown its email list from zero to more than one million opt-in addresses. According to Starzan, "75 to 80 percent of all subscribers come from this pop-up." The team has effectively used humor that is consistent with its brand to ask for email subscribers.

Thrillist is another company that uses humor both in its emails and on its website, thrillist.com. It delivers what it calls, "the best of what's new in your 'hood and on the web," emails every day. Even its help page under the "Emails" section offers a bit of humor. One FAQ reads, "How do I unsubscribe? Thrillist is ruining my life." When you click that link, the first sentence on the new page reads, "If you've signed up for Thrillist and you're not receiving emails, it's not your fault."

However, the language on its email opt-in form is what really caught our attention. Again, it's one of those things that jumps out at you, makes you pause, maybe even makes you say "Holy cow. This is awesome!" It reads, "Thrillist is the free daily email that sifts through the crap to find the best new spots to eat, drink, and shop in your 'hood."

This type of plain language is all over its site. Thrillist's About page, the one that talks about who the company is and encourages new email signups, says, "Each weekday, we'll drop you a must-have recommendation, from the best of what's new, to deeply under-the-radar goodness. We're talking absinthe-only cocktail spots, eateries that dish up BBQ Rattlesnake Salad and Reindeer in Bourbon Sauce, and ATMs whose currency is marijuana—handy, although after making a withdrawal, you'll feel even more paranoid about the stocking repercussions of consuming Santa's only friend."

That page ends with the following:

"So, should I get on the list? Oh, hell yes." (This links to its email sign-up form, of course.)

Funny or Die and Thrillist might be a couple of the better examples of organizations that use clever writing or creativity to draw people in to subscribing. However, growing your list can also happen because of the type of technology you use to do so.

Using Technology: QR Codes and Smartphone Apps to Grow Your List

Escaping technology is hard. Seemingly everywhere you go, someone is using a smartphone—texting, checking the scores on ESPN, playing Angry Birds, updating a Facebook status, tweeting, or maybe even emailing. This all-pervasive nature is one of the many reasons that using technology, specifically a smartphone, to help grow your email list can be a very effective tactic.

LockerGnome founder Chris Pirillo has more than 200,000 subscribers and more than 128 million video views on YouTube. He runs a publishing network and a highly regarded technology conference. He also uses technology, namely QR codes, to grow his email list (see Figure 2.5). Pirillo tacked on a QR code to the bottom of his YouTube videos for a few weeks in December 2011 and saw his list grow. Scanning the QR code with a smartphone opens a mobile-optimized landing page (website) with an email sign-up form for the LockerGnome email newsletter. Awesome!

http://goo.gl/lr8L0.qr

Figure 2.5   *The QR code that Chris Pirillo included on the bottom of his YouTube videos for a few weeks in December 2011 (http://goo.gl/info/lr8L0).*

 Note

For those unfamiliar with a QR (Quick Response) code, it's simply a type of barcode, like a UPC label. Today, more and more marketers are using it in various media: television, billboards, magazines, storefronts, in email marketing campaigns, and so on. In fact, DJ has dedicated the entire back of his business card to a QR code. When the code is scanned with a smartphone device (using a QR code scanner), a webpage opens in the phone's browser, as shown in Figure 2.6.

Notice also that LockerGnome saves subscribers time by allowing the option to sign in with Facebook.[6] If you are already logged into Facebook, the email form in Figure 2.6 opens pre-populated with your name and email address. All you have to do is click the Register button to be added to the list. Talk about easy, right? *Note: A bit of web development is necessary to ensure this feature works properly.*

Pirillo included the QR code in more than 130 videos from December 12 to December 28, 2011. Over that time period, his QR code was scanned more than 4,500 times. We asked him how many of those scans resulted in additional email subscribers to his LockerGnome list. His answer: "a few hundred." Although this result is not earth shattering, we would argue that many marketers would be thrilled with a few hundred additional email subscribers over a two-week period.

Overall, as smartphone and QR code use become more mainstream, we expect to see more marketers leveraging this technology to help grow their email lists. Considering the relatively low cost (even free in some cases) and minimal time and effort to set up, we advocate for marketers to test this approach to determine whether it's worth it as an additional list growth channel.

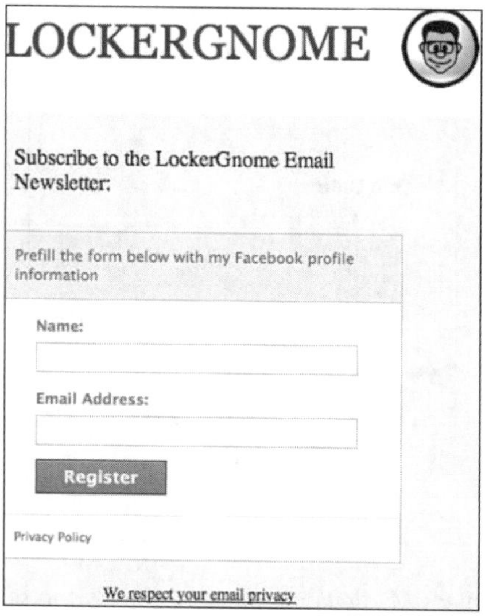

Figure 2.6 *This is the mobile-optimized landing page for Chris Pirillo's QR code as it appeared on most phone web browsers. Notice how simple and easy the page is to complete. Just enter your name and email address and register.*

Another great example of a company using technology to grow its email list comes from the folks at BabyCenter. When DJ learned that his wife was pregnant with their second child, he immediately grabbed the My Pregnancy Today app from the iTunes store and downloaded it to his iPhone.

If you've ever installed an app on your smartphone, you know it usually involves some sort of setup process (see Figure 2.7).

DJ was asked to enter his Due Date—in this case, his wife's due date. However, as an email marketing guy, the next part of the set-up process is what really caught his eye. The app included an option to "Sign up for the weekly newsletters about your pregnancy." Brilliant!

BabyCenter made the email sign-up process easy and obvious. It asked for a sign-up response and was a bit creative in the technique used to do so. It set proper expectations around content ("newsletters about your pregnancy") and frequency ("weekly"). While it did not promise an incentive such as a discount, in this case it was not necessary to secure an opt-in. After all, the email newsletter was free! What's really nice about these weekly emails is they are customized based on the due date entered during opt-in. Well done.

Figure 2.7   *BabyCenter's My Pregnancy Today iPhone app setup screen is not only the first step in using the application, but also includes an easy opt-in email form.*

Not every business is going to have a smartphone app, but if yours does, don't miss the opportunity to capture users' attention and sign them up for your mailing list. If you build an app that takes off and is downloaded by 50,000 users, won't you feel silly if you don't wind up with the email addresses of many of them?

Use Social Media

As you likely know, social media is a hot area of marketing. The rate of growth in participation, activity, and products and services is astounding. However, in regard to integrating social media into other marketing channels, too often we see one person managing social media while another person is in charge of Search Engine Optimization (SEO), and still another is responsible for all things email marketing. In some cases, due to unique skill sets and differing strategies for various online channels, this approach might make sense. However in other instances, due to limited resources or employees with more complete skill sets, combining efforts to ensure a cohesive, consistent message might be a better approach.

As more companies and individuals are learning the social media ropes, we hope they consider integrating their social media efforts with email marketing, specifically to grow their email lists. We discuss more about the integration of social media and email in Part IV, "Batman (Email Marketing) and Robin (Social Media)."

If you think about social media as another marketing channel, the opportunities for cross promotion are plentiful. Consider Twitter: Let's say that you are getting ready to send out your next, amazingly awesome email campaign. You have a strong following on Twitter. Why not take advantage of this free channel to invite your followers to subscribe to your email newsletter? That's exactly what C.C. Chapman does occasionally, as shown in Figure 2.8.

Figure 2.8   *C.C. Chapman sends out a tweet inviting his followers to subscribe to his email newsletter.*

Notice how Chapman keeps this tweet short, direct, and to the point. He includes a short URL to make retweeting easy and entices his followers with a simple call-to-action question: "Want it?" Another approach Chapman has is that he isn't all sales, all the time. Not only is this particular tweet casual and friendly, but he mixes it in with his normal banter and chit-chat with people on Twitter, sharing links to other people's great content and the like. The occasional call to action then comes across as a soft-sell and genuine in its intent, rather than just another sales pitch.

Don't forget Facebook! We bet that you ask questions and post links to content that you and others in your industry have produced. Maybe you even have conversation with your fans, prospects, and customers. However, are you taking advantage of your Facebook status updates to encourage your fans to engage with you on other channels? Notice in Figure 2.9 how CruiseDeals.com leveraged Facebook to help in growing its email list.

Similar to Chapman's tweet, this update includes a question as the main call to action, the incentive to sign up for email alerts. CruiseDeals.com references a well-known publication, the *New York Times*, as part of its invitation to subscribe. It also clearly lists what an email subscriber will receive by signing up (deals, guides, tips, and reviews).

Speaking of Facebook, be sure you are taking advantage of its "apps" feature, which allows developers to build custom applications such as an email opt-in form. Notice how Park City Mountain Resort (PCMR) takes advantage of this feature to grow its email list (see Figure 2.10).

Figure 2.9   *CruiseDeals.com updates its Facebook status to include a link to its email subscription form.*

Figure 2.10   *Park City Mountain Resort collects email addresses on its Facebook page using an application specifically designed to feed that information into its email database.*

The beauty of including an email sign-up form on your Facebook page is that it gives you an easy opportunity to convert your Facebook fans (those who "like" your page) into email subscribers. PCMR has tens of thousands of Facebook likes. It can reference this page on other social networks such as Twitter, LinkedIn, or

Google+ (or even directly on its Facebook page), and invite people to sign up for its email newsletter.

Providing Incentive (WIIFM—What's In It For Me?)

When asking someone to opt-in to your email list, telling her why is critical. Also known as "What's In It For Me?" (WIIFM), this language is often the push that encourages a possible subscriber to enter her email address and click the Subscribe button.

Clearly, appealing to the WIIFM mindset is not limited to email marketing. Any good marketing campaign takes advantage of WIIFM. A television commercial, a billboard, an in-store sign—anything that asks people to provide their information—usually explains what they will get in return. Sometimes it's something tangible ("buy now and receive a free gift") or an item of value ("order today and shipping is free!"). Other times it's simply a promise, like CruiseDeals.com's statement, "Sign up now to get all the deals, guides, tips, & reviews."

Either way, including some type of incentive to prospects to enter an email address in an opt-in form is often an effective way to grow your list. You give me something. I give you something. Easy.

Marcus Sheridan, also known as the "Sales Lion," is the owner of a swimming pool company in the Washington, D.C., area. In 2008, when the economy took a turn for the worse, he was forced to embrace a new way of marketing: *inbound marketing*. This term is defined as creating valuable content, becoming a trusted source for that content, and being found online—your leads come to you rather than your having to go find them. Before long, Sheridan's swimming pool site, in his words, "dominated the entire industry."

Now along with his swimming pool site, he's started TheSalesLion.com where he teaches other businesses how to experience huge increases in web traffic and sales through the power of inbound and content marketing. One of the methods Sheridan uses to teach his audience about inbound marketing is through his eBook, *Inbound & Content Marketing Made Easy*. This eBook has also been useful in growing his email marketing list.

Sheridan attributes most of his list growth on TheSalesLion.com (from 0 to more than 2,000 email addresses in just a few short months) to the clear, obvious, incentive-based sign-up forms that are plastered all over his website (see Figure 2.11).

We asked Sheridan why he uses this eBook as his main incentive to grow the list. He said, "Doing this was one of my best moves ever because it allows me to say at the end of a presentation, conference, or webinar, 'Hey everyone, in order to read much, much more of what you heard today, you need to go to my site and download my eBook right way. It's FREE and it's AWESOME.' It also makes for a much, much better call to action when doing a guest post as, well, having something tangible to offer."

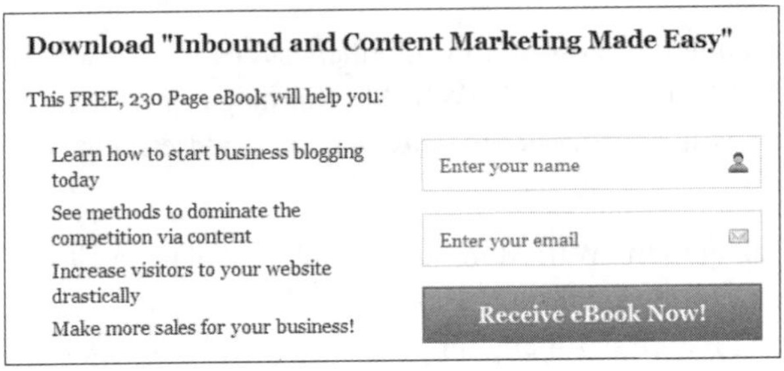

Figure 2.11   *The email opt-in form on the homepage of TheSalesLion.com provides subscribers a 230-page eBook as an incentive to sign up.*

We love it.

Even better, it works. Sheridan believes that his list growth has occurred at double the rate it would have otherwise, by simply including an incentive. As he told us, "Numbers don't lie." List building is the number-one goal of his website. As such, having the opt-in be front-and-center in his website's experience makes perfect sense. Sheridan also reports that the form generates about 60 percent of his list's opt-ins.

Chris Garrett also effectively uses an incentive to grow his email list. Garrett is a digital marketing consultant, speaker, and educator. He blogs about new media and online marketing on chrisg.com to educate small businesses on how to create content, provide value to their audience, and build trust and loyalty.

Garrett is what you would call an early adopter of email marketing. He said, "My first email broadcast list was in the early 1990s. It was to distribute jokes that got sent to me in the Fw: Fw: Fw: fashion. After it got to a serious size I cobbled together an automated system using the Pegasus email client filtering rules to allow people to subscribe and unsubscribe."

Today, he has graduated from Pegasus to using an email service provider (less cobbling, more seamless automation). His list is growing at a fairly steady clip. If you navigate to chrisg.com, the first thing you'll notice is the opt-in in Figure 2.12.

Garrett had been providing similar incentives to subscribe to his blog posts via RSS from early on. So when it came to his launching his email newsletter in February of

2007, "it just seemed the sensible thing to do, and it worked." In fact, in the first 7 days after adding the incentive (as seen in Figure 2.12), Garrett's list grew from 0 to 500 subscribers.

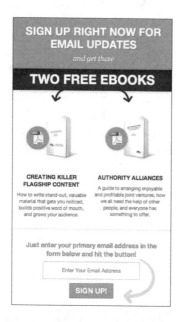

Figure 2.12   *The chrisg.com email opt-in form emphasizes the incentive rather than the sign up, making readers feel like they're getting great value in exchange for that email address.*

Like some of the other examples we mentioned in this chapter, Garrett not only provides incentive to opt-in, he ensures his form is the main part of his site. Why? "You have to remember my site is not just a blog, it is the main marketing vehicle for my consulting and coaching business," he said. "So, yes, people do type in the URL to get my latest updates, but people who visit the homepage are in the minority.

"If you like my content then you subscribe and probably never see the homepage again! I want people to check out certain things when they first visit but *most of all I want people to stick around, so I give people a big obvious reason to do that*" (emphasis ours).

Notice how consistent Garrett's message is with what both Laura Roeder and Carley Knobloch said about the importance of collecting email addresses.

Growing Your Email List Offline

For some reason, offline is the channel that gets the least amount of love in regard to growing your email list. However, if used effectively, it can be one of the most powerful methods. The issue is that many companies just slap a pad of ruled paper on the counter and hope customers will add their email addresses to the list. This certainly covers the "make it easy" part of an email opt-in; however, it's usually far from effective.

Consumers see offline email opt-ins everywhere. Restaurants provide cards on tables asking diners to sign up for their email program. Some even include a link or website address on the bill or receipt. Everyone has seen fishbowls at the hostess stand where people can drop their business cards (with a valid email addresses) for a chance to win a free meal.

Effective opt-in campaigns don't have to happen online, either. Where DJ lives in Salt Lake City, his local dry cleaners—Red Hanger—has a clipboard next to the cash register. The clipboard has a book of Post-It notes on the right-hand side with a simple message: "Want an email when your order is ready? Jot it down and you're set!"—see Figure 2.13. (*Note: DJ captured this image with his iPhone one day when picking up the three freshly starched dress shirts he owns*).

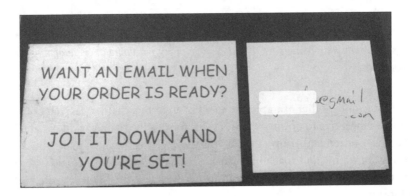

Figure 2.13   *Red Hanger collects email addresses in its store using a Post-It note (Salt Lake City, Utah).*

What makes this clipboard signup even better is its location. Strategically placed on the counter, you would have to never once look down to miss it, which certainly is possible if you were using your smartphone to send a quick email. However, if you are signing a credit card receipt, you actually use the clipboard to write on!

Other than the fact that the messaging is written in Comic Sans—a font that is usually reserved for child-related copy—the call to action is simple and clean. There are no fancy graphics or edgy copy, just a clear "here's what to do" message.

Finally, we love the use of the Post-It note. It solves many of the possible privacy issues of the ruled pad of paper that exposes everyone's email address. The cashiers can also easily rip off each Post-It note immediately after the customer leaves the store for data entry into their system later on.

The arts and crafts (and framing) store, Michaels, also does a nice job collecting email addresses in its stores. The Michaels store DJ frequents near his house features a big green box that advertises where customers can sign up for the store email. The green box also stores those customer email addresses (see Figure 2.14).

Figure 2.14   *The Michaels in-store customer email sign-up box in Salt Lake City, Utah, is a great example of on-premise email list building.*

If you let your imagination run a bit, the lime green box, held together with duct tape, almost looks like an early computer. Other than the manual data entry process that someone has to do, it almost is like a computer! This "computer" is located at the front of the checkout line. Similar to the Red Hanger clipboard discussed earlier, it's quite difficult to miss.

A word of caution: Although neither the Red Hanger nor Michael's examples require consumers to provide their email address, some businesses do mandate employees collect customer email addresses when they check out. If you choose this approach, be sure you are monitoring it closely because the possibility exists that your staff might input fake email addresses to pad their stats and meet quota. If you make it a requirement, you risk having a significant number of invalid email addresses, which ultimately impacts your overall email delivery and jeopardizes all email programs.

We used these examples because they can inspire you to think of creative, yet simple, ways to capture email addresses of your customers or prospects. Many other ways exist to build your list, too. Whether online or offline, we hope you'll start tackling a few of these suggestions to see which ones work best for you. Test. Deploy. Iterate. Test again.

 Note

> Also keep in mind that technology continues to evolve and some list growth tactics are still in their early phases of development. For example, at the end of 2011, Google began experimenting with "email subscription ads," essentially allowing companies to include an email opt-in form within their paid ads. If a user is logged into Gmail at the time this ad is served, the email address box will be pre-filled. This feature makes it that much easier (one-click) to opt-in to receive email from that company. As of this writing, the program was still in "small experiment" phase with only a handful of companies testing it out.

These tried-and-true ways to grow your email list are a great way to get started with email marketing.

Think back to the exercise we asked you to do at the beginning of this chapter. What you likely found was that most marketers do not make it easy to opt-in to their email list. In some cases, the subscribe form is at the bottom of their website. In other instances, it simply blends into the rest of the page. If you are not making your email sign-up form easy to locate and easy to complete, you are missing an opportunity to grow your list. If your opt-in form looks like everyone else's, you're less likely to stand out from the crowd.

We encourage you to test new ways to grow your list—using QR codes or smartphone apps, adding a bit of humor to the process. Some methods will be more successful than others. Test. Try. Learn. Adapt. However, whatever you do, be sure that you're dedicating the time and effort needed for growing your email marketing list.

Now it's time to get a bit more technical. But don't worry! We're not going to start speaking in IT department code. We need to walk through some of your email marketing setup to ensure you're making it super easy for people who want to subscribe to your offerings to do so.

Endnotes

1. "View from the Digital Inbox 2011," *Merckle*, http://www.merkleinc. com/sites/default/files/whitepapers/WP-DigitalInbox_11Jul_0.pdf accessed on February 15, 2012.

2. http://www.tastingtable.com/about accessed on February 11, 2012.

3. Mashable, *How a Niche Email Newsletter Grew to a Million Subscribers [VIDEO],* January 10, 2012. http://mashable.com/2012/01/10/ video-tasting-table/

4. http://digitwirl.com/about-digitwirl

5. Falls, Jason, "Why Businesses Struggle With Social Media...And What To Do About It," *Social Media Explorer.* December 20, 2011. http://www.socialmediaexplorer.com/social-media-marketing/ struggling-with-social-media/

6. "Sign in with Facebook," https://www.facebook.com/about/login/ accessed on February 22, 2012.

3

Let's Get Technical

By this point in the book, the secret is out. We guess you could say it's no longer a secret. Growing your email list is the most important first step of email marketing. Chapter 2, "How to Grow Your List," provides several tactics to take your list from zero to more than zero or from some to more. Congratulations—you are on your way to email marketing success!

It's now time to get a bit more technical, but not with heavy-duty math or computer programming stuff. No way. In this chapter we share with you some of the little intricacies of your email software's set up and execution that are often overlooked or taken for granted yet that can make a huge difference in growing your email list and gearing up to kick off your email program.

To Pre-check or Not to Pre-check

To pre-check or not to pre-check: That is the question. By *pre-checking*, we are referring to pre-selecting the check box that opts people in to receive your emails. See Figure 3.1, which shows a dialog box from the Apple Store, for an example of what we mean.

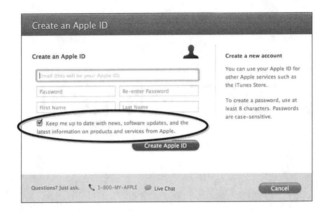

Figure 3.1   *In this account creation form from the Apple store, the email opt-in box is pre-checked. If you do not want emails from Apple, you need to uncheck the box.*

The box on the bottom with the check mark in it that reads, "Keep me up to date with news, software updates, and the latest information on products and services from Apple," is an example of a pre-checked email opt-in box.

Generally speaking, using a pre-checked box on your web page grows your list faster than an unchecked box. Why? The answer is simple. Most people either do not notice the box—not realizing they are opting in—or see the box but don't want to take the extra step to uncheck it.

The downside to using a pre-checked box is that your list quality often suffers. If people who are opting in are doing so without really knowing they are, or are simply being lazy and not unchecking the box, they are less likely to be invested in your emails. This, in turn, could lead to fewer opens, click-throughs, and conversions. They might unsubscribe when your welcome email comes or mark it as spam.

So the question remains: to pre-check or not to pre-check?

Looking at it from the other side—leaving the opt-in box unchecked—you are likely to have a more engaged list, subscribers who open, click, and (hopefully) convert. These are people who had to take a proactive stance. These subscribers who are raising their virtual hand saying, "Sign me up!"

"If you pre-check the box, at least 70 percent of people will leave it checked," Gretchen Scheiman, who was a partner and director Digital Dialogue at OgilvyOne for nearly five years, told us. "If you leave the box unchecked, at best 30 percent of people will check it. I usually see closer to 20 percent, and sometimes as low as 15 percent."

However, based on the size of your list, it can be a numbers game. Using the stats from Scheiman above with various list sizes, consider the following scenario:

1,000 people land on the email opt-in page. List A, with the pre-checked email opt-in box, gains 700 new subscribers. List B, with the un-checked box, gains 300 new subscribers (at best).

List A is likely less engaged so their open rates and click-through rates will be lower. For argument sake, let's say of the 700 emails sent, List A averages a 10 percent open rate (70 opens) and a 2 percent click-through rate (14 clicks).

List B is more likely to be engaged as they proactively opted-in. Their open rate is 25 percent (75 opens) and click-through rate is 5 percent (15 clicks). As the disparity between open and click-through rates gets greater per list, the difference between total opens and click-throughs becomes more pronounced.

The question of whether to pre-check a subscribe box comes down to two factors: the total size of your list (larger the list, the less the overall impact) as well as your email marketing moral code. Do you err on the side of driving numbers or do you err on the side of putting your audience in complete control? No right or wrong way exists because the audience does have the option to uncheck a pre-checked box. Whether to pre-check the box is just one of those decisions you'll have to consider and make for yourself.

So, can a pre-checked opt-in box work? An online community site that asked to remain anonymous has 18 million members with an annual email list growth of around 3 million per year. It uses a pre-checked subscription box on its account creation form. It has tested an unchecked opt-in box, and the results showed that the list growth plummeted and negatively impacted all the numbers it tracks. This company also makes unsubscribing easy to do. Because of this, it is able to maintain good email deliverability rates and not have its emails sent straight to spam.

Email is essential to this company's business. It sends nearly 100 million emails per month that are all segmented to different lists and in different categories. It does not take email lightly, especially as it's still the number-one driver of traffic to its site by a wide margin.

However, you still have to be careful. Currently in the United States, pre-checking an email opt-in box is not against the law. However, this is no longer the case in Canada. As of December 15, 2010, "express consent" is required for all email opt-ins.[1] In other words, the subscriber must take an action (that is, check a box) to opt-in to your email list. Passive opt-ins no longer fly.

While we're neither soothsayers nor lawyers, the general consumer and regulatory trends lead us to believe similar guidelines might have legs in the U.S. and other countries soon. Ensuring that your methods not only meet any regulatory guidelines of your industry or various governments, but also the expectations and preferences of your audience, is always a diligent practice. If you are unsure of what's on- or off-limits, please consult an attorney familiar with the presiding law in your area, specifically this new provision if you're in Canada. We wouldn't want you to get in trouble.

Explain the Email List Sign-Up Process

Chris Penn is the Director of Inbound Marketing at WhatCounts, a co-host of the Marketing Over Coffee podcast, and an active blogger at Awaken Your Superhero (christopherspenn.com). He frequency speaks on the intersection of marketing and technology. Most importantly, Penn does a lot of experimentation with email marketing;[2] specifically, testing out new ways to grow his list and engage his subscribers. He also breaks the rules of email marketing—often. We talk more about him in Part III, "Breaking the Rules."

Penn has been growing his email list since he sent his first newsletter in 2007. At the time of this writing, Penn's list has grown to more than 13,000 subscribers.

"On average, it grows 68 percent (compound growth rate) per year, from an initial seed list of 1,000 to today. Some years have obviously been better than others," Penn told us.

We sign up for a lot of emails—some for personal reasons, others for business, and some as research for this book. Of all the emails we've ever signed up for, Penn's does a great job in regards to setting proper expectations. On his newsletter opt-in landing page, he includes the following text:

> "So you're interested in subscribing to my newsletter? Good for you! Let me take a few moments to explain what you get by signing up for the newsletter. My newsletter, Almost Timely, is a roundup of the best stuff that's crossed my desk in the last week or so, from blog posts I've written to tool tips on Facebook to news I've shared on Twitter, plus the occasional career tip. I also share details about fellow newsletter subscribers you should meet and follow.

> "So, why would you want a newsletter when you could just read the blog or follow me on Twitter or become a fan on Facebook? Well, I know you're busy. I know you've got a million things to do, a lot going on, and

have a million different items vying for your attention every day. The newsletter provides a nice roundup of the week's stuff, stuff you don't want to let slip through the cracks. That's why you should subscribe to it."

Penn concludes the text on that page with the following: "Complete this short form and you'll begin receiving my newsletter. You'll get the most recent back issue as well." He tells his subscribers what to do and what they should expect after they click Submit.

Notice a few things that Penn does really well:

- He confirms that the reader is on the right page ("...subscribing to my newsletter.").

- He explains what the contents of the newsletter will include ("best stuff that's crossed my desk").

- He answers the one question that most people are likely to be thinking about ("why would you want a newsletter when...").

We asked Penn why he chooses to dedicate so much copy to explaining the sign-up process.

"Telling people what to expect and then meeting their expectations is the single best way to keep subscribers," he said. "If you say, 'hey, I'm going to email you three times a day with gigantic emails' and [they] still hit the subscribe button, then [they] expect three emails a day. I also explain why the newsletter exists in the first place, and if [they] agree with that logic, [they] sign up."

It's as simple as that.

Penn told us his email opt-in page is fairly active. "The page gets about 50 visitors a day. Of the people who visit that are new visitors (about 75 percent), about 25 percent subscribe." Although 25 percent might not sound like a super large number, in regard to conversions—especially email opt-ins—it's actually quite high.

Chris spends quite a bit of time promoting his subscription page and is adamant about ensuring the messaging is spot on.

"We live or die on our database," says Chris. "It's the only thing that's ours. Social media is nice and I'm an avid user of it, but at the end of the day, if we don't get people into a database of our own, then we're at the mercy of private corporations like Facebook and Twitter for our networks. That's not a super comfortable place to be. Having a newsletter means having control of your assets and network, and that in turn makes the subscription page and subscription mechanisms absolutely vital to get right."

Send a Welcome Email

Remember the exercise we had you go through in the beginning of Chapter 2? In case you forgot, we asked you to opt-in to emails from four different companies— one being your own. We also asked you to save any emails that you might have received. Hopefully you did!

Please go to the folder you saved those emails in and open them up. You have at least at few emails, right? If so, how many of those emails were sent to you the same day that you subscribed to that company's list? How many of those emails were what you would call a "Welcome" email? How many thanked you for sub- scribing and welcomed you to their email program?

We would venture to guess that at least one, and maybe even two or three, of those companies did not send a welcome email.

In 2008, Return Path, an email delivery services certification and scoring firm, found that 60 percent of the companies from the retail, consumer goods, travel, and media/entertainment industries that they researched did not send a welcome message to new subscribers.[3]

That's right—only 4 out of 10 companies are sending welcome emails. Said another way, 6 out of 10 are not taking the time to welcome their new subscribers with an email.

Who cares? Why does this matter? The answer is simple: The welcome email tends to have a much higher open rate compared to other emails in a campaign. In fact, according to some analysis done by the Experian CheetahMail Strategic Services Group, "Welcome emails generate four times the total open rates and five times the click rates compared to other bulk promotions."[4]

If you consider that the overall email industry average open rate is somewhere around 20 percent,[5] this figure is quite impressive.

A welcome email is a critical component of getting your email program off to a good start. It sets the stage—the tone—for the rest of the emails you will send. Not sending a welcome email equates to not thanking someone for a gift—it's bad form, bad karma. More importantly, a welcome email can increase your business and help you better understand your new subscribers.

Derek Halpern is the founder of Social Triggers, a blog that shows you how to attract leads and make sales by leveraging proven psychological principles on your website and in your email list. When we asked him which email has been his most successful, Halpern did not hesitate. "My welcome email. Not only does it tell me exactly who subscribes to my list, it also entices people to tell me what their prob- lems are...and how I can help them.

"This research is PRICELESS," Halpern continues. "I learn what my subscribers' problems are, and what they're struggling with, in their own words."

The following is the copy of the email Halpern sends. Notice that it's all text. We come back to that (and Halpern) in Part III of this book.

> *What's up {!firstname}?*
>
> *Thank you for signing up. Every week, you'll receive valuable advice that shows you how to turn web traffic into leads and sales.*
>
> *And if you're not getting traffic, I have advice for that too.*
>
> *Right now, I want you to do two things.*
>
> Thing #1:
>
> *Reply to this email and tell me what you're struggling with right now. Even if it's something really small, don't hesitate.*
>
> Thing #2:
>
> *Prepare yourself. I whipped together some great stuff for you, and you'll receive it soon, so keep an eye out.*
>
> *I look forward to hearing from you.*
>
> *Talk soon,*
>
> *Derek Halpern*

Besides the welcome message being all text, notice how conversational it is. Halpern believes this tone is why people respond. He says the answers he receives are sometimes pages long.

However, sending a welcome email is more than just the courteous thing to do. It also provides good data about deliverability. If you send an initial email and it bounces (does not get delivered) due to a bad email address or some other factor, you might have an issue with your opt-in process. The possibility exists that you are using pre-checked boxes and people are typing in false information. It's crazy, we know. However, we also know that it happens—intentionally or not.

If you find that a high percentage of your welcome emails are bouncing, you might consider putting extra measures in place to ensure the email address is valid. Many ways are available to do this validation. The one we see used most often asks people to type in their email address in one field and then confirm it (re-enter) in another. Services are also available that will validate email addresses in real time, and not let someone continue with the opt-in process with a bad email address. Either way, the welcome email provides this bounce data and informs you whether you need to change some processes.

Moreover, the welcome email is a chance to continue setting expectations about what your new subscriber will receive from you going forward. It should be consistent with the promise that you gave during the opt-in process. You did offer some type of promise, right? Some welcome emails also include a call to action, such as to sign up for a webinar, download a whitepaper, buy a product, click a link, and so on. Still others provide a link to the incentive that was promised during signup.

Another example of a well-done welcome email is from SkyMall. DJ opted in to the SkyMall email list in December of 2011, after purchasing a gift for his wife. (See, those in-flight SkyMall magazines do work!) SkyMall not only has its email sign-up form prominently placed on its homepage, right at the top, it also includes a bit of the "what's in it for me" tactic by adding the phrase, "exclusive offers." Moments after entering his email address and clicking the Sign Up button, DJ received the welcome email from SkyMall shown in Figure 3.2 in his inbox.

Figure 3.2   *This welcome email from SkyMall.com does a nice job thanking the new subscriber and telling her what she will get in return for the opt-in.*

The SkyMall.com welcome email does a few things very nicely. It includes a big header with its logo and a "Welcome to our email list" graphic. It also its new email subscriber and confirms the opt-in:

Thanks for joining our email list. You are now signed up to receive the latest and greatest from SkyMall.

Just below that message is a link back to the SkyMall.com website, a call to action to get you back to its website, where you can continue shopping! Skymall also does a nice job telling new subscribers what they will now receive as a result of their joining the program.

Even better is that the email marketing team from SkyMall fulfills its promise as outlined in the welcome email ("weekly emails with offers up to 30% off"). Since receiving the welcome email, DJ has gotten a weekly email from SkyMall with discounts ranging from 15 to 30 percent. SkyMall's frequency around the holiday season certainly picked up a bit more, but has since settled into seven to nine emails per month. DJ has yet to be automatically entered into a contest or sweepstakes (not that he's aware of, at least); however, this is not a huge deal for him.

Welcome emails can also be used to gain additional subscriber segmentation information. What calls-to-action subscribers click on in the welcome email can provide further insight into their interests. This data can be used to send an automated (triggered) email or put them on another list or segment to target in future email campaigns.

For example, in the SkyMall email in Figure 3.2, let's say the bullet point "Automatic entries into contests and sweepstakes" had been a link. SkyMall could put everyone who clicked that link into a new list called "interested in contests and sweepstakes." Then, when its next contest was beginning, it could send an email to that group as a "sneak peak" exclusive email.

We've also seen welcome emails asking subscribers to "tell us more about you." Folks who take the time to update their preferences get more targeted, relevant email delivered to their inbox.

Using an incentive is a nice way to grow your email list. If you promised an eBook, like Garrett did, be sure to include a link to download it in your welcome email. If you are a business-to-consumer (B2C) company, consider using your welcome emails to provide new subscribers a reason to return to the store (in-store coupon) or shop online (10% off next order). In the SkyMall example, it could have modified the main call to action to read: "As a thank you for subscribing, we'd like to offer you 10% off on your next order. Simply use Coupon Code 'WELCOME' when you check out. Shop Now to redeem your discount!"

One caution on welcome emails: Be careful that your first communication with your new subscriber is not overwhelming. Trying to include all of the examples listed above may clutter the email.

Remember, Make a Good First Impression

Whether you use a pre-checked box that drives more people to your list, clear instructions and information on what signing up for that list gets them, a welcome email that also lets them know what they're getting into, or a combination of the preceding, you must carefully consider the value a good first impression has in your email marketing life. Just throwing together an opt-in call to action and using the default welcome message your email marketing provider has might mean the difference between your audience feeling good about you, or thinking you're a weird neighbor with a staring problem.

The opt-in language you use with a check box or call to action, the explanation you give on your website or even in a video description of your newsletter, and the wording used in your initial welcome email does two powerful things for your email marketing and you:

- It sells you and the newsletter one last time.
- It establishes expectations for your audience.

Making your sign-up process cumbersome or confusing can force subscribers to give up. Clearly explaining to them what they'll get and how awesome it will be puts the icing on the cake of the sales job you've done so far in getting them interested. A great explanation of your newsletter or welcome email is like the car salesman handing you the keys, pointing out ahead of the car and saying, "The open road is yours, my friend! Drive it!" That extra kick in pants makes you take that first drive with a smile on your face.

Do that with your subscribers, too. Tell them how much smarter they're going to be when they start reading that newsletter. Reassure them that you're on the other end should they ever have any problems. Heck, even tell them how thankful you are they decided to join. They'll appreciate the warm welcome.

That warm welcome sets a tone for what's to come. They'll grow to expect that kind of friendly service, inspiration, or down-to-brass-tacks directness. However you write your welcome email or opt-in verbiage, whatever tone and voice, and whatever promises you make to your audience is what they'll expect email in and email out. Now your challenge is to deliver on that promise.

Before you do, though, you need to know a little more about emails, starting with the actual construction of one.

Endnotes

1. Parliament of Canada, Bill C-28, http://www.parl.gc.ca/
    HousePublications/Publication.aspx?Docid=4901869&file=4 accessed
    on March 11, 2012.

2. DJ worked with Chris at Blue Sky Factory in 2009 and 2010.

3. "Creating Great Subscriber Experiences: Are Marketers Relationship
    Worthy?" *Return Path*. http://www.returnpath.net/downloads/
    resources/GreatSubscriberExperiences.pdf accessed on March 11, 2012.

4. "The welcome email report: Benchmark data and analysis for engag-
    ing new subscribers through email marketing," *Experian Marketing
    Services*. http://www.experian.com/assets/marketing-services/
    white-papers/welcome-email-report.pdf accessed on March 14, 2012.

5. "Epsilon Q1 2011 EMAIL TRENDS AND BENCHMARKS, Average
    Volume Per Client Up Almost 40% Over Previous Year," June 2, 2011,
    http://www.epsilon.com/apac/download/q1-2011-email-trends-and-
    benchmarks accessed on March 17, 2012. **Note:** Open rates fluctuate
    greatly depending on industry, list source, and type of email. The 20
    percent figure is an overall average.

4

Examining an Email's Body Parts

At this point you might be thinking, "Wait. The title of this book is The Rebel's Guide to Email Marketing. *When do we start breaking the rules, raising all sorts of havoc, and winning?"*

Fair question.

We promise we are getting there. However, before we start mixing it up and ruffling some feathers, being on board with the fact that email is not dead is important. Understanding how to grow your email list is also critical so you have someone to read those rule-breaking emails of yours. Finally, you must be clear on the various components (parts) of an email marketing message because we'll be referencing them often in Part III, "Breaking the Rules."

In this chapter, we cover the structure of a typical email—from the "top" (Subject line and From name) to the "bottom" (footer)—and we outline the main sections that are included in most email marketing messages.

An email marketing message is made of up of many components, much like the human anatomy. Each of these parts plays a unique role, and each is critical to the makeup of the overall email.

Figure 4.1 shows an email from REI, a national store for outdoor activists and enthusiasts. We'll be referring to various components of this email throughout this chapter and Chapters 5–7 as we explain the different parts of an email marketing message. Note: Each number in Figure 4.1 corresponds to a section of the email detailed next.

Figure 4.1   *This email from REI shows all of the components of a well-written marketing message.*

The Subject Line and From Address

You make your first impression with the first thing subscribers see in their inbox. Quick. Without thinking too hard, what part of the email do you see first, before you open it? If you guessed the From name (sender name) or Subject line, you are correct! *Go to Appendix A for your prize.* These two components of the email are the two most important factors for determining whether or not an email gets opened.

Looking at Figure 4.2, we can see that REI does a nice job identifying itself using those two critical elements. Its From name, "REI Gearmail," clearly reflects the company name/brand (REI) as well as a qualifier for the name of its email campaigns (Gearmail). Additionally, the Subject line alerts subscribers to the contents of this email. Combine those two parts of the email, and a subscriber can decide if she wants to open that REI email.

| REI Gearmail | Skis, Boards and Expert Advice + Save on Fitness Gear at REI-OUTLET.com |

Figure 4.2 *Having an effective From name ("REI Gearmail") and Subject line ("Skis, Boards and..."), as shown in this REI email, is critical for achieving high open rates.*

As you'll learn in Chapter 5, "The First Impression," the Subject line and From address are critical for one primary metric you'll be interested in: open rates. Although we don't want to establish any "rules"—this is *The Rebel's Guide*—generally, no one wants to open an email that has a headline that screams, "I'm really boring," and is from CompanyABC@CompanyABC.com. You want one that screams, "If you don't open this right now, you're going to miss out on something awesome...like free chocolate!" And people probably feel better knowing the sender—at least enough to not need the incentive of free chocolate to entice them to open it.

The Preheader

Figure 4.3 shows the preheader (#2), the snippet of text that comes immediately before the header image or first line of copy in the body of an email. In many email clients such as Gmail, it's the line of text that you can see in the preview, next to the Subject line. An effective preheader can set the stage for the rest of the email as well as drive some clicks and conversions.

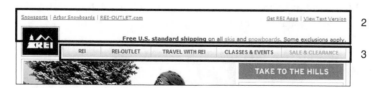

Figure 4.3 *Preheaders (#2) give the reader a bit of a tease in most inboxes and can lead readers to open more frequently if planned correctly.*

Whether you're offering free shipping, like in REI's example, sharing an inspirational quote, or teasing the main content to come, the preheader is just another reinforcement for your open rate efforts. If your email were an image, this would be its caption. Think about this real estate and how you can use it to make people say, "I think there really is free chocolate in here. I'd better open this email."

The Header

Moving down the email a bit, you find the header (#3), shown in Figure 4.4. Often a company logo or an image of some sort, this is the first visual that subscribers will see when they open your email. Not all emails include it because it takes up valuable real estate (or they simply forget to add it). Some headers include a navigation bar—one that has a similar look and feel to the sender's website, often with links back to that particular section.

Figure 4.4   *Assuming a preheader does not exist, the header (#3) is often the first thing a subscriber sees after opening the email.*

REI's header is narrow and mimics the company's website navigation with active links that send people to the homepage. Some companies replicate the masthead or banner from their website. Still others use large images that establish a mood or tone for the communications. Think of the header as the place you can whet the reader's appetite with a picture of the free chocolate, or show them where to click to find more information about your company, like how you make the chocolate.

The From name, Subject line, preheader, and header are the four components of an email that your readers see first. If you miss the boat here, you might never get a second chance to make a first (email) impression.

Table of Contents

Now we come to the main body of the email, where in traditional email newsletters, we often find a table of contents (TOC). Typically, a TOC is included in emails that are sent out less frequently (monthly) and have enough content to warrant a place to categorize what's included in the newsletter. Many traditional media companies that are making the transition to email marketing include a TOC. Some habits are hard to break. We're not suggesting a TOC is good or bad; just that sometimes it's part of an email, and sometimes it's not.

The TOC is a good idea if you pack a lot of information in your newsletter, as MarketingProfs does (see Figure 4.5). Having multiple sections, stories, coupons, or information requires a bit of navigation, so a TOC helps users find what they're really interested in. Using anchor tags, which most email marketing software companies enable you to add to an email, the link in the TOC will actually scroll the user's browser down to that section. The email might appear as if it is a microsite in and of itself, but nonetheless helps the reader get where they want to go. We'll talk a bit more about anchor tags in Chapter 6, "The Meat and Potatoes."

Figure 4.5 *This newsletter from MarketingProfs has a table of contents that links to different sections in the email.*

Keep in mind that, outside of a newsletter format—like the MarketingProfs example—very long emails (one where a reader has to scroll and scroll and scroll) are becoming less popular these days. Most people will not dedicate the time or effort to read through a 17-page email. Although long emails can still work in the business-to-business (B2B) "newsletter" space, they typically are not successful in a business-to-consumer (B2C) setting. However, you could always "break the rules" and test a long copy approach to see if it works for your audience. Be a rebel!

Main Call to Action

Just below the table of contents (or header if no table of contents is present), is the main call to action (#4), as shown in Figure 4.6. Also known as the CTA if you're hip, this is the action you are hoping subscribers take after opening the email. It's the strategic reason the email exists. It's what often matters most. Nearly every single email should include it.

Figure 4.6 *A call to action is the single-most important reason you're sending the email. REI does a nice job with this using the "Shop all snowsports" button (#4).*

Essentially, the main call to action is the single-most important reason you're sending your email. To know what to place in it, ask yourself these two questions:

- Why am I sending this email?
- What do I want people to do after reading it?

The answer to those questions, particularly the second one, will tell you what your primary call to action should be. We cover the main CTA more in Chapter 6.

Secondary Calls to Action

Below the main CTA are your secondary and tertiary CTAs, as shown in Figure 4.7 (#5). These calls to action are nice to include as long as they don't cannibalize the main call to action too much. Remember, the goal of most emails is to get a subscriber to take an action. In some cases you might want them to do more than one thing—click on a few links, click a few buttons, buy a few products, and so on—but be careful not to overdo it!

Figure 4.7 *Secondary and tertiary CTAs (#5) can be located below the main CTA or somewhere nearby. In this example, they are on the right side and below.*

Speaking of CTAs, should they all be buttons? What about links? Images? Images that are clickable? We discuss and answer these questions in Chapter 6.

Sharing Your Email

As we wrap up today's introduction to anatomy class, let's discuss one last component often included to finish off the email. Moving down the body of the message, you often find social sharing and social connection options, as shown in Figure 4.8 (#6). Including these links (or buttons or icons) can be a great way to expand the reach of your message and encourage your email marketing subscribers to follow you or your company on your social networks. We think this is so important that we've dedicated an entire part of the book to it—see Part IV, "Batman (Email Marketing) and Robin (Social Media)."

Figure 4.8 *Adding social sharing and connection elements (#6) to your emails makes it easier to grow your list and increase the reach (more views) of your email.*

Social sharing and forwarding buttons don't have to be at the end. (We realize we've not gotten to this part yet, but you'll soon learn we're not into rules.) Jason's emails from Social Media Explorer have sharing buttons at the top, which he believes (from testing them in other parts of his emails) encourages more people to click and share the emails. But for the sake of your anatomy class, we're covering it here because that's where many commercial email newsletters choose to place these buttons.

The Footer

Finally, we come to the bottom of the email—the "feet" if you will. The very bottom of any email, the footer (#7), is where marketers include disclaimers, their physical address (required by the CAN-SPAM Act), preferences center, and the unsubscribe link. Part III covers more about the unsubscribe link and whether it should always be in the footer, but typically, that's where it's found—in the bottom, somewhat obscure, sometimes hard to find. Can you find it in Figure 4.9?

Keep in mind that, like the social sharing and forwarding elements, the unsubscribe link and other parts of an email won't always be in footers, at the end of the body copy and so forth. As we'll discuss in later chapters when we dive a bit deeper

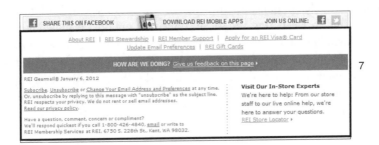

Figure 4.9 *The footer—as can be seen in this email from REI (#7)—contains important information, including the unsubscribe link (usually).*

into the anatomy of an email, sometimes sharing buttons can be more effective at the top of the email, spattered throughout, or next to each section or article. Sometimes, unsubscribe buttons are better used near the top. But don't fret about these things yet. We just want you to know an email's elements before we start dissecting them.

Now you know the anatomy of an email, let's start operating. Okay, maybe that's a bit too gory of an analogy. Let's go through these elements and talk about the strategies you could use with each one to optimize your email marketing programs. We'll start where your audience starts—the first impression.

5

The First Impression

If you lived through the '80s and '90s in the United States, it's likely that you've seen the famous Head & Shoulders dandruff shampoo television commercials that ended with the catchy phrase, "You never get a second chance to make a first impression." These first impressions are pretty important in both the offline and online worlds. If you navigate to a webpage or blog and the creative (graphics) or content (text) does not draw you in immediately, it's likely that you will be gone—never to return. The same holds true with email.

The first impression in the email marketing world is typically delivered in the form of the Subject line, From name, preheader, and header. When you optimize those four areas to make your subscribers notice the email and either trust that it is worth opening or feel curious to know what's in the communication, your open rates go up, as do your subscribers.

This chapter discusses those various components of an email marketing message—the parts that are imperative to have well thought out as they are the first your readers will see. Get them right and you'll keep subscribers coming back for more. Miss the boat, and you may have lost them.

From Name and Subject Line

If we were to pick two areas that are the most important to generating an open, they would be the From name and Subject line. When paired together, they are like a good shampoo. You don't want someone ignoring, deleting, or marking your email as spam because of a bad first impression. In other words, you don't want dandruff.

Think about your own personal email experience. When an email lands in your inbox—whether it be on your desktop, laptop, smartphone, or tablet—what do you see? *Hint: It's not a pretty image, a company logo, or a compelling offer/call to action.* Nope. In most email clients, only two components of an email message are visible before it's opened: the From name and the Subject line. Other than the pre-header (snippet text), which we cover later in this chapter, that's it!

Making the most of both of those components is critical. The From name, some-times called the "From line," "Sender," or "Sender name," is simply the name of the person/company/brand that is sending the email. Best practices would dictate the From name should be clear and recognizable. In other words, if your company name is Best Buy, the email should come from Best Buy—not Richard Schulze (the founder of Best Buy). However, if the email is personal, the From name is usually the name of the person sending the email. In the case of an email marketing mes-sage, the From name is usually the company or brand name. In other instances, the From name is a combination of a person's name as well as the company name. Sometimes, the From name is a word such as *marketing,* or *info,* or even the dreaded *donotreply.*

Let's once again revisit those emails you subscribed to back in Chapter 2, "How to Grow Your List." Of those companies who sent a welcome email, what did they use as their From name? What does the From name of your company's email market-ing message look like?

A quick scan of some emails in DJ's inbox revealed the From names shown in Figure 5.1.

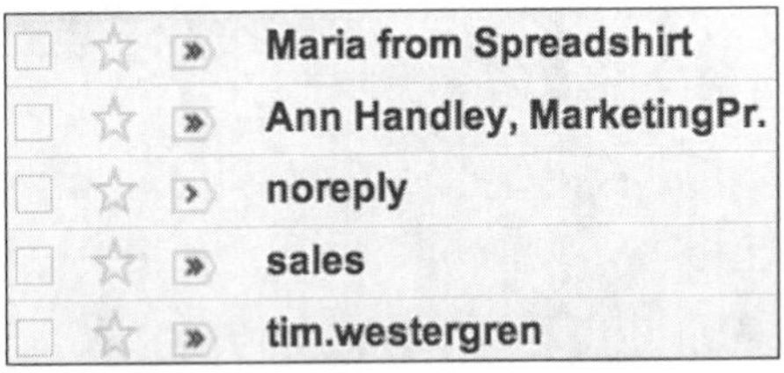

Figure 5.1   *Some of the From names in DJ's inbox are hard to tell who they're actually from.*

Which From names in Figure 5.1 are clear and recognizable? If those marketing emails were in your inbox, which ones would you be more likely to open? Which ones might you skip over or delete before reading? What if we told you that Tim Westergren was the founder of Pandora and "sales" in this case was really from GoDaddy? How about if we said "noreply" was an email from Sprint? If you had seen an email from Pandora or GoDaddy or Sprint (versus Tim Westergren, sales, and noreply) would you have been more likely to recognize it?

The From name is that first impression. It's a chance to introduce yourself to a potential reader, an opportunity to build trust and recognition. Can you imagine walking into a party and saying, "Hi. My name is sales."? The From name is super important. Before you click Submit on your next email marketing message, be sure you know what the From name is.

Equally as important as the From name is the Subject line, which most often describes what subscribers can expect when they open the email. It's the headline, not all that different from a headline in a newspaper or magazine (or blog post title for that matter). In regards to email marketing, the Subject line can range from the generic, such as "February 23,[1] 2012 Newsletter," to the more descriptive, such as "20% Off Our Entire Fall Catalog," to the teaser, such as "Spoiler Alert: You're Only a Click Away From..." Along with the From name, the Subject line is one of the first things your eyes are drawn to when scanning your inbox.

The email marketing purists will tell you some best practices exist in regard to Subject lines, such as ensuring the optimal length and number or characters as well as avoiding certain words. However, the truth is different things work for different people. We talk more about breaking the "rules" of Subject lines in Part III, "Breaking the Rules."

Once again, take a look at the Subject lines of the emails you received from Chapter 2's exercise. Our guess is that they're all over the place. Some likely have the word "welcome" or "thanks" somewhere in them, while others omit those types of words. Some might be quite generic and vanilla, while others are more descriptive and intriguing.

What do your company's email marketing Subject lines say? At what end of the continuum do they fall—generic or descriptive?

Many of the email marketing practitioners would suggest that Subject lines should be short, descriptive, and enticing enough to get someone to open. Although that may work for some audiences, it certainly is not the case for all. We'll talk more about breaking the rules of subject lines in Chapter 9, "My Word! You Must Read This Now!," but for the purposes of this chapter, let's keep an open mind while we look at some of the email Subject lines in DJ's inbox (Figure 5.2).

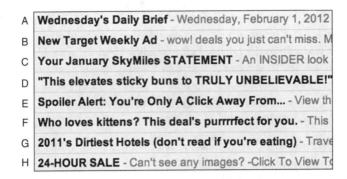

A	**Wednesday's Daily Brief** - Wednesday, February 1, 2012
B	**New Target Weekly Ad** - wow! deals you just can't miss. M
C	**Your January SkyMiles STATEMENT** - An INSIDER look
D	**"This elevates sticky buns to TRULY UNBELIEVABLE!"**
E	**Spoiler Alert: You're Only A Click Away From...** - View th
F	**Who loves kittens? This deal's purrrrfect for you.** - This
G	**2011's Dirtiest Hotels (don't read if you're eating)** - Trave
H	**24-HOUR SALE** - Can't see any images? -Click To View To

Figure 5.2   *From this list of Subject lines in DJ's inbox, which one would you be most likely to open?*

If the emails in Figure 5.2 were in your inbox, which ones would you be most likely to open? Which would you delete before even reading? Which jump off the page and which blend in and get lost?

Let's take a little quiz to see whether you can figure out who sent which of those emails. Look at the subject lines A through H in Figure 5.2. Now see whether you can match each with the company that sent it by drawing a line from the letter representing the Subject line to the company you think it belongs to:

A	Delta Air Lines
B	Overstock.com
C	Target.com
D	The Huffington Post
E	Fabric.com
F	The King Arthur Flour Company
G	TripAdvisor
H	BustedTees

Now back to analyzing the Subject lines. To be clear, we are not telling you which Subject line is the *best in all instances*. Nor are we saying that one Subject line is always more effective than another. In fact, you might be surprised by which of the Subject lines performed best for various senders. The bottom line is this: The Subject line is another critical component in getting a subscriber to open your emails. Take time to think about what works best for your audience. Test it. (Chapter 9 talks about testing Subject lines in more detail.)

Keep in mind that the From name and Subject line are paired together, side by side, for every email. Most people look at one or the other, but some scan both. If

Answers: A—The Huffington Post; B—Target.com; C—Delta Air Lines; D—The King Arthur Flour Company; E—BustedTees; F—Fabric.com; G—TripAdvisor; H—Overstock.com.

your From names are easily recognized and trusted and your Subject lines generate an open, you've successfully navigated an important step in an effective email marketing program.

If you've made it this far, either your Subject line, From name, or a combination of the two, has enticed someone to open the email. That's pretty important because if they don't open your email, other than the brand impression the From name and Subject line can leave, not much else in the email really matters. An unopened email can't be read. Other then being forwarded, it can't be shared. It can't have links or buttons clicked, and it's unlikely to get you anywhere near the $40.56 average return on investment (ROI) figure.

BREAKING THE RULES: THE SUBJECT LINE

Industry best practices have always said that your Subject line should be unique and stand out. LockerGnome Founder, Chris Pirillo, nailed this "rule" when he sent an email with the Subject line, "Snellipg, Lkie Puncttaliuy, Cnuots." His entire email introduction for that message was delivered using the Cambridge University theory that the human mind doesn't need a word to be spelled correctly in order to decipher it. Only the first and last letter need be correct. Pirillo hit the catchy, unique subject line squarely on the head for this communique.

But you don't have to be as clever as Pirillo to deliver a good Subject line. In fact, you don't even have to use one that's all that interesting. Message Systems, a company that offers—wait for it—email and text messaging services, has a quarterly newsletter that is informative and entertaining for customers and similarly interested audiences of the company. Yet, the Subject line for its winter 2012 offering was, "Message Systems Winter 2012 Newsletter." Yawn.

Boring as the Subject line might seem, the email performed fairly well, generating nearly a 20 percent open rate. Provided the content in your newsletters is good and the audience expectation is there, a dud of a headline can still come with high open rates and even buzz around your content. The expectations of the audience are what matter most.

BREAKING THE RULES: THE FROM NAME

Message Systems is also an example of a company breaking the rules in the From name field. Its winter 2012 newsletter had a From name of "The Team," which offers nothing at all personal. "The Team" seems so vague and non-committal. It might even turn off a potential reader. However, Message Systems bucked the "rule" and was still successful—that email generated nearly a 20 percent open rate.

Conversely, MoveOn.org is an organization that, like Pirillo with the Subject line, staked its claim on a unique use of the From name. In a February 6, 2012, email from MoveOn.org to its email marketing list, the From name was actually that of a guest writer who contributed the copy of the email. Frederick Raven was a member of MoveOn.org, but not an employee or staff member. The From address was a help account at MoveOn.org, too, further signifying that the organization was simply using a third-party author's content as its email newsletter.

What this name strategy does is create an immediate sense of credibility for and gives a human touch to the marketing effort. Logically, let's hold true the argument that most people are more likely to open an email with a person's name in the From field than that of a company or organization. MoveOn.org is increasing its chances of its email effort being seen by humanizing that data point. The fact the email pays off by being a personal letter from Raven to other MoveOn.org members only enhances the effort by making the message more personal.

Whether Subject line or From name, the rules don't always have to apply for you to have email marketing success.

Preheader

The preheader, sometimes called the snippet text, is the part of the email that is immediately above the header. It's often the first text that you see when you open an email. Also, in many email clients, such as Gmail, the preheader is the few words of introductory text that are visible before you open an email (see Figure 5.3).

| Nike.com | Off-the-Court Gear in Tournament Colors | Our latest basketball-inspired collection Plus: Take an extra 20% off clearance. Can't see . |

Figure 5.3   *The preheader is visible in many email clients before opening the message. We've highlighted it here with a box.*

Many email marketers use the preheader space for reminders, such as

- "To view this email in your browser, click here" or "Can't see images? Click here."

- "Please add xxx@xxx.com to your address book" or "Don't forget to add us to your whitelist." (Contacts added to a whitelist have a better chance of getting delivered to the inbox and not sent to spam.)

Angie's List, as you can see in Figure 5.4, includes the ability for its subscribers to view the email with images in a browser by using the "Go here" link. It also makes an easy task of sending the email to a friend (via the "Invite a friend" link) or adding its email address to your address book. Finally, Angie's List includes a way for its readers to update their email preferences and unsubscribe from these types of emails—all in the preheader.

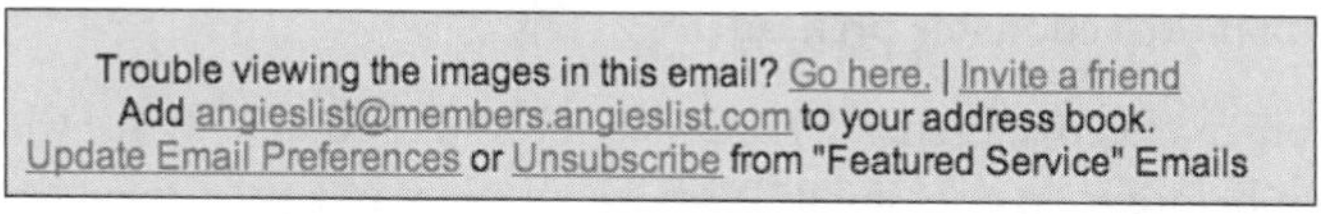

> Trouble viewing the images in this email? Go here. | Invite a friend
> Add angieslist@members.angieslist.com to your address book.
> Update Email Preferences or Unsubscribe from "Featured Service" Emails

Figure 5.4   *This email from Angie's List has a fairly standard, traditional preheader.*

Over the past few years, many email marketers have realized how valuable the preheader real estate can be. Instead of using it to just alert their subscribers about viewing the email in their browser or adding them to their address book, many marketers are now adding actionable text and links. Often, these links are used to generate more conversions. See Figure 5.5, from an REI email.

Figure 5.5   *This email from REI includes a preheader that uses links as calls to action. Denoted as #2 in this image.*

Notice how REI's preheader includes links to its snowsports and Arbor snowboards sections on REI.com as well as a link to the REI OUTLET online store. But that's not all. The top right of the preheader includes links to access REI apps and view the text-only, mobile-friendly version of the email.

REI has taken the preheader a step further than most companies—really taking advantage of the real estate—and included links to free shipping on its ski and snowboard sections of its website. It hopes its subscribers click on those links, go directly to specific pages on its website, and purchase items (convert).

Many marketers are finding pretty good success by spending time focusing on the preheader:

"[We saw] a 35 percent click through (of the opens) [increase] to...a 51 percent click through after optimizing the preheader," said Andy Thorpe, Deliverability and Compliance Manager at Pure360, an email service provider. "The preheader call to action was the third most clicked link, behind the text link in the header and the text link at the bottom."

Take a look at those emails you opted in for in Chapter 2. Do any of them include preheaders? We would venture to bet that most of them do; however, it's likely they're the standard "view in browser" or "add to address book." Are there any emails with more actionable preheaders?

Simply put, an effective preheader allows a subscriber to quickly see what the email is all about before even opening it. It's the equivalent of a preview pane. It has the potential to increase open rates, click-throughs, and conversions. It also can reduce spam complaints.

With more people reading emails on their mobile devices, a well-designed pre-header is becoming increasingly important. If you think real estate is limited in an email that lands in someone's inbox, try comparing that to the amount of visible text when an email is viewed on a smartphone with a much smaller screen!

Many marketers craft their preheader message to be consistent with the Subject line and main call to action. The preheader serves as an extension to the Subject line. This approach ensures a smooth transition from Subject line to preheader to call to action. The repetitiveness reinforces the action that marketers want their subscribers to take, often resulting in more opens, clicks, and conversions. To be clear, consistent and repetitive does not necessarily mean you use the same wording in all three parts of the email, although you could.

It's also worth testing a different approach. Instead of having the preheader call to action be the same as the call to action in the body of the email, we've seen some marketers use that space to promote a secondary or tertiary call to action (more about calls to action in Chapter 6, "The Meat and Potatoes").

Another effective technique to use in preheader text is to keep the language creative and enticing. For example, instead of "view with images" try using "Click here for free shipping." Basically, you are giving subscribers a reason to view the email in their browser. You are giving them a reason to click through. Also, try using creative language such as "Can't see this? Turn images on!" to keep the email light and fun, something that can help your email stand out in a crowded inbox.

BREAKING THE RULES: THE PREHEADER

WhatToExpect.com is an information resource for expecting parents. In addition to scads of neat resources on its website, the company also produces an e-newsletter that includes two very peculiar items, one in the preheader, another in the header, that break the mold of what email marketing best practices have always been.

The WhatToExpect preheader (see Figure 5.6) tells subscribers why they're receiving the newsletter (because they subscribed), but then gives them an opportunity to unsubscribe before they ever get to the content! The traditional marketer would scoff at such a notion. Why would you ever want to make opting out of your newsletter obvious or easy for someone? Because you want to be a good steward of their attention, that's why.

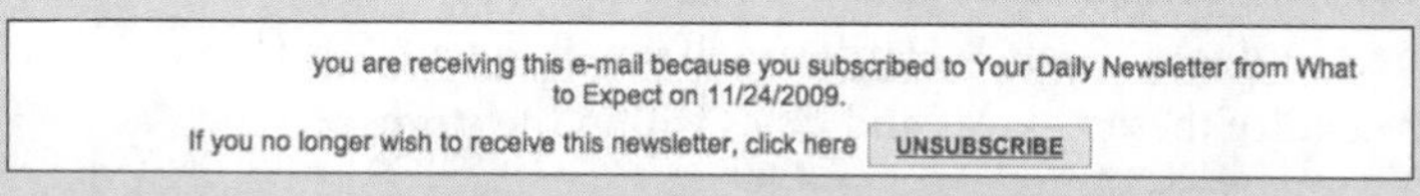

you are receiving this e-mail because you subscribed to Your Daily Newsletter from What to Expect on 11/24/2009.
If you no longer wish to receive this newsletter, click here   UNSUBSCRIBE

Figure 5.6   *The WhatToExpect preheader includes a prominent option to unsubscribe.*

By placing an unsubscribe link in the preheader, WhatToExpect.com is making sure its audience knows it has control over whether or not the company can continue to market to them through email. Making unsubscribing easy and obvious is a subtle way to build trust from the audience as well. Plus, it helps keep your open rates strong because those who aren't really interested in the emails anymore can simply opt out. We dive deeper into unsubscribes in Part III.

If you think slapping an unsubscribe link in the preheader goes a little against the grain, wait until you see what WhatToExpect.com does with the header of its email.

Header

As we continue through this anatomy lesson, we arrive at the head, er...header of the email. Note that when we refer to a header, we are not talking about the more technical definition of an email header—the one that includes Delivered To, Received by, Received from, Authentication-Results, DKIM and SPF information, and other email delivery terminology. Instead, we are referring to the first part of an email that subscribers see after they open your message—assuming a preheader does not exist.

Head back to your inbox and pull up some of the emails you subscribed to in Chapter 2. After you open the email, what is the first thing you see at the top? If it's an image (like a company logo) or a combination of an image with text, then you are likely viewing the header.

In addition to an image or logo, many email marketers choose to include some form of navigation that is consistent with the navigation on their website. This navigation is in the form of a series of tabs at the bottom of the header. However, these tabs are actually links back to specific areas on the company website or blog. If the company is a business-to-consumer (B2C) organization, these links often point to a specific product category. For example, as you can see in Figure 5.7, The Home Depot's navigation buttons are linked to Appliances, Bath, Lighting, Fans, Flooring, Outdoors, Tools & Hardware. If you frequent The Home Depot, you'll likely recognize these as areas and aisles within the store.

Figure 5.7 *The Home Depot does a nice job of making its navigation buttons in its email consistent with those on the website.*

Bonus

The Home Depot is also using this email as an opportunity to grow its email list. Assuming someone is reading this email through a social share or "forward to a friend," The Home Depot provides him with a way to sign up for "exclusive savings." Nice!

Including navigation buttons in the header is an easy way to direct subscribers back to your website, a place where (you hope) they will ultimately buy something. If they buy enough, you start to inch closer to that $40.56 ROI number we discussed in the Introduction.

Some B2C companies use the header navigation to highlight a link to their sale or discounted items section of their website. In this case, the "sale" link or button usually stands out in some way, possibly appearing in a larger font or red type instead of black (See Figure 5.8 from chiasso).

Figure 5.8 *chiasso uses the header navigation to highlight its sale center (in red in the original color email).*

Some marketers use the header space to include social sharing or social connection icons. We talk more about this topic in Chapter 7, "The Finishing Touches."

The header is an important part of any open email message. It's often what readers' eyes are first drawn to. It's an opportunity for brand recognition and to earn trust—assuming they have a favorable impression of your company, brand, or you as an individual.

And don't forget the animated header. Animated images were the rage in the mid- to late 90s. It would seem they are making a comeback. While somewhat challenging to show in a printed book, Figure 5.9 is a static version of a Starbucks reminder email that uses an animated image.

Figure 5.9 *Starbucks includes an animated image in this email. The stars are moving as if is falling from the sky!*

Close your eyes. Imagine that logo had confetti in the shape of stars weaving in and out of it, almost falling from the sky. Now you have a pretty good idea of what this animated header image from Starbucks looked like. We're not necessarily suggesting that you create animated headers, or use animation at all, for all of your email campaigns, but it might be worth trying. It certainly caught our eye and got us to click. Success!

BREAKING THE RULES: THE HEADER

So are you ready to hear what WhatToExpect.com does with its header? Can you believe it uses the space to place a banner advertisement for someone else's product (see Figure 5.10)? It's true. Frankly, it's valuable real estate, so if you follow an advertising model and can sell the space and build a nice sized list, well, you have a revenue source.

Figure 5.10   *The header of a WhatToExpect.com email shows a banner advertisement for someone else's product.*

In most cases, we wouldn't recommend putting someone else's product or service ahead of your own in your email list, but keep in mind that WhatToExpect.com is actually a media resource for soon-to-be-parents that is largely supported by advertising. So in its business model, using the header for advertising makes sense. What the approach dictates, however, is that WhatToExpect.com must produce such great content with the rest of its email newsletter that its audience will still open and consume it, despite the advertisement and potential distraction of someone else's product or service.

You Don't Need a Second Chance Do You?

Remember that you don't get a second chance to make that first impression. Through your Subject line, From name, preheader, and header, you're essentially reaching out your hand, smiling, and introducing yourself to your audience. And you're doing it in email after email, day after day. Unless or until people absolutely know and trust your email is going to be ultimately useful to them, you're making that first impression each time you click the Send button.

So now let's focus on making that email content so good that whether to open it isn't even a question for your audience. The content you provide might not make people open the email at first, but it should after they get used to the value you provide there. This content, whether it's information, entertainment, or even coupons or promotions, is what we call the meat and potatoes of your email.

Endnote

1. This happens to be DJ's birthday. Yes, he's still accepting presents.

6

The Meat and Potatoes

So, you made the first impression. It was successful. Your email was not deleted, archived, marked as spam, or otherwise ignored. Instead, it was opened. Congratulations.

One could argue that getting someone to open your email is one of the most difficult parts of email marketing. Most people receive a ton of email every day. Many delete much of that email without ever reading it. In fact, according to Merckle, a customer relations marketing agency, "subscribers that receive promotional permission email estimate that they delete 55 percent without opening."[1]

Couple this 55 percent of emails that are deleted without opening figure with the industry averages open rate near 20 percent—if people are opening your emails consistently, you are doing something right.

However, getting someone to open an email is just the beginning. Ultimately, we all want our subscribers to actually read our emails. Depending on the type of email, we also are hoping for subscribers to take some action—click a button or link, download a whitepaper, view a video, sign up for a webinar, or buy a product.

Now let's move the discussion from the From name and Subject line (external to the email) and the preheader (external/internal) and the header (internal) to the meat and potatoes of an email. This part of the email helps to drive action and is what we'll cover in this chapter. For some emails, this call to action starts with the table of contents.

Table of Contents

A *table of contents* (TOC) is typically what you see in a book (like this one) or a magazine. It lists the contents of the document, broken into the order they appear—Introduction, Chapter 1, Chapter 2, and so on. Magazines often have a type of TOC that includes a bit more of a teaser about each article or section. Either way, the point of a TOC is to give readers an idea of what information the book or magazine contains.

Email marketing messages that include a TOC are not much different. Email TOCs range from the basic, such as a list of the various sections within an email newsletter, to the more advanced—such as a format that enables readers to quickly scan the top of the email and click a link to jump to the section in which they are most interested. In online marketing speak, the "jump" refers to what's known as an *anchor* link. Clicking on this link takes the reader to that particular section in the email.

Not every email will or should have a table of contents. It's utilized most often by more traditional media and/or publishing companies. Additionally, if an email is extremely long (more than a few printed pages), then including a TOC to break up the copy and enable subscribers to read just those sections they are most interested in is common.

Zappos's Digest TOC Email

Online retailer, Zappos, is one such company who includes a TOC in some of its emails. On occasion, they send a "digest" email—one that highlights many of their items for sale—that includes an "IN THIS ISSUE" section. This functions as a TOC, as shown in Figure 6.1.

As you can see in Figure 6.1, the Zappos "IN THIS ISSUE" TOC informs its subscribers of what's included in the email. It's one of the more basic TOCs out there. Zappos doesn't use anchor links or make the email fancy in any way. Instead, it chooses to keep it simple and direct. You'll find out more about mostly text emails in Chapter 10, "The Perfect-Looking Email."

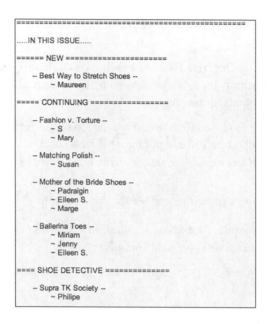

```
=========================================================
.....IN THIS ISSUE.....

====== NEW =======================

    -- Best Way to Stretch Shoes --
          ~ Maureen

===== CONTINUING ==================

    -- Fashion v. Torture --
          ~ S
          ~ Mary

    -- Matching Polish --
          ~ Susan

    -- Mother of the Bride Shoes --
          ~ Padraigin
          ~ Eileen S.
          ~ Marge

    -- Ballerina Toes --
          ~ Miriam
          ~ Jenny
          ~ Eileen S.

==== SHOE DETECTIVE ===============

    -- Supra TK Society --
          ~ Philipe
```

Figure 6.1   *This digest email from Zappos includes a very basic table of contents. This email is also mostly text.*

MarketingProfs's Approach to Email Table of Contents

MarketingProfs, with a list size of nearly 500,000 subscribers, has been doing email marketing since the turn of the millennium. Email marketing is a critical part of its business model.

As Ann Handley, Chief Content Officer at MarketingProfs and co-author of *Content Rules* (Wiley, 2011) said, "From its early incarnation, email is the Gorilla glue that helps cement relationships with our subscribers. With every bit of emailed content we send out, I hope to deliver great information, useful know-how, excellent content, and top-shelf advice. My job—in a big way—is in service to our email subscribers, our members. Because to paraphrase country music's Tracy Byrd... *'When they ain't happy, no one's happy.'*"

MarketingProfs's VP of Marketing, Anne Yastremski, says that email marketing is the company's main source of revenue and at the center of all marketing-related campaigns. It sends close to one million emails each week (not including e-newsletters). "As you can imagine," says Yastremski, "the marketing team spends the majority of each week on email campaign planning, creative, segmentation, list management, and reporting to make sure we get the most return from our investment in email marketing."

When it relaunched *MarketingProfs Today* as a daily email in January 2011, the team saw it as an opportunity for redesign. According to Handley, the team chose to include a table of contents for two reasons:

- Newsletter headlines and content would appear "above the fold." In other words, subscribers would not have to scroll down to access the day's content (and it could be seen in many email client preview windows).

- In one quick glance, a subscriber can see the day's offering.

"We know a daily email equals a lot of communication—this was our attempt to make it less weighty, more accessible," said Handley.

However, the MarketingProfs's TOC is not your average one, as shown in Figure 6.2.

Figure 6.2   *MarketingProfs's daily email has a table of contents whose links go to specific landing pages.*

In contrast to the Zappos email, MarketingProfs uses its TOC as an opportunity to get more subscribers to click through to an article or blog post on its website. The MarketingProfs TOC serves a few purposes, one of which is to list the various content blocks (sections) of the email. This allows readers to skim what's "in this issue" and quickly decide what's most interesting to them. However, these links are not the traditional anchor tags that are often utilized in an email TOC. Instead, each link redirects to a specific landing page—an article, a blog post, and so on—on one of the MarketingProfs websites.

"We didn't want to force our subscribers to click or scroll more than necessary," said Handley. "An anchor link would necessitate a second click (once to the in-newsletter headline, then a second click through to the site). That's unnecessary, and you risk annoying (or losing) readers along that path."

Besides making it easier for readers to quickly access the content, another advantage of this approach is that the email service provider (ESP) can track the click-through numbers and provide MarketingProfs rich data on which and how many subscribers are taking action on each link in the TOC. This allows MarketingProfs to segment its users based on links they click and make some educated guesses on which content is most appealing to each reader.

In the first quarter of 2012, the top-ten content links in terms of unique website page views were all from the table of contents links. In fact, among the top 400 content links in the *MarketingProfs Today* daily email, the table of contents links accounted for 63 percent of the unique website page views.

Open a few of the emails you opted in for in Chapter 2, "How to Grow Your List." Do any of them contain a table of contents? If so, what does it look like: the more traditional one listing what's in the newsletter, or topics linked like the MarketingProfs example? Does your personal or company email newsletter contain a TOC?

BREAKING THE RULES: TABLE OF CONTENTS

Can you think of an email that wouldn't need a table of contents? Sure you can. If your email content is a daily deal or coupon or just a short update with one big idea rather than a lengthy newsletter-style communication, you won't need one. AppSumo, a daily deal email for technology and software specials, makes its email offers super simple by offering just the deal of the day and a big button (View Deal) to click through to its website and purchase the deal (see Figure 6.3). Because of the simplicity and length, a table of contents isn't necessary.

The table of contents is more convenient for readers if there are multiple sections of content they might want to skip ahead to, or if so much content is in the email they might want to come back and read through the email later. AppSumo is not only a nice example of an email that uses few words, but also one of presenting a main call to action.

Figure 6.3   *AppSumo doesn't need a table of contents because its email contains one big idea rather than many small ones.*

Main Calls to Action

Let's now move to the actual body of the email. The main call to action (CTA) is the purpose of your email marketing message. It's what you want your subscribers to see, read, click, or do. It's the action you want them to take. Ideally, you make the offer so compelling (*"Holy cow! This is great!"*) that they have no other choice but to click.

In many cases, the main CTA is similar to the Subject line and can be an extension of it. Remember: The goal of the Subject line is to get someone to open your email. If the Subject line includes a promise of "Free Shipping" or information on an upcoming webinar, ensuring that the main CTA is consistent is important. Make it easy for your subscribers to quickly respond to your message.

An email CTA is not all that different from any other CTA. Let's compare it to a few more traditional and new media examples:

- **Television commercials:** Think back to the last TV commercial you watched. What was it about? What did the advertiser want you to do? Go to a website? Call a super-special number? That website or phone number is the call to action.

- **Outdoor billboard:** Considering many billboards are located on the side of highways, they have to get their point across quickly and succinctly. Similarly to a TV commercial, many include a website or phone number as their main call to action, or the simple instruction to exit now and eat!
- **Social media updates** (Tweets, Facebook status updates, Google+ posts, and so on): When using social media for marketing purposes, you have a limited number of characters to get someone to take action. Most often, a link is that main call to action, directing your community to a website or landing page where they can learn more.

Look at the emails you opted in for in Chapter 2. Do they all have a main call to action? Is it clear and obvious what the goal of the email is, what action the sender wants you to take? If you are having trouble answering that question, the email likely lacks a call to action.

Think about the call to action in your email campaigns. Is it working? Are your subscribers clicking through? Are they reading that article you point them to? Are they buying the product you want them to? If not, it's worth considering running some split tests, keeping one email the same and changing the other in some way. Most email marketing providers will allow you to test one email's creative (copy and/or artwork) against another. Try setting up a few tests, such as these:

- **Size of button:** Test a large button versus a smaller one.
- **Placement of button:** Test the button left justified versus centered versus right justified in your email layout.
- **Frequency of button:** Test putting the same button in multiple places in your email.
- **Button versus link versus images:** Test different types of calls to action.

Digitwirl founder Carley Knobloch, whom we first introduced in Chapter 2, relies heavily on email marketing to drive website and video views. She told us that her typical open rates are between 45 and 55 percent—well above industry averages. Additionally, her click-through rates average around 20 percent. Not bad.

"I completely credit [these high rates] to fantastic content...content [that] is solving a problem...making it very relevant," she said. "We only produce one show per week so we always try to 'knock it out of the park.' The email is no more than three to four sentences long with a prompt to click on the video."

That prompt is her call to action.

Check out an example of the Digitwirl email in Figure 6.4. Can you spot the main call to action?

Figure 6.4 *This Digitwirl email has a simple call to action—a red Read More button.*

If you guessed the Read More button, give yourself a high five. However, notice that this email also includes a link call to action ("last-minute planning") as well as an image call to action (an iPhone with "Love You" on it). If clicked on, all three of these CTAs send subscribers to the same landing page, which details Digitwirl's weekly tip and includes the embedded video.

Whatever method you choose to showcase your call to action, it is the authors' strong belief that every single email marketing message needs one. Why bother sending out an email if you don't have a purpose to fulfill, a goal to achieve, or an action you want your subscribers to take?

What's important is to test. What works for some subscribers might not work for others. Try sending out the exact same email with one small change: Instead of using a button as your main call to action, replace it with a link. See what happens. How does that change impact your click-through rate? Your social shares? Your conversions?

BREAKING THE RULES: CALLS TO ACTION

An email without a call to action, at least from a marketing perspective, is more than likely a wasted effort. Sure, it might be nice to email your customers from time to time and say, "We appreciate you. That's all." But even then, you'll probably include a subtle CTA for email recipients to check out the latest catalog or share the email with friends.

The general rule in email marketing has always been to make your call to action big, obvious, and in many cases red (or orange). Above the fold is better than below it, and placing the main CTA throughout the email in a few places is also said to work well. But what about those emails that are intended to be informative or educational rather than sales driven? What about the occasional note from the CEO that just expresses some level of gratitude or information to the audience? In some, albeit rare, cases, a CTA can be a distraction from the point of the email.

AirTran's email newsletter sent to its A+ Rewards customers (see Figure 6.5) after the announcement the airline would merge with Southwest Airlines became a platform to inform customers of how service and their relationship with AirTran would change. Communicating the information effectively was imperative to retain the company's loyal customers as they made the transition to a new brand. Slapping a big CTA in the middle of these communications could have distracted the audience from the real point.

Figure 6.5   *AirTran subtly placed its CTA in its emails to customers about its integration with Southwest Airlines. (Image not meant to be read in detail.)*

AirTran placed only one main call to action in the email and placed it at the bottom of the communication so as to not distract the audience from the important instructions and information in the meat of the email. Notice that Figure 6.5 has a dotted line in the middle as well. The actual AirTran email was rather lengthy, so we had to crop out much of the image so it would fit here. The chances that many people actually saw the CTA, much less clicked on it, are far less than if AirTran had placed it at the top of the document, made it bigger, and called more attention to the request. But the point of the email—to communicate key changes in the customer experience—was met because it broke the rule of CTAs being big and obvious.

Secondary and Tertiary Calls to Action

As we introduced briefly in Chapter 5, "The First Impression," the secondary and tertiary calls to action are typically less prominent in the email. They are often "below the fold" (meaning you have to scroll down a bit to see them). Sometimes they are on the sidebar or closer to the footer of the email (see Figure 6.6). Suffice it to say, these calls to action are not usually the first thing that catches a reader's eye.

Figure 6.6   *An email from REI shows a secondary call to action (#5), both on the right sidebar and below the main call to action.*

This is intentional.

If the main CTA is the action you want your subscribers to take, then consider the secondary and tertiary calls to action as bonus areas. To be clear, we are not saying they are less important or that you don't want your subscribers to take action on these other calls to action, only that they are not as prominently featured for a reason—the marketer really wants you to click on the main call to action (that's why it's featured!).

In the REI example (see Figure 6.6), the main call to action (#4) is on the left side, above the fold. This area is typically where a reader's eyes are drawn to first. REI's main goal is to have subscribers click through to the snowsports section of its website ("Shop all snowsports").

Moving to the right is where you find the secondary calls to action (#5). Notice how they are significantly less prominent: The imagery is smaller and the calls to action are less noticeable links compared to the large image and big blue button in the main call to action.

Continuing down the email are the tertiary calls to action, which appear below the fold: In other words, subscribers are forced to scroll to see the rest of the email. In this area, REI encourages subscribers to "Check out Arbor" snowboards and shop at its online outlet store. Although the call to action is still quite strong and large, you can tell it's not the main call to action because of its placement below the fold.

Although REI would not object to having customers click through—and ultimately purchase—items in the secondary and tertiary areas, the main goal of the email is to have readers click through to snowsports. The reason for adding additional calls to action is to give readers some options—especially those who are not enticed by the main call to action.

Secondary and tertiary calls to action can be very important to the success of an email; however, they don't appear in every email. Some marketers choose to include only a single CTA in their emails. This approach can work if your email has a single goal such as to register for a webinar, save 20 percent on all merchandise, or read a blog post. In this case, you don't want to distract your subscribers with any extraneous information. Your goal is to get them to take one and only one action.

Buttons vs. Links vs. Images

Email marketing CTAs come in many flavors. Sometimes a simple link serves as the main call to action, as shown in Figure 6.7. In other cases, a big button (see Figure 6.8) or an image does the trick. Some marketers use a combination of links, images, and buttons (see Figure 6.9).

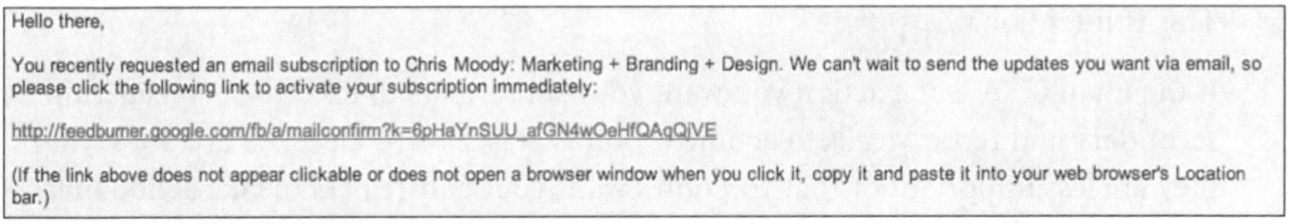

Hello there,

You recently requested an email subscription to Chris Moody: Marketing + Branding + Design. We can't wait to send the updates you want via email, so please click the following link to activate your subscription immediately:

http://feedburner.google.com/fb/a/mailconfirm?k=6pHaYnSUU_afGN4wOeHfQAqQjVE

(If the link above does not appear clickable or does not open a browser window when you click it, copy it and paste it into your web browser's Location bar.)

Figure 6.7   *An email from Feedburner shows a simple link as the main call to action (no buttons, no images).*

If you've ever subscribed to receive blog post updates via email from Feedburner, you'll recognize the email shown in Figure 6.7. This email is known as a "double opt-in" email. In other words, to start receiving Chris Moody's blog posts via email, the subscriber needs to click the link within the email. In this case, a single, link-based call to action is appropriate. What action the sender wants each reader to take is very clear (click the link!).

BustedTees also includes a clear call to action in its Deal of the Day emails. However, as opposed to a single link, its emails have a big "View This Deal" button, as can be seen in Figure 6.8.

Figure 6.8   *An email from BustedTees uses a big, orange button as the main call to action.*

BustedTees doesn't bother with secondary or tertiary calls to action nor does it add any other distractions to the email. The email is simple and straightforward: a picture of a man modeling the "Keep Calm and Move Along" t-shirt, the discounted price ($12.00), the date and time the deal ends, a brief product description, and the big "View This Deal" button.

Similar to the single link call to action in Figure 6.7, BustedTees's "big button" approach makes it very clear what action it wants its subscribers to take. The only way to learn more about the offer is to click the "View This Deal" button.

One of our favorite examples of an email that includes one main call to action with a variety of CTAs is from MarketingProfs.

Figure 6.9 *An email from MarketingProfs uses many different tactics—links, buttons, and videos—for its main call to action.*

How many different types of calls to action can you find in this email? How many total CTAs do you count? Let's see how much you've learned so far in the "Anatomy of an Email" part of the book. If you are the type who writes in books, grab a writing utensil and circle all the calls to action in this email.

Let's see how you did.

Starting from the top, you can see a call to action link (Save $300) in the pre-header. That's one. Moving down just a bit to the header is a clickable image with a "Register today!" call to action. That's two. Continuing down the email, the opening paragraph provides readers an introduction to the SocialTech 2012 event as well as the main call to action link: SocialTech 2012. That's three. Next, there is a bulleted list of six reasons to attend the March event. This section has four clickable links as well as a clickable image of a video. Toss in the "see you in Seattle" link, and the email contains nine total calls to action. Breaking this down by call to action "type," it has seven clickable links (one in the preheader), one clickable image in the header, and one clickable video image.

What's really great about this approach is it enables the MarketingProfs community to engage with the content in whatever way appeals most to them. Whether it be a link that catches a subscriber's eye or the video that draws them to take action, it doesn't matter to MarketingProfs. As long as the subscriber clicks through to the landing page (and registers), MarketingProfs is happy.

What's the best type of call to action? Should it be a button or a link or an image? Part of the answer comes through proper testing, but it also depends on what type of marketing message you are sending. For example, if you are an online retailer who sells men's and women's clothes, say Ibex Outdoor Clothing, showing pictures and images of your products is important (see Figure 6.10).

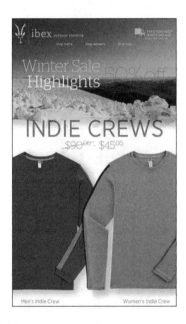

Figure 6.10   *This email from Ibex Outdoor Clothing features men's and women's long-sleeve crew shirts appears to be one big image, but is actually sliced into multiple images.*

The Subject line of this Ibex email is "Get Our Indie Crew for Your Crew—50% off!" Notice that the main call to action in Figure 6.10, a clickable image, is very consistent with that Subject line. The big image features a snowy landscape with pictures of both a men's and women's Indie Crew shirt. The text on top of the image reinforces the Subject line and the imagery.

Even better, when a subscriber clicks anywhere on this image, he is sent to an Indie Crew product landing page.

Contrast the Ibex "image CTA" with the one from Help a Reporter (HARO), which sends out an email to its subscriber base three times per day with simple links as its main call to action. See an example of one of those emails in Figure 6.11.

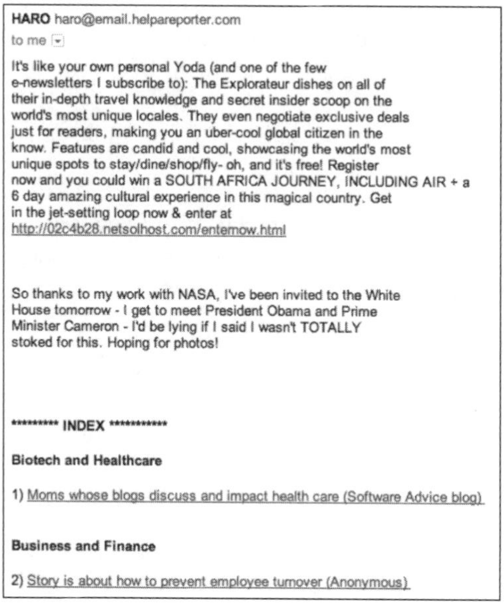
HARO haro@email.helpareporter.com
to me

It's like your own personal Yoda (and one of the few e-newsletters I subscribe to): The Explorateur dishes on all of their in-depth travel knowledge and secret insider scoop on the world's most unique locales. They even negotiate exclusive deals just for readers, making you an uber-cool global citizen in the know. Features are candid and cool, showcasing the world's most unique spots to stay/dine/shop/fly- oh, and it's free! Register now and you could win a SOUTH AFRICA JOURNEY, INCLUDING AIR + a 6 day amazing cultural experience in this magical country. Get in the jet-setting loop now & enter at http://02c4b28.netsolhost.com/enternow.html

So thanks to my work with NASA, I've been invited to the White House tomorrow - I get to meet President Obama and Prime Minister Cameron - I'd be lying if I said I wasn't TOTALLY stoked for this. Hoping for photos!

********* INDEX ***********

Biotech and Healthcare

1) Moms whose blogs discuss and impact health care (Software Advice blog)

Business and Finance

2) Story is about how to prevent employee turnover (Anonymous)

Figure 6.11 *HARO's email digest of public relations pitches and journalists' story resource needs is all text and only presents calls to action in link form.*

Considering the HARO email is mostly text (intentionally), its main calls to action are simple links; nothing fancy, just links. This email generates a high amount of response from its audience. Reporters and public relations professionals actively read and click through the links to see which reporters need help with stories and what pitches might resonate with a media outlet's audiences. HARO is a perfect example of a highly successful email marketing effort that breaks all kinds of rules. It has no images; multiple calls to action with none called out as primary; and it is incredibly long.

Like preparing meat and potatoes for your family at dinner, preparing this part of your email marketing gives you lots of options. You can use images, buttons, or links for your call to action. Or, you can have lengthy emails that inform, assuming your audience will intuitively know to click through and buy things. You can deliver one message per email or compose a more traditional "newsletter" style email with many different content elements. You can forego sending the email to everyone on your list and segment your email list and send specific messages to specific types of customers. The key to having this part of the anatomy of your email as successful as possible is creating content (deals and coupons, informative articles, beautiful pictures, entertaining videos, and so on) that your audience finds irresistible: Readers become insatiable for your emails. When you accomplish that, your CTA metrics will impress you.

However, having delicious meat and potatoes in your email doesn't mean the meal is finished. You have to have dessert, right? So let's put some finishing touches on these campaigns.

Endnote

1. "View from the Inbox 2009," Merckle. http://www.customerinsight-group.com/marketinglibrary/wp-content/uploads/2009/04/view-from-the-inbox-2009.pdf

7

The Finishing Touches

This is the final chapter of the email anatomy lesson. In case you were worried, no, there will not be a test at the end of this chapter. Instead, you'll move on to Part III, which covers ways to break the "rules" of email marketing and still be successful.

This chapter covers the finishing touches: the bottom section of an email marketing message. This part is usually not a priority for email marketers when it comes to designing an email. Often, this is not a huge deal as the footer tends to be ignored by many subscribers. After all, who scrolls to the bottom of an email these days? Who has that kind of time or patience? However, it's an important component of the email from a legal perspective as well as an opportunity to extend your message.

The bottom of an email is where you often find social sharing and connecting buttons, disclaimers, the unsubscribe and manage preferences links, and the organization's physical address. As covered in detail in Part III, however, not all of these parts of an email must be in the bottom of the message.

Social Sharing and Social Connecting

Before reading this section, let's review the differences between social sharing and social connecting:

- **Social sharing:** This is when a marketer includes an option for subscribers to share the entire email or a specific content block with their social network(s).

- **Social connecting:** This is when a marketer asks email subscribers to like an organization's Facebook page, follow it on Twitter, subscribe to its YouTube channel, circle it on Google+, "pin" an image on Pinterest, and so on.

As social media continues to gain steam, marketers are taking every opportunity to have people connect with them on their social channels: Facebook, Twitter, LinkedIn, Google+, Pinterest, and [insert social-network-of-the-day here]. Additionally, the smart marketers are allowing subscribers to easily share sections of content as well as the entire email with their social media followers/friends/connections.

These social sharing options are an important feature of your emails. Although some email marketers have social sharing and connecting options near the top of an email or next to each content block, most still choose to locate them near the bottom of the email, just above the footer, as Lands' End does in Figure 7.1.

Figure 7.1   *This email from Lands' End shows Twitter and Facebook sharing icons as well as a "Fan Us" on Facebook image.*

This email from Lands' End includes both social sharing and social connecting icons in the footer of its email. What we like about the company's use of the Twitter and Facebook icons is it actually tells subscribers why they're there! Notice the language: "Share the savings! Click the icons to post to Facebook or Twitter, or simply forward this e-mail."

If a subscriber clicks on the Twitter icon, a tweet automatically pre-populates the text box, as shown in Figure 7.2. (Note: You must be logged into Twitter for this feature to work).

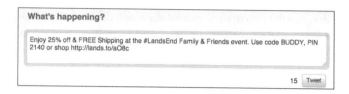

Figure 7.2 *Lands' End's Twitter button pre-populates a Twitter message with its coupon or deal of the moment.*

What's great about this auto-generated tweet is it's consistent with the Subject line, preheader, and main call to action of the email. Additionally, the social sharer does not have to think too much before posting that tweet. Assuming he's logged into Twitter, in two quick clicks (on the Twitter icon in the email and the Tweet button) he's posted this update for the world to see. Users can edit the default tweet to their liking, but can also just click "Tweet" and post it, as is.

If a subscriber chooses to share this email on Facebook, he simply clicks on the Facebook icon, and similarly to clicking the Twitter icon, a status update with pre-populated content is auto-generated, as you can see in Figure 7.3.

Figure 7.3 *As with the Twitter auto-generated message, Lands' End produces the same type of message for Facebook.*

Lands' End also includes an image in this update that's consistent with the image in the email. Can you tell the company has thought through this a bit? From the social sharer's perspective, all he needs to do is add a short note (in the "Write something..." box) and click the Share Link button. Again, two clicks. Easy.

If a subscriber clicks on the social connecting Fan Us Facebook icon in the lower right (see Figure 7.1), he is redirected to the Lands' End Facebook page. One more click (on the Like button), and Lands' End's Facebook friends grows by one.

The biggest difference between the social sharing and the social connecting options is that the first has the potential to extend the reach of the email—more people will potentially see the original email. The second simply allows subscribers to like (Facebook), follow (Twitter), or subscribe (YouTube).

Footer

Much like the Subject line and the From name, every single email marketing message has a footer. Conveniently located at the bottom (or "foot") of the email, the footer is usually a catch-all for all the things that are not critical components of an email, yet still need to be there.

Think of the footer of an email as the fine print on a television commercial or legal advertisement. You know—the text that is nearly impossible to read even with 20/20 vision.

Not all footers are created equal, however. Some are simple (see Figure 7.4) and only include a mechanism to unsubscribe as well as the physical address, which is a CAN-SPAM requirement. Others are more complicated (see Figure 7.5), loaded with disclaimers, privacy statements, and terms and conditions; messaging about how and when a subscriber opted in; links to manage your email preferences; as well as other methods to contact the sender.

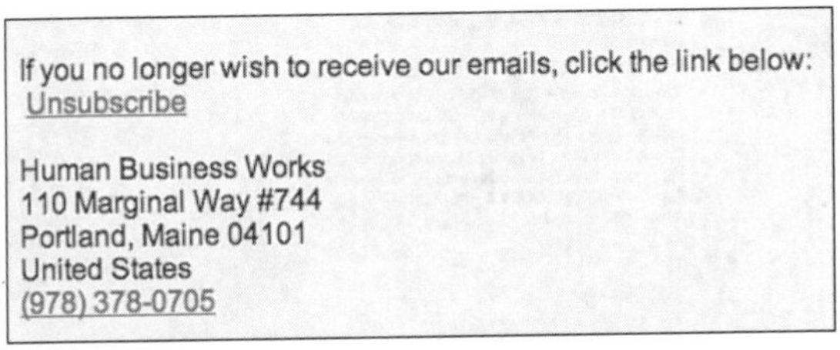

If you no longer wish to receive our emails, click the link below:
Unsubscribe

Human Business Works
110 Marginal Way #744
Portland, Maine 04101
United States
(978) 378-0705

Figure 7.4 *Chris Brogan's Human Business Works emails include a simple footer with just an unsubscribe link and a physical address.*

We are not suggesting that one footer is better than the other. They are simply different. Brogan's simple email footer (Figure 7.4) gets the job done. Even though it does not contain a lot of information, it's certainly easy on the eyes.

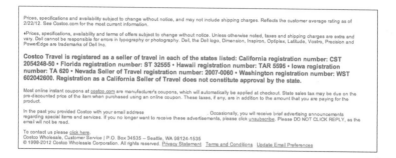

Figure 7.5 *Costco's email footer is quite a bit more detailed compared to Chris Brogan's one in Figure 7.4.*

The majority of the more detailed footer from Costco (Figure 7.5) is made up of legalese and disclaimers. However, also notice the sentence immediately following the unsubscribe link: *"Please DO NOT CLICK REPLY, as the email will not be read."* The CAN-SPAM Act of 2003 states that all commercial email must contain a "clear and conspicuous" opportunity to opt out. Although this email complies with the law by including the unsubscribe link, adding (in all caps) "DO NOT CLICK REPLY" is not likely to send warm fuzzies to the subscriber. Remember that some people will simply click Reply to an email out of habit, if they have a question for the sender. As an email sender, you must be ready to honor that opt-out request if someone asks for it, no matter what method he chooses.

Another use of the footer is to include messaging around when and where subscribers opted in to your email list and campaigns. The footer of an email DJ received from *Funny or Die* included the following paragraph: *You were added to the system October 20, 2011. For more information click* here. When he clicked the "here" link, he was redirected to a landing page that showed the source information for his email address (Figure 7.6).

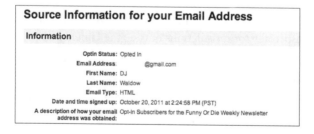

Figure 7.6 *Funny or Die's landing page shows where and when DJ opted in, offering proof in case he forgot.*

Although it's not all that likely that the average subscriber will see this information in the footer, or even care about it, including it as proof (if it's ever needed for legal purposes) of opt-in is a nice feature.

No matter how much you choose to include in the footer, it's pretty much guaranteed that it will exist in every single email you send. This is especially true if you are sending your emails through an email marketing company because it will often put the required CAN-SPAM information in this area.

Providing Unsubscribe Options

You've finally made it to the end of the anatomy lesson. Is there a better way to finish than by discussing the unsubscribe link? Enabling your readers to unsubscribe is not only required by CAN-SPAM, it's also a best practice to keep your subscribers happy that they are in control of their inbox and your visits to it. Having clear unsubscribe options for people is good business.

But back to the law: CAN-SPAM Act of 2003 requires that all email marketing messages sent to U.S. residents include an opt-out (unsubscribe) mechanism. If you choose to send your email marketing messages through a reputable email service provider, it will most likely include this opt-out information by default. You can usually modify it to fit the look and feel of your email campaign; however, having it is still a requirement.

Even if you are not sending commercial email through a third party, you are still required to provide your subscribers an opt-out method. This unsubscribe method can be "old school"—having subscribers write a letter or call the company to opt out. It can also be as simple as having them reply to the email indicating that they no longer want to receive emails from your company. The "reply to this email" option is why we don't recommend including "DO NOT REPLY" messaging in the footer as used in the Costco example (refer to Figure 7.5). Again, this phrasing is not illegal, just not advisable if your goal is to build trust with your subscribers.

Please consult legal council if you have specific questions around any email marketing laws, especially for jurisdictions outside the United States.

Most often, the unsubscribe link is located in the footer of an email. In some cases it's actually below the footer, almost as if it's tacked on as an afterthought. Why would a marketer plop it all the way at the bottom, sometimes in smaller font, in a somewhat obscure place? Most likely it's because marketers don't really want you to unsubscribe. They've worked so hard to court you and entice you to subscribe to their email list. Why would they let you leave so easily?

See Chapter 10, "The Perfect-Looking Email," which covers the topic of individuals and companies that choose to not only *not* hide the unsubscribe link in the footer, but instead bring it all the way to the top of the email and make it prominent.

However, the far majority of email marketers stick with the default: an unsubscribe link in the footer. As mentioned earlier, if you're sending email through an email service provider (ESP), it will likely require you to use its opt-out mechanism. It does this not to punish you, but instead to protect you. ESPs automatically process unsubscribes and remove them from your email list.

Some ESPs, such as Emma, use a third party to manage their unsubscribes. Emma uses TrueRemove, a service that manages unsubscribes for all Emma clients. By clicking the "opt out using TrueRemove™" link, the subscriber will be removed from the sending organization's email list immediately.

Other ESPs, such as Constant Contact, have their own branded opt-out mechanism. SafeUnsubscribe "guarantees the permanent removal of a contact's email address when he or she selects to opt out of all mailings through the unsubscribe link."[1] It can most often be identified in the footer of an email with the following: "Instant removal with SafeUnsubscribe.™"

When the unsubscribe link is clicked, users are redirected to a landing page that looks something like what's shown in Figure 7.7.

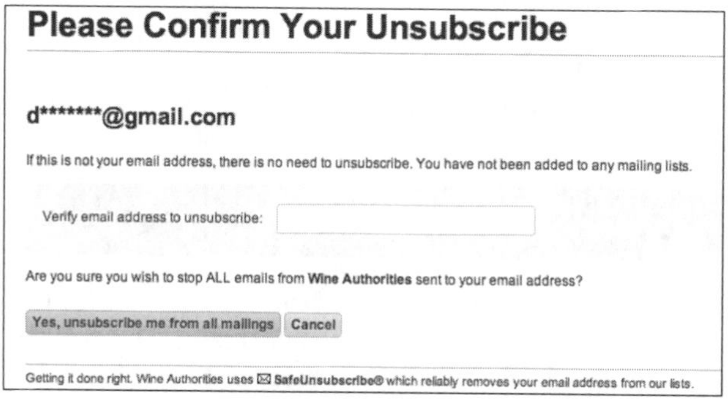

Please Confirm Your Unsubscribe

d*******@gmail.com

If this is not your email address, there is no need to unsubscribe. You have not been added to any mailing lists.

Verify email address to unsubscribe:

Are you sure you wish to stop ALL emails from **Wine Authorities** sent to your email address?

Yes, unsubscribe me from all mailings   Cancel

Getting it done right. Wine Authorities uses ✉ **SafeUnsubscribe®** which reliably removes your email address from our lists.

Figure 7.7 *Constant Contact's SafeUnsubscribe landing page asks users to confirm their email addresses to unsubscribe from the mailing in question.*

After getting to the unsubscribe page, a subscriber must verify his email address by entering it in the box provided. Then, after he clicks the "Yes, unsubscribe me from all mailings" button, his email address will be permanently removed or marked as "do not send" from the sender's database (unless, of course, he chooses to opt-in again at a later date).

BREAKING THE RULES: THE FOOTER

As if you haven't noticed by now, you can find exceptions to every rule and the footer is no different. Social sharing, social connecting, and even unsubscribe and physical address requirements can be placed anywhere in an email. Some email marketing campaigns might even elect not to include social sharing or social connecting (though we typically don't recommend it). The unsubscribe and physical location information is legally required, but it's not legally required to be in the footer. It can be anywhere.

Emma, the email marketing provider mentioned earlier, actually adds social sharing options by default at the very top of emails sent from its system as can be seen in this genConnect email (Figure 7.8).

Figure 7.8   *The genConnect email newsletter presents social sharing options at the top of its emails which encourages people to share immediately, rather than after consuming the email.*

There is probably no better example of breaking the "rule" of hiding the unsubscribe link in the bottom of an email than in Christopher Penn's Almost Timely Newsletter. After fielding a few complaints that his unsubscribe link was hard to find, he changed the email's first few paragraphs to look like the screen shown in Figure 7.9.

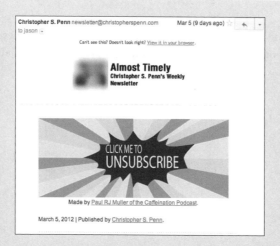

Figure 7.9 *Just below the header of Christopher Penn's newsletter is a huge, colorful graphic that draws attention to the opt-out or unsubscribe option (shown how it looked as of this writing).*

So far, this book has covered a lot of ground. You now know various tips and tricks to build your email list and have a Ph.D. in anatomy—of emails. You're familiar with some techy terms like preheader, the initials CTA, and the basic requirements of the CAN-SPAM Act (bonus points if you know what the acronym CAN-SPAM stands for). You have an idea of whether or not you should pre-check your email opt-in box. We even touched on Twitter and Facebook—social sharing and social connecting. After all, what's a marketing book without at least a mention of social media?

You've also seen examples from Ibex, MarketingProfs, HARO, Chris Penn, Zappos, Digitwirl, and REI, to name a few. The foundation has been laid, the groundwork set. You are on your way to becoming an email marketing veteran.

With only a few exceptions, however, we haven't really started breaking the rules. What's a *Rebel's Guide* without a little rebellion, right? Now it's time to dive into the rules so you can know which ones are breakable and how to break them while still delivering quality emails that get opened, get read, and drive business. So get pumped, put on your leather jacket and shades, and let's dive into to Part III, "Breaking the Rules."

Endnote

1. Constant Contact Resource Center, "Frequently Asked Questions."
    http://constantcontact.custhelp.com/app/answers/detail/a_id/351/~/
    what-is-safeunsubscribe%3F

8

Are Best Practices Really "Best"?

"We know best practices, but we don't always follow them. When everyone follows best practices, you've merely redefined mediocrity."
Part of the email signature from Andrew Kordek,
Co-founder and Chief Strategist at Trendline Interactive

Best practices.

Best practices.

Best practices.

In DJ's first few years at Bronto (an email service provider), he lived and breathed that mantra. Best practices or bust. There was only one way to do it right. As a salesperson, he reminded potential clients that if they were not following the tried-and-true email marketing best practices, they would not find success as a client. As an account manager, he informed his clients that if they wanted to get emails delivered, opened, read, and acted on, following all email marketing "best practices" was important.

In 2008, DJ was promoted to a new role within Bronto. His title read "Director of *Best Practices* & Deliverability." The evolution continued. With that kind of title, preaching anything other than best practices would have been somewhat of a challenge—and quite hypocritical. If you wanted to know the "best" way to grow your email list, the "best" way to ensure your emails were delivered, opened, read, and clicked on, DJ was your man.

In those early years, 2005–2008, many of the best practices that were floating around included things such as

- Never include ALL CAPS in a Subject line.
- Never send an email with one big image.
- Never use the words "free" or use punctuation in a Subject line.
- Never send all-text ("ugly") emails.
- Never (ever!) buy an email list.
- Subject lines should be no more than 50 characters in length.
- The unsubscribe link should always be at the bottom of your email, in the footer.
- Double opt-in is the best way to collect email addresses.
- Never send an email late at night or on the weekend.

Notice that nearly all of these best practices include the words "always" or "never." Absolutes. Extremes. Black or white. Right or wrong. More on this view later.

In 2009, DJ moved to another email service provider, Blue Sky Factory. In his new role as Director of Community, he began to soften up his "all best practices all the time" line of thinking. He started to become aware of clients who did not follow all of the rules, clients who intentionally (or unintentionally) broke the rules of email marketing and yet still, somehow, found success. It was around this time DJ created and adopted a new theory on email best practices.

In this chapter, we're going to share with you our combined theory of best practices. It's one that takes into account "rules" and breaks them but still helps you apply best practices. Our philosophy accounts for what other people have tested and declared the "right" way and shows you how to prove them right or wrong and develop your own best practices...because that's what ultimately makes you a better email marketer.

Best Practices Are Practices That Are Best for You

In January of 2009, Morgan Stewart (then of email service provider ExactTarget) wrote:

"I am exhausted by the overuse of the term 'best practices.' It's a crutch and frankly, when people use it incorrectly, it makes me want to poke them in the eye."[1]

We are in no way advocating poking people in the eye; however, we agree with what Stewart said. It's a phrase that's overused and, in some ways, outdated. When you perform a search for the phrase *email best practices,* some of the information returned is, frankly, old. Some of the "rules" that were in play five years ago are no longer applicable, yet thanks to high search rankings, they continue to surface.

In that same writing, Stewart continued:

"There is no one size fits all answer. The only honest answer is, 'it depends.' It depends on your business, it depends on your goals, and it depends on your value proposition. It just depends!!!"

We agree.

The problem is most marketers hate that answer. Sometimes you just want to be told what to do. You want the case study that corroborates what you believe to be true. You want the easy answer. You want to just hit the easy button and make it all work out just fine. "It depends" forces you to test some of those best practices to uncover what is best for your audience. "It depends" makes you do a bit of work to see how your subscribers will respond.

"It's important to remember that not all best practices are as black and white as many experts present them to be," wrote Spencer Kollas, director of delivery services at StrongMail.[2] "In fact, after working with some of our customers we found through testing that not all best practices help them achieve their business needs and goals. On the contrary, some have actually seen better results by not following a conventional best practice."

That last sentence is what this section of the book is all about: individuals and companies seeing "better results by not following a conventional best practice." As DJ started to believe in 2011, many email marketing rules are meant to be broken. The key to breaking them and still being successful is to properly test.

Test and Test Often

Most email marketing solutions have testing capabilities built right into their applications, yet for some reason they are not used as often as they should be. Does testing take more time then just hitting send one time? Most likely yes. However, testing forces you to think about alternatives. We recommend testing as often as you can as what works today may not work tomorrow. The payoff is usually worth it.

We encourage you to test Subject lines, copy, and creative. Test buttons versus links and big images versus few images. Try a test of an HTML email against one with mostly images. Try including a screenshot of a video with a big play button on it. In one test use ALL CAPS, and in another use all lowercase. The testing possibilities are endless.

However, before you go on a testing spree, be sure you're mapping your desired goal with the strategy or tactic that influences it most. In other words, if you are not happy with your email list growth, test various strategies and opt-in forms—single versus double opt-in, long forms versus short, offline versus online. If you are hoping to increase your open rate, it's important to test the From name and/or the Subject line. If click-throughs are not as high as you'd like them to be, be sure you are mixing up your email creative by testing emails with different content blocks and/or images. If conversions are suffering, consider testing the call(s) to action in your emails.

If your email provider has the capability to do multivariate testing, you can set up a test with a few different variables and determine the "winner" based on the combination that leads to the more desirable outcome (more email opt-ins, higher open rate, more click-throughs, more conversions).

Sometimes it makes sense to test with your best customers, those who engage with your emails the most, spend the most money, or sign up for the most events. Try a new tactic on a portion of that list to see how it impacts their behavior. Other times, it may be better to run tests with your least engaged audience, those who are not opening, clicking, or converting. Test to see if subtle (or dramatic) changes will alter their behavior.

Testing can be very case-by-case specific. What works best for your audience may not work for others. What works for you today or tomorrow may not work next week or next month.

Either way, our view is simple: Whenever you see the words "always" or "never" tied to email marketing advice, it's probably worth investigating further. Test these "best practices" and see what happens. Look at your key metrics (you do have metrics, right?). Do open rates plummet? Do unsubscribes or complaints shoot through the roof? Do you get more click-throughs and conversions?

What to Expect

Now that you have all the tips and tricks to grow your email list and have passed your (email) anatomy lesson, it's time to move to the rebellious part of this book. It's time to unlearn everything you've ever heard, read, or been told about email marketing best practices.

The next three chapters take a deep dive into many of these email marketing best practices in hopes of convincing you to break some of the rules—flip them on their heads—and see what happens. We'll provide examples of companies and individuals who have found success doing just that.

However, you don't have to break all the rules, all the time. Instead, just be open to trying a few of these "rule breakers" to see whether they can work for your audience.

Chapter 9, "My Word! You Must Read This Now!," covers why longer Subject lines might actually outperform shorter ones. You also learn why it's okay (maybe even good) to use ALL CAPS, the word *free*, and even to drop in some punctuation in the Subject line of your email.

Chapter 10, "The Perfect-Looking Email," continues with the "pretty" theme and dispels the myth that sending an email with one big image is a bad thing. We'll also look at the opposite end of the spectrum, showing examples of companies who send all (or mostly) text emails and then find that they outperform HTML emails. We'll dispel the myth that the unsubscribe link belongs in the footer. The chapter closes by talking about emails that you may find ugly, yet actually perform.

Chapter 11, "The Best Way to Grow Your List," provides examples of people who use the dreaded, evil popup to collect email addresses—and grow their list at an incredibly fast rate. The chapter covers double opt-in versus single. Is one better than the other? You'll also see examples of companies that send email without explicit permission and still find success. Chapter 11 ends with a discussion about companies that send nonpermission emails and touches on when it's okay to buy an email list. This topic is certain to be the most controversial one covered in the book.

Now it's time to break some rules.

Endnotes

1. Stewart, Morgan, "Your opinion is not 'Best Practice!' (and mine isn't either)." January 21, 2009. http://blog.exacttarget.com/blog/morgan-stewart/your-opinion-is-not-best-practice-and-mine-isnt-either.

2. Kollas, Spencer, "Why you should ignore some email best practices." July 25, 2011. http://www.imediaconnection.com/content/29599.asp.

My Word! You Must Read This Now!

This will be the most incredible chapter you've ever read. Okay, perhaps not, but that headline and first sentence got your attention, didn't it? That's an example of the mentality behind writing a Subject line. No, you shouldn't exaggerate to the point of lying, but your job is to make readers open the email. The Subject line has to grab them by the collar and scream, "OPEN ME!"

Even better than just having an attention-getting Subject line is making the From address complement the crafty Subject line by illustrating the message is from a trusted sender. Maybe the email comes at the same time of day or same day of the week consistently (like HARO—three times per day, fives days per week). Or perhaps it has a certain style of Subject line the receiver comes to expect (something witty and eye-catching).

Think of how excited you'd feel if you received an email from one of your favorite companies (Apple)—the Subject line announcing the newest iPhone, the one for which you've been waiting several months. Think of how likely you are to open an email from your favorite shoe store, the Subject line promising an impossible-to-say-no-to discount for that pair of cowboy boots you've been swooning over.

However, if you're an Android fan, the Subject line of that iPhone email might not be all that interesting to you. What if you prefer tennis shoes to cowboy boots? Does the subject's promise of a discount matter? Is there such a thing as the perfectly written email Subject line?

We don't think so. It all depends on the subscriber. What is a perfect subject line to get you to open an email might not be for your co-worker sitting three feet from you in the next cubicle. The types of Subject lines that grab your attention might be the same ones that your significant other ignores, deletes, or marks as spam.

This chapter examines two email marketing best practices you've likely read about at some point, both involving the ideal Subject line:

- Never use ALL CAPS or the word *free* in the Subject line unless you want to end up having your email land in a spam folder.
- Subject lines should be between 30 and 50 characters to get the best results.

Email Subject Line Words to Avoid

Ready for a quiz? Guess how many search results will be returned by Googling the following phrase (without quotes):

email subject line words to avoid

What do you think? Thousands? Tens of thousands? Hundreds of thousands? Millions?

Now, put this book down for a minute, grab your computer, and see how close your guess was. If you guessed "in the millions" you were correct. In fact, when we did that search, it returned more than ten million results, as shown in Figure 9.1.

A ton of content is floating around online that has to do with words you should avoid using in email Subject lines. It seems that everyone has something to say about which words trigger spam filters.

Interesting, but who cares? It matters because many of those articles and blog posts about which words to avoid in an email are just flat-out wrong. In fact, if you click through on many of those search results a few words pop up over and over as words to never (ever) use in an email Subject line.

Figure 9.1   *We got more than ten million Google search results for the phrase "email subject line words to avoid" (no quotes).*

The ones we found in many of the "top words to avoid" lists include

- Free
- Never
- Limited time
- Anything that looks like you are YELLING (all caps)
- Deal

Take a look at your own inbox right now. (Yes, you'll have to put this book down, but just for a second.) Search for emails that use any of the preceding words or phrases that many blog posts and articles say you should avoid. Are there any emails with *free* in the Subject line? How about *never* or *deal*? Do any Subject lines include one or more words in all caps?

The answer is likely a resounding YES!

If you subscribe to any business-to-consumer or brand emails that use email to sell, we're pretty certain that you'll see the word *free* in the Subject line, most likely followed by the word *shipping*, or the phrase *limited time offer*. If you have opted in for deal-of-the-day sites, you quite possibly have in your inbox some Subject lines with the word *deal* in them.

When DJ searched his inbox for the word *free*, the results (shown in Figure 9.2) showed many emails using that forbidden word. Most of those emails were from well-known companies and brands, and none of them were in his spam folder.

Red Hanger Cleaners	New coupon, plus win $100 in FREE cleaning - ... Day, you're never far from a parade. The f
Solutions	Free Shipping + New for spring! - ... CATEGORY | NEW ARRIVALS | DEAL CENTER | CLIC
Lands' End	Share the savings: 25% off + free shipping - limited time - ... also modify or cancel your sub
Wine Anthology	Insane Low Price and Free Shipping - ... such a great deal that we are offering FREE SHIPP
Lands' End	Limited time - save 25% + free shipping | including Men's - ... also modify or cancel your su
Wine Library	95 Pt Blockbuster. 44% off Release Price: Was 54 now 29.99 with free ship on 3 bt orders
Lands' End	Everyone saves 25% + gets free shipping | limited time - ... 53595 Subscribe, modify, or uns
My Starbucks Rewards	Free Starbucks tasting cup with whole bean purchase: limited time and quantity - ... it fron
GearBuzz	50% Off Rugged, Weather-Proof iPhone Case: Plus FREE SHIPPING - ... Price $25 Plus FR

Figure 9.2   *DJ's inbox is full of emails with Subject lines that include "spammy" words (such as free).*

You know the old saying, "Don't believe everything you read (or hear)?" It also applies in the online world. If you were to believe what you read on the Internet, you would never use the word *free*, include ALL CAPS, or have punctuation in the Subject line because doing so would trigger spam filters. These rules were true— more than five years ago.

Karen Rubin wrote the following about email spam trigger words in a January 2012 blog post:[1]

"One of the easiest ways to avoid SPAM filters is by carefully choosing the words you use in your email's subject line. Trigger words are known to cause problems and increase the chances of your email getting caught in a SPAM trap. By avoiding these words in your email subject lines, you can dramatically increase your chances of getting beyond SPAM filters."

Although it's true some of these words might "increase the chances of your email getting caught in a SPAM trap," it's less likely than the article makes it sound. Chad White, Research Director at Responsys and author of The Retail Email Blog left a comment on Rubin's blog post: "Content filtering hasn't been a big component of spam filtering algorithms for nearly a decade. Sender reputation and, increasingly, engagement metrics are way more important. Any marketer with half-decent permission and list management practices will be able to use these words and phrases without worry."

According to Laura Atkins, founding partner of the anti-spam consultancy and software firm Word to the Wise, the truth likely lies somewhere between those two extremes:

"Naïve content filtering (filtering on 'FREE!!' in the subject line[2]) hasn't been a big component for nearly a decade, but content filtering...a much more complex and subtle style of content filtering, one that looks at the words in the subject lines and how they relate to the words in the body...is where filtering is going," she wrote on her blog in response to Rubin's post and White's comments. "Content matters, don't think it doesn't. But don't let word lists like the above frighten you off from crafting good subject lines."[3]

Take a look at your spam folder now, but not those emails you proactively mark as spam. Instead, look at the emails that are automatically filtered as spam. (Note: Depending on which email client you are using—Gmail, AOL, Hotmail, Outlook, Yahoo!, and so on—they'll either be in a "spam" or "junk" folder.) What do those Subject lines look like?

As you can see in Figure 9.3, which shows a screenshot of DJ's Gmail spam folder, the spammy Subject lines include

- Mentions of the drugs Viagra and Cialis
- The phrase *Investment inquiry*
- Two Subject lines in a language other than English
- Re:UPSNotification Package_delivery-failure 06...

Delivery-Confirmation	Grab it now! $1000 Visa gift card! - Congratulations! You Are Today's W
Delivery-Confirmation	You could get $1000 to shop at the Walmart® in your area - Congratul
Romeo Club	Join Romeo Club and let the money start rolling in - Whether you're a
Mr. John Mario	investment inquiry. - Dear friend, Compliments. We've been trying to rea
me	Соберем для Вас по сети интернет базу данных потенциальных к
NOW 20% OFF	BUY NOW VIAGRA CIALIS !!! - USPS - Fast Delivery Shipping 1-4 day L
NOW 20% OFF	BUY NOW VIAGRA CIALIS !!! - USPS - Fast Delivery Shipping 1-4 day L
Delivery-Confirmation	Grab it now! $1000 Visa gift card! - Congratulations! You Are Today's W
NOW 20% OFF	BUY NOW VIAGRA CIALIS !!! - USPS - Fast Delivery Shipping 1-4 day L
drugsonline_68787	Overnight packing of Viagra - http://rieswitt.ri.funpic.de/n2.html
朱容菁	-一成为上司的得力助手，使之沟通及协调等工作更加专业化。n83wb - 请d
Fox News:	Unemployed? Fox News investigates. - I actually make $3000 to $7000
6090993_United Parcel-Se.	Re:UPSNotification Package_delivery-failure 06de5a521e3a9b7d9. - _55

Figure 9.3 *DJ's Gmail spam folder shows what spammy Subject lines really look like.*

Note the sender or From names on those emails. As you can see, the vast majority do not come from individuals or companies. Instead, they are from "Delivery-Confirmation" or "NOW 20% OFF" or "6090993_United Parcel-Se."

Those are spam.

Now let's take a look at some of the companies and individuals who break the rules and include words such as *free* or who craft emails with ALL CAPS in the Subject line—all with incredibly positive results.

King Arthur Flour: Achieving Higher Sales Using All Caps and FREE

Founded in Boston in 1790, King Arthur Flour (KAF), kingarthurflour.com, is not only the oldest flour company in the United States, it's one of the country's longest-standing companies, period. When it started more than 220 years ago, its main (and only) product was flour. Today, it sells top-quality baking products and serves as a baking resource through its blog and social media properties on Facebook and Twitter. Email marketing is an integral part of its online business and a main driver of sales, too.

In 2012, on February 29—a date that only comes around every four years—it decided to have some fun with the number 29. KAF sent an email to its list of more than 600,000 subscribers with the following Subject line:

29¢ shipping TODAY ONLY

As you can see in Figure 9.4, the incentive was "29¢ shipping on your order of $29+." The offer, of course, ended on February 29 at midnight. Did you happen to notice anything "rule-breaking" about the Subject line?

Figure 9.4 *An email sent by KAF on February 29, 2012 has the Subject line, "29¢ shipping TODAY ONLY."*

It used ALL CAPS! The next question you have (we think) is, "Yeah. Great. But did it work?" According to Halley Silver, Director of Online Services at KAF, this email resulted in the top sales day at KAF ever. EVER! KAF tends to break a lot of rules in regard to email marketing. What's unique about it, however, is it doesn't just break the rules for the sake of breaking the rules. Instead, the company is voracious about testing.

"We do tests all the time—two to three per month. Sometimes subject line, sometimes creative," Silver said.

As you dive more into the "Breaking the Rules" part of this book, you'll notice that the word *testing* appears more and more. This is not by accident. Like any effective marketer, testing is usually a critical component of a successful campaign. Sure, sometimes you'll get lucky. Sometimes you'll try something and it will just work. However, as you'll see over the next several chapters, most successful marketers performed some type of test to determine what worked best for their audience. Remember: *Best practices are practices that are best for your subscribers.*

Back to KAF and its 600,000 person email list. With its list that large and that accounts for a large portion of the company's digital marketing revenue, KAF takes email marketing pretty darn seriously.

"It's incredibly powerful," Silver told us. "Our email program is a top driver of traffic and the number one driver of revenue to our site."

See—we told you that email marketing was not dead. In fact, KAF might be to "blame" for that $40.56 ROI of email discussed in the Introduction. If we had to bet, its ROI is quite a bit higher than the average.

KAF sends an email to its list two to three times per week, a number that jumps up during the holiday season. In addition to its full-list mailing, KAF also sends a monthly email to its retail and wholesale list. Finally, it sends a "please rate/review your recent product purchase" email once per week.

In 2011, it decided to test the email shown in Figure 9.5.

The entire email shown in Figure 9.5—the preheader, header, copy, creative, and call to action—were identical for both test groups. The only part of the email that was different was the Subject line:

- **Subject Line A:** Ends Thursday: FREE SHIPPING
- **Subject Line B:** Hawaiian Pizza—the secret's in the crust...

Notice that Subject line A, mentioning free shipping ending Thursday, is only reiterated in the head of the actual email. Compare that to Subject line B, about the Hawaiian pizza, for which there is a picture (looks good, right?) as well as a short note about it. The email copy and creative is much more an extension of Subject line B than it is of A. Finally, most would agree that Subject line B is more interesting. It almost leads the subscriber into the email—entices them to open it—to find out more about this pizza and the "secret" of the crust.

Figure 9.5   *KAF split this 2011 email and sent to different portions of its list, each receiving a unique subject line.*

If you had to describe Subject line A, you might use adjectives such as *boring* or *non-descriptive*. Don't worry; you're not alone. We agree. Looking at Subject line A, it's nearly impossible to tell what the contents of the email will include—other than the fact that the "free shipping" deal ends on Thursday.

Which Subject line do you think was the winner—garnering the most opens, clicks, and conversions?

If you guessed A, you are correct. However, if you guessed B, you are also correct. How is that possible? They both are winners?

It depends, of course, on what the winning criteria are for your Subject line test. Check out the results in Table 9.1.

Table 9.1   King Arthur Flour Subject Line Test Results

Version	Subject Line	Open Rate	Sales
A	Ends Thursday: FREE SHIPPING	27.2%	386% higher than version B
B	Hawaiian Pizza—the secret's in the crust...	31.8%	

As you can see, although email B—the one with the more creative, enticing, descriptive Subject line—had a higher open rate (31.8 percent versus 27.2 percent), the sales for the email with the "boring" Subject line had sales that were nearly 400 percent higher. Better yet, the winning Subject line, according to sales numbers, was the one that broke two email marketing rules in one shot! That Subject line not only used the word *FREE* but also had it in all caps.

If you were running the email marketing at your organization, which result would you rather have? Assuming part of your compensation was tied to revenue, clearly the answer is A.

"As my colleague put it, customers open an email with a plan," Silver shared. "Based on the subject line, the user goes in with an intent." In this case, their intent was to take advantage of the free shipping. By including *FREE SHIPPING* in all caps, the Subject line stood out in subscribers' inboxes. Note that KAF has worked extremely hard over the years to earn the trust of its customers. This trust likely contributed to the high open and conversion rates as well. The "sales" type of emails can also have a long-term effect. Have you ever saved an email from an individual or company to use later when you needed it? We have. So have our wives and our friends.

One of the strategies KAF employs to ensure its subscribers save their emails is to include recipes in every single one of its emails. "It's very intentional that every one of our emails has a recipe in it," Silver said. "People save them for the recipes."

Tumbleweed: More Opens and Click-Throughs Using All Caps and Free

Tumbleweed Tiny House Company (tumbleweedhouses.com), a company founded by Jay Shafer, builds tiny houses, some less than 100 square feet. Tumbleweed tests its Subject lines often using a test feature in its email service provider's software. This feature allows the company to easily test one Subject line against another to determine which has a higher open rate.

In one test,[4] it pitted the following Subject lines against each other:

- **Subject line A:** It's FREE. All the tiny houses on our site and more
- **Subject line B:** It features all the houses on our website plus more...

Not only did Subject line A (with the word *FREE* in all caps) win, it won by a large margin—26 percent more opens compared to Subject line B. Crystal Gouldey, an Education Marketing Associate at Aweber (Tumbleweed's email service provider), believes that "People love free things, so using the word 'free' right up front may have been key here. Other than that, the subjects are very similar. Just one word can cause a huge difference."

In another test Tumbleweed used the exact same Subject line in each version; however, version A was all caps:

- **Subject line A:** SOLAR LIVING GOES TINY
- **Subject line B:** Solar Living Goes Tiny

The criteria for the winning Subject line were opens as well as click-throughs. While many business to consumer (B2C) companies, such as KAF, measure success by the number of conversions (sales, registrations, and so on), this is not always the case. Tumbleweed was more interested in sharing its story and spreading its message.

We know what you are thinking: There is *no way in the world* version A—the ALL CAPS one—even came close in a head-to-head Subject line test. It's not like Tumbleweed just used one "all caps" word in its Subject line. Instead, it capitalized every single word, as seen in Table 9.2.

See for yourself.

Table 9.2   Tumbleweed Subject Line Test Results

Version	Subject Line	Open Rate	Clicks
A	SOLAR LIVING GOES TINY	13.8 percent higher than version B	30 percent higher than version B
B	Solar Living Goes Tiny		

Version A received nearly 14 percent more opens and 30 percent more clicks than version B.[5]

Did these results surprise you? We're guessing your first reaction to version A was something along the lines of "ALL CAPS! THAT'S SPAM!" You might have even yelled that very phrase at the top of your lungs. But here's the thing: Tumbleweed tested it. It intentionally broke the rules and found success. It performed a similar test comparing "Amazing New Photos" to "AMAZING NEW PHOTOS." Once again, the all-caps Subject line was the clear winner: 21 percent more opens and 31 percent more clicks than the other Subject line! Clearly, the Tumbleweed audience responds better to an all-caps Subject line.

Keep in mind that using all caps in your emails might not work for your audience, but now you have seen examples of case studies where it has worked for others. Whether you follow or break the rules depends on your audience. The only way you can know if they like or dislike all caps in their email Subject lines is to test.

The Proper Length of a Subject Line

Pinpointing exactly when the best practice of using a short subject line was first introduced is difficult, but it's one that seems to live on (and on, and on). Somewhere, sometime, someone stated: "Email subject lines should be short."

Dela Quist, CEO of Alchemy Worx (alchemyworx.com) suggests this advice originally came from email clients such as AOL who "truncated the subject line at 40 characters."[6]

That theory seems quite logical and very possible, but where the original source of this advice came from is still unclear. Either way, it's one of those best practices that has prevailed over the years. In a 2007 report, MailerMailer, an email marketing service, came right out and said, "Always use short, descriptive subject lines."[7]

In a 2008 blog post, email service provider MailChimp concluded that, "Shorter subject lines seemed to work better than long subject lines (the difference in open rate was more noticeable when they differed by 30 characters)."[8]

To be fair to both MailerMailer and MailChimp, these quotes are from 2007 and 2008, respectively. But this is the Internet. Four or five years is an eternity and, yes, times have changed. In June of 2011, MailChimp stated, "The *general rule of thumb* in email marketing is to keep your subject line to 50 characters or less. Our analysis found this to *generally* be the rule. The exception was for highly targeted audiences, where the reader apparently appreciated the additional information in the subject line"[9] (emphasis is ours).

Others in the industry simply believe that the optimal subject line depends. "We have clients [who use] short and to-the-point subject lines (think VIP invitations with clear and concise benefits/calls to action) and others where lengthy subject lines tease you into reading the email and acting,"[10] said Simms Jenkins, author of *The Truth About Email Marketing* and CEO of BrightWave Marketing.

Data and metrics aside, one of the reasons many email marketing folks argue that "shorter is better" in regard to email Subject line length is because of readability.

The problem with longer Subject lines is they often get truncated in many email clients, as shown in Figure 9.6.

HuffPost Media	Andrew Breitbart Dead: Conservative Blogger Dies Suddenly - ... passed away. Get HuffPost Media On Twitter and Facebook ! Know somethin
HuffPost Media	Top Cable News Programs Of February 2012 - ... last year. Get HuffPost Media On Twitter and Facebook ! Know something we don't? E-mail us
HuffPost Media	WATCH: Chris Matthews Turns Mitt Romney Into 'The Artist' - ... verbal gaffes. Get HuffPost Media On Twitter and Facebook ! Know something
HuffPost Business	Former Top Halliburton Exec Heads To Prison For Bribery - ... one-man play, media coverage of his work and the broadcast of a one-hour versi
HuffPost Media	Moore's Romney Critique Gets Personal, Fox News Host's Surprising Admission, Buchanan V...	Tuesday, February 21, 2012 WATCH: Moor
The Huffington Post	Friday's Daily Brief - ... We're Simpletons' MEDIA Murdoch Announces Sun On Sunday BLOG POSTS Elena Halicizar: HuffPost Launches Social I
HuffPost Business	Detroit Baffled By Romney - ... events, used social media and crafted multiple iterations of our resume based on each new blogger's opinion. Then
HuffPost Business	Fannie And Freddie To Underwater USA: Drown - ... technology and social media who won't open their societies are Humpty Dumpty. Once tech

Figure 9.6   *This Subject line from HuffPost Media was cut off due to its length.*

As you can see in this very long (93 character) Subject line from HuffPost Media in Figure 9.6, the last few characters are cut off. The Subject line ends with "Buchanan V…" Is that the first initial of Buchanan's last name or is it the start of a new word? Although it's not necessarily problematic, depending on where your Subject line gets truncated, it could make a difference in context.

As you can see in the following example, when cut off at 26 characters, the entire meaning of this Subject line is lost. As Mark Brownlow said, "…sometimes, frankly, you just have to smile."[11]

Full Subject line: *Get up to 70% off children's fashion*

Subject line truncated at 26 characters: *Get up to 70% off children*

Character length on smartphones can be even more pronounced. Take the iPhone, for example. Depending on your individual settings, the average Subject line can max out at 35 characters, as you can see in Figure 9.7.

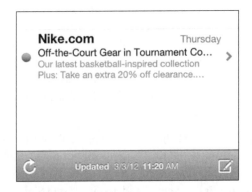

Figure 9.7   *The Subject line of this Nike email got cut off on an iPhone after 35 characters.*

In addition to lost meaning, another argument against long Subject lines is that, in the age of social media, brevity rules. SMS (Short Message Service or simply "text messaging") is limited to 160 characters, whereas Twitter has a 140-character limit. Many of us seem to have a short attention span. Assuming that applies to email marketing, shorter likely is better.

However, as we've stated before, it depends on what metric is most important to you. According to Mark Brownlow, it's actually quite easy to write Subject lines for high open rates: "Segment by gender and send this [subject line] to your male subscribers: *Free beer as a thank you for subscribing.*"[12] However, if you want click-throughs, be sure the email copy contains a simple way to redeem that free beer.

In all seriousness, if your goal is more opens, using a short, catchier Subject line might be better. If you are trying to get your subscribers to take some kind of action (click-through or convert), using a more direct, possibly longer Subject line might be the answer.

Or maybe it's just the opposite. Again, it depends on your audience.

Measuring Success

Too often, marketers measure the wrong things or don't measure anything at all. Always keep the goal of each and every email you send in mind. Is success determined by open rate? Click-throughs? Clicks-to-opens (the number of clicks divided by number of opens)? Conversions/sales?

Consider the following scenario: You've been reading this book that keeps suggesting to test all aspects of your email campaigns to determine what works best for your audience. You decide to do a test based on Subject line: 50 percent get Subject line A; 50 percent get Subject line B. Group A gets an email with a short, direct, to-the-point Subject line. Group B receives one with a Subject line that's so long it gets cut off in most email clients.

Forty-eight hours after both emails are sent, you observe the following statistics:

- **Subject line A:** 20 percent open rate
- **Subject line B:** 10 percent open rate

Which Subject line is the winner? A (the shorter one) or B (the crazy long one)? Based on open rate alone, you would be silly (or not that great with numbers) unless you said "A" was the winner: 20 percent versus 10 percent. Group A's open rate was twice that of Group B's.

However, now consider the following metrics:

- **Subject line A:** 500 clicks
- **Subject line B:** 1,000 clicks

Using the same logic as earlier, Group B is the clear winner.

Now, taking the example one step further, let's look at conversions (sales):

- **Subject line A:** $10,000 in email-related sales
- **Subject line B:** $20,000 in email-related sales

Looks like "B" wins again.

The bottom line is this: Depending on the goal of your email campaign, a different (possibly longer) Subject line might outperform another (shorter).

But that's just a made-up scenario. How about a test using real client data?

Evidence in Favor of Long Subject Lines

Although many people have thought the short Subject line is the rule for several years now, many studies have been published to contradict that mentality. Instead, as discussed in this section, a longer Subject line might be the answer to more clicks and increased sales.

Alchemy Worx is the United Kingdom's largest full-service email marketing agency. It helps clients with everything from copywriting to design to testing and provides delivery and deployment services as well as reporting and analysis consulting. Its clients work with a full range of email service providers. This means, as an agency, it is ESP-agnostic (in other words, they do not favor one ESP over another). This helps when sharing testing results because it displays no bias towards one provider.

In a 2008 study,[13] Alchemy Worx ran a test similar to the earlier fictional scenarios; however, it used actual client data. Alchemy Worx analyzed 646 Subject lines across 205 million messages sent over nearly five years. Its conclusions were interesting. The first was that the longer the Subject line, the lower the open rate. As you can see in the chart in Figure 9.8, an inverse relationship exists between open rates and Subject line length (determined by number of characters).

All of those in favor of email marketing best practices just rejoiced with a big, resounding, "See. We told you!"

However, that's only the first part of the study results from Alchemy Worx. The agency also discovered the longer the Subject line, the higher the click-to-open rates. But that's not all: The click-through rate (clicks divided by delivered) also increases. In other words, you get more clicks with fewer opens!

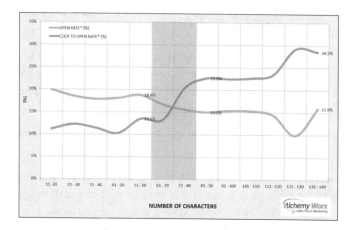

Figure 9.8 *An Alchemy Worx study shows the inverse relationship between open rates and the number of characters in the Subject line.*

Dela Quist, CEO of Alchemy Worx, believes that the key to Subject lines is meaning. "The shorter the subject line, the less likely you are to convey meaning. People have to open your email [to understand what it means]."

An example of a company who is notorious for sending emails with creative (and short) Subject lines is Urban Outfitters (urbanoutfitters.com). It intentionally writes its Subject lines to entice its audience to open the email to uncover the content. The following are a few actual Subject lines from Urban Outfitters:

- Top This
- A Dress For...
- Color It In
- 5, 4, 3, 2, 1...
- Introducing...

Consistent with what Quist said, conveying meaning with Subject lines that short is hard. They certainly tend to pique interest, thus leading to an open. However, as evidenced by the Alchemy Worx study, a higher open rate does not necessarily mean a higher click rate.

On the complete other end of the spectrum from Urban Outfitters is Groupon. Although certainly not always the case, some of its Subject lines tend to be on the long to very long side. In a February 16, 2012 email DJ received, the Subject line read:

One Oil Change, Three Oil Changes with Inspections, or a Four-Wheel Alignment (Up to 78% Off) | 10 or 20 Gym Passes (Up to 69% Off) | Salon Package with Cut, Style, and Two-Color Highlights; Shellac Manicure; or Acrylic Nails (Up to 51% Off)

Coming in at a whopping 42 words and 241 characters, this Subject line is in the very, very, VERY long category, possibly the longest we've ever seen. As you can imagine, it was truncated in Gmail to *"One Oil Change, Three Oil Changes with Inspections, or a Four-Wheel Alignment (Up to 78...."*

"With a longer subject line, the person can decide if the email is relevant. Although fewer emails are opened, those who open them are more qualified," said Quist.[14]

While we agree with Quist on this point, this Groupon Subject line might actually be too long to determine relevance. If you were in need of a car-related service, you would be more likely to open and click through on this email. However, if this email landed in your inbox and you were interested in gym passes or a salon package, due to the super-long nature of this Subject line, you would never know they were also being offered.

The Alchemy Worx study also found similar relationships when looking at number of words rather than number of characters. Subject lines with more words had a higher click to open rate compared to those with fewer words. It concluded this was true because words often are more important when conveying concepts compared to characters.

Alchemy Worx suggests that if you want to maximize open rates, using ambiguous (like Urban Outffiters does) or somewhat misleading Subject lines, which are often the shorter ones, is best. However, you have to be careful with deceptive Subject lines because they are illegal under the CAN-SPAM Act (it's what spammers do!).

To summarize, the Alchemy Worx study came to the following three conclusions:

- Shorter Subject lines generate higher open rates, a measure of reader interest, but much lower click-to-open rates.
- Longer Subject lines earn a much higher click-to-open rate, an indication of real relevance.
- The open rate and click-to-open rate curves intersect at about 60 to 70 characters, a "dead zone" where neither metric is optimized.

To muddy the waters a bit, studies have also shown longer Subject lines lead to higher open rates, among other things.

One of our favorite websites in regard to performing split tests is WhichTestWon. com. Founded by Anne Holland in 2009, WhichTestWon.com has more than

150 test case studies ranging from web to email to direct mail. It adds a new test every week and allows readers to vote on which option (A or B) they think is the winner.

In its 2011 "Long vs. Short Email Subject Line Test,"[15] WhichTestWon.com asked its members to guess which email received more opens and webinar registrations in a test for Sonic Foundry. The company sent an email targeting information technology and audio-visual decision makers. The split test featured only the Subject line as the differentiator. Everything else was the same.

- **Subject line A:** January 25 webinar: Enterprise Webcasting for High-Profile Clients
- **Subject line B:** January 25 webinar: Webcasting High-Profile Clients

Subject Line A was eight words and 66 characters long whereas its counterpart (B) was only six words and 51 characters. Any guesses which Subject line led to more opens, more click-throughs, and more webinar registrations? Humor us and forget for a minute that you're reading a book about breaking the rules of email marketing. If you guessed Subject line B, you would be in the majority, along with 63 percent of the site visitors on WhichTestWon.com who voted. Only 37 percent guessed that Subject line A was the winner.

However, even if you guessed A was the winner, we think you'll be surprised by how much it won by. Compared to Subject line B, A's open rate was 58.9 percent higher, its click-through rate was 224 percent more, and—most importantly for Sonic Foundry—webinar registrations jumped by 279 percent.

To be fair, a test like this is not as black and white as it might seem. Although it would appear that Subject line A won because it was longer, this might not be the case. After all, as the team at Sonic Foundry noted, the inclusion of the word *Enterprise* in Subject line A possibly was the reason for the higher numbers. Subject lines are something Sonic Foundry now tests on every webinar invite it sends.

The Most Incredible Chapter Ever

So this probably wasn't the most incredible chapter you've ever read. But it was vitally important in understanding how to approach email marketing like a rebel. Just because the madding crowd is running off the cliff with their aversion to ALL CAPS and propensity for short Subject lines doesn't mean you have to join them. What you're learning is that ALL CAPS and using certain spam trigger words, such as *free* and *limited time* and *deal*, are only a bad idea after you've tested Subject lines containing them with your audience and gotten bad results.

Even if you've proven through testing that they don't work with your audience, you can still pull them out and have them prove effective. Try a random FREE

SHIPPING email now and then and see whether you notice a jump in your success metrics, even if your tests show ALL CAPS are a turn off. If the current gold-standard case study for an email marketing success story, Groupon, can use a Subject line that is 42-words long, well, the shorter is better thing becomes null and void, too. Still, tossing out a short, teasing email Subject line will likely produce more opens or clicks, even when your tests show longer Subject lines are what the audience prefers.

In true rebel form, there are no rules—not even when you think there are. And that truth starts with Subject lines, but also applies to the design, or how your emails look.

Endnotes

1. Rubin, Karen, "The Ultimate List of Email SPAM Trigger Words." January 11, 2012. http://blog.hubspot.com/blog/tabid/6307/bid/30684/The-Ultimate-List-of-Email-SPAM-Trigger-Words.aspx

2. Waldow, DJ, "Words to Avoid in a Subject Line." March 7, 2012. http://waldowsocial.com/words-to-avoid-in-a-subject-line/ (update to blog post based on Laura Atkins email)

3. Atkins, Laura, "Content, trigger words and subject lines." January 11, 2012. http://blog.wordtothewise.com/2012/01/content-trigger-words-and-subject-lines/

4. "Why Should You Split Test Email Subject Lines?" http://www.aweber.com/blog/email-marketing/why-should-you-split-test-email-subject-lines.htm

5. WhichTestWon, "Email Subject Line Test: ALL CAPS vs Initial Caps." http://whichtestwon.com/email-subject-line-test-initial-caps-vs-all-caps

6. Alchemy Worxs Whitepaper, "Subject lines — length is every-thing." 2008. http://www.alchemyworx.com/Alchemy%20Worx%20Subject%20lines%20-%20length%20is%20everything.pdf

7. MailerMailer, "Email Marketing Metrics Report. JANUARY–JUNE (H1) 2007. http://cdn.mailermailer.com/documents/email-marketing-metrics-2007h1.pdf

8. MailChimp blog post, "A/B Split Testing — Does it Help Email Marketing?" August 28, 2008. http://blog.mailchimp.com/ab-split-testing-does-it-help-email-marketing/

9. MailChimp support article, "Best Practices in Writing Email Subject Lines." Updated June 22, 2011. http://kb.mailchimp.com/article/best-practices-in-writing-email-subject-lines

10. Jenkins, Simms, "4 Surefire Ways to Get Your Emails Read." August 25, 2011. http://www.clickz.com/clickz/column/2103830/surefire-emails-read

11. Brownlow, Mark, "Truncation traps: 3 more subject line lessons." June 4, 2010. http://www.email-marketing-reports.com/iland/2010/06/truncation-traps-3-more-subject-line-lessons.html

12. Brownlow, Mark, "5 lessons from a typical subject line test." August 26, 2011. http://www.email-marketing-reports.com/iland/2011/08/subject-line-test.html

13. Alchemy Worx Whitepaper, "Subject lines—length is everything." 2008. http://www.alchemyworx.com/Alchemy%20Worx%20Subject%20lines%20-%20length%20is%20everything.pdf

14. McDonald, Loren, "Guest Q&A: Dela Quist on Managing Inactives, Subject Line Length and Marketers' Fear & Self-Loathing." January 20, 2012. http://www.silverpop.com/blogs/email-marketing/dela-quist-subject-line-length.html

15. WhichTestWon.com, "Long vs Short Email Subject Line Test." February 9, 2012. https://whichtestwon.com/long-vs-short-email-subject-line-test

10

The Perfect-Looking Email

Think for a minute about the ugliest email you've ever received—an email that made you recoil in disgust. If you are having trouble thinking of just what that email looked like, put this book down for a minute and jump over to your email inbox. Scan through some recent emails and pick one that makes you say, "Yuck—this is one ugly email" out loud.

What were the characteristics of that email? Perhaps it was mostly text. You were appalled the sender didn't make the effort to include some pretty images or at least include the copy in an attractive template. Maybe the email was just one big image. You did not have images enabled by default, so the email looked like a whole mess of nothing. Maybe it had a bunch of different font sizes and types or one with so many colors it hurt your head to look at.

We all can think of a thing or two that drives us nuts about email marketing messages. For some, HTML (or website code) in email is the best thing that's ever happened. It allows senders to create aesthetically pleasing messages, ones that are easy on the eyes as well as make clear what action they want subscribers to take. However, for others, HTML in email is not so good. These are people who we believe should never be allowed to design emails or be in charge of email marketing programs. Okay, maybe that's a bit harsh, but you get the point.

In 2012, one would think marketers have matured from mostly text emails or emails with one big image. There is no excuse for sending ugly emails in the second decade of the twenty-first century. Unfortunately, this is not true. Email marketers break these "rules" all the time. Examples of "ugly" emails are everywhere, in every inbox across the world.

How can that be?

You have to remember that beauty is in the eye of the beholder. What you think is ugly might be gorgeous to someone else. This adage applies to more than just email marketing, of course, but is also true in the inbox. Also keep in mind that one company's target audience or customer base is different from another's. What looks appealing for a retail company focused on teenagers might not be the best format for a business-to-business (B2B) firm targeting chief financial officers.

Despite these rules, many companies are successful sending emails that are far from perfect looking. These people send mostly text or mostly images emails. They make opting out easy for their subscribers by placing an unsubscribe link or button at the top of their emails. They send what many would call "ugly" emails.

Are these folks crazy? Maybe. But that's another book altogether. What's interesting is that most of them are intentionally breaking the rules of email marketing by sending "ugly" emails and still finding a great deal of success. In this chapter, we're going to get ugly, but successful, and show you how the beautiful ones aren't necessarily the chosen few in email marketing.

It's Okay to Send Mostly Text Emails

Although Jameson Lopp might have been a bit extreme with the tweet shown in Figure 10.1, it's similar to a question we often hear: Why in the world would I send an all or mostly text email when I have the option of sending an HTML email with images?

Before we address that question, let's take the time machine back to the end of the twentieth century. In the late 1990s, as the Internet and email were first starting to become more accessible and mainstream, many people were still using modems with slower-than-molasses dial-up connections. Due to these slow speeds, images took forever to load on websites as well as in your email client (think: America Online and "You've Got Mail"). Additionally, not all email clients could read HTML. If you wanted your email to load quickly and have the best chance of being read by most of people, a text-only email was your best option.

Figure 10.1   *In a tweet, Jameson Lopp admits to reading email in plain text format.*

One argument in favor of mostly text emails has to do with how HTML emails render (or display). Litmus is a company whose software allows you to preview your HTML emails in actual email clients and mobile devices before sending your message, allowing you to see how the message renders. Then, based on what you discover, you can go back to your email and modify it accordingly.

As you can see in Figure 10.2—a screenshot using the Litmus software—the same email can look very different depending on the email client (Gmail, Hotmail, AOL, Lotus Notes), browser (Internet Explorer, Firefox), smartphone (BlackBerry, HTC, iPhone), or tablet (iPad 2) your subscriber is reading it on.

Sending a plain text email nearly guarantees your email will look the same on every device. Even though most smartphones can read HTML emails, BlackBerry devices continue to have rendering problems with them (as seen in Figure 10.3). Email service provider MailChimp published a support document[1] that listed several reasons why you should still create plain-text emails. One confirmed what Lopp tweeted: Some people just prefer plain-text emails. Another one focused on security concerns. Many modern email programs warn their users about potential threats of privacy and *phishing*. This is when someone sends an email that appears to be from a legitimate source, such as a bank, to get the recipient to respond with personal information such as his account password, Social Security number, and the like.

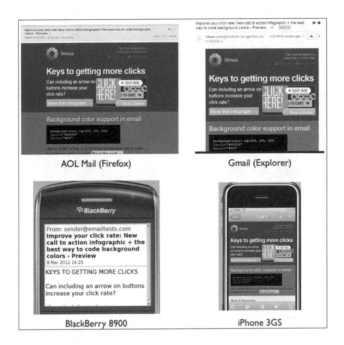

AOL Mail (Firefox)   Gmail (Explorer)

BlackBerry 8900   iPhone 3GS

Figure 10.2   *A preview of one email (using the Litmus software) looks very different depending on the email client, browser, and smartphone being used.*

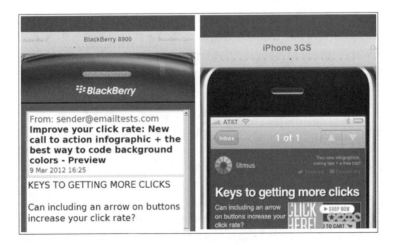

Figure 10.3   *The same Litmus email viewed on a BlackBerry 8900 (left) and an iPhone 3GS (right). Which one is most likely how the sender intended it to look?*

It's safer to use plain text emails because HTML is often preferred by scam artists. A plain text email also streamlines the amount of code, or technical information, that is contained in the email file. Smaller file sizes can help your email clear spam filters and appear safer to your recipient's email service provider.

Finally, plain text email can seem a lot more personal—more one-to-one. When was the last time a friend, family member, significant other, colleague, or co-worker sent you an HTML email? When was the last time they dropped you a note that was in a template with images and various styles? Unless you signed up for that person's email list, probably never. For personal communications, everyone is much more accustomed to seeing emails in plain text.

However, the key to success is to test. What works well for one audience might be totally different for another. Your goals and success metrics might look quite different than someone else's.

Some Subscribers Prefer Simple Text Emails

Derek Halpern, who does marketing at DIYthemes and is the founder of Social Triggers, is big on testing. Through blog posts, articles, podcasts, webinars, and live presentations, Halpern shares insights on how to use psychology to better understand what makes people tick.

In less than a year, Halpern has grown Social Triggers into one of the leading destinations for online marketing advice. As of April 2012, he had attracted more than 20,000 subscribers to his site. Email marketing has historically been, and continues to be, a big reason for Halpern's rapid growth.

"I've experimented with both simple text and fancy HTML, and in all my experience, simple text generates the best results," Halpern said. Knowing that his emails are mostly text, we asked him to clarify how he determined best results.

"Not only did I average more click throughs, I also had lower unsubscribes and more interaction," he said. Halpern even asked his subscribers to share their thoughts about simple text versus fancy HTML email in a survey. The results:

- 55.1 percent of respondents said they preferred simple text.
- 19.7 percent preferred HTML.
- 25.2 percent of respondents responded with "Kind of..." (which really means that they like text, but there was something else bothering them like the width of the email).

Those who responded in favor of the simple text emails shared a bit more about why:

- "Clean"
- "Much easier to read"
- "The new format tended to make me feel as if I were a tried and trusted confidant—and that was welcomed"
- "It's clean and easy to read. Call to actions are also clean and easy to follow."

Halpern told us that focusing on simple text emails has been extremely effective. "On one email I sent out to more than 10,000 people," he said, "I saw a 74.2 percent open rate and a 25.1 percent click-through rate." He's able to measure this open rate because his email, while mostly text, is still written in HTML, thus allowing the email service provider's invisible image to record an open. (For an explanation of the invisible image approach, see the following sidebar on open rates.)

"This all depends on how you condition your subscribers," Halpern explained. "Also, it depends on how great your content is. Just because text emails work for me, doesn't mean they will work for you. However, don't let that be your excuse for not trying them. Smart email marketers test, and they test often. What's true today may not be true tomorrow."

Halpern believes, and we agree, that one of the keys to email marketing is to take widely accepted assumptions (best practices) and ensure they're true in your business. In other words, *best practices are practices that work best for you and your subscribers.*

A NOTE ABOUT OPEN RATES

One of the challenges with sending text-only emails is that accurately measuring open rates is difficult. Email service providers include a small piece of code in every email, one that's invisible to the viewer. When a recipient enables (turns on) images in an email, that image is downloaded and the email provider is able to record that occurrence as a unique open. Although it's far from a perfect tool, it does provide a fairly accurate measure of true open rate.

Therefore, sending a plain-text email, which has no links and no image, makes measuring open rates impossible. Without any images to download, that tiny snippet of code is never displayed, and the email provider has no way of knowing whether the message was opened.

One way around this problem is to send an "HTML-lite" email. This email is written in HTML and allows for some basic text formatting, yet does not have images, or none that you can really see. They're there, but small, unobtrusive to the point of being invisible, and used for tracking purposes. This method allows an email provider to track opens (assuming those images are enabled), yet still ensure that the email has a text-only look and feel.

Writing Letters Versus Pamphlets

Jason Keath is a social media speaker and analyst. He is an entrepreneur as well as Founder and CEO of Social Fresh, a social media education company. Keath produces high-level social media conferences and training across the country and online, for the marketing perspective. Keath has been doing email marketing for nearly six years. Like Halpern, email plays a critical role in his business.

"(Email is) our most direct line to our fans and customers. If we want to let our stakeholders know when we are launching a new event or product or websites, email reaches ten times what we can get through Facebook, Twitter, and our blog combined," Keath said.

In 2011, Keath decided to switch his email campaigns from well-designed, "pretty" HTML emails, to mostly text with a few links as the main calls to action. He cited several reasons, including more efficient production time, the emails are more easily read on mobile devices, and the new format allowed him to build more of a personal connection with his email audience. He said the transition was, "like writing letters as opposed to mailing out pamphlets."

The personal touch and community connection aspect of mostly text emails is the most important one for Keath. Considering Social Fresh advocates the personal connection, this approach makes sense. Equally as important, he's seeing great results. Opens and click-through rates on Keath's mostly text emails are higher than his more traditional, HTML template emails with images. Since making the switch, Keath has seen open rates rise from 18 percent to 21 percent, whereas click-through rates have jumped from under 6 percent to more than 8 percent.

Like Halpern, Keath also stressed that the content of his emails, more than the format, is the real driver in success. "Very timely topics get high click-throughs. Talking about Facebook when they are in the news or topics related to broader newsworthy topics like Christmas or the Super Bowl [generate more clicks]."

Text Emails Have a Clean Look

Chris Brogan is the president of Human Business Works, a media and education company. He's also a consultant, professional speaker, and bestselling co-author of the book *Trust Agents* (Wiley, 2010). Brogan and his team at Human Business Works have been sending a weekly, mostly text, email newsletter to their list since 2010. In late 2011, they switched to a new email service provider and really began focusing on list growth. The result? An 86 percent growth in their email list in a short 11 weeks.

Rob Hatch, Chief Operating Officer of Human Business Works, attributed this rapid growth to four main factors:

- Useful content written in a personal way; connecting with people in a human way and being helpful

- Consistency of delivery; generally delivered on Tuesday mornings at 10:30 a.m.

- Asking people in a simple, direct and clear way to subscribe. And to do so in many places.

- Asking for referrals, recommendations, and shares at the end of emails

As you can see in Figure 10.4, Brogan's email is nearly all text, with a few links here and there. It's written 100 percent by him and has averaged a 34 percent open rate since the company began sending on a more consistent (weekly) schedule.

Figure 10.4 *Professional speaker Chris Brogan sends emails written in HTML, but they are mostly text.*

In case you missed that last part, it's worth repeating: The Human Business Works mostly text email averages a 34 percent open rate—almost double the industry average!

So why send mostly text emails, especially when Human Business Works uses an email platform that makes creating HTML emails in a "pretty" template easy?

"We like the clean and direct look of a text email," Hatch explained. "Your friend doesn't send you emails in a nice template, I'm not sure we need to. I really believe plain text appearance (done in HTML for tracking) makes for easy reading on all devices and gets right to the point with the reader, which is to be helpful."

Early on in 2010, the company sent templated HTML emails. Hatch said, "We didn't see them as useful or necessary for the community of folks who subscribe to our newsletter."

Text Works for B2C Marketers, Too!

The preceding three examples are from service-related businesses or consultancies, but mostly text emails also pop up on occasion in the business-to-consumer (B2C) world. Chad White, Research Director at Responsys, said that sometimes companies mix up their normal messaging style to provide a "wake-up slap." He said subscribers to your email newsletter can get bored by opening the same type of email again and again.[2]

The company 1-800-Flowers.com mixed up its regular style email (see Figure 10.5). Although it still included its logo and color template in the header of this message, the rest of the email is rich text with a few calls to action links. That's it.

White believes this type of email, when mixed in with your typical, image-heavy HTML emails, can provide enough of a double-take to get subscribers to pay attention and take action.

"This [1-800-Flowers] email is a big deviation from their usual design, so subscribers are more likely to pay attention," White said. "The brief, text-heavy arrangement also screams urgency, which is exactly what you want with a deal email like this."

Help A Reporter Out (also known as HARO) does not use the "wake-up slap" approach. It never sends pretty HTML emails. In fact, none of its messages contain images at all. They are comprised of a whole bunch of text, a few anchor links as well as many, custom email address links.

To be fair, HARO is not your average company. Although it's in the media relations business, it takes a very different approach than the industry standard of reaching out to media and hoping for a response. HARO reverses the process, collecting the coverage needs of journalists who submit them.

Figure 10.5   *1-800-Flowers.com deviated from its normal, HTML, image-heavy messages. This "wake-up slap" tactic helps capture subscriber attention.*

Founded by Peter Shankman in 2008 and purchased by Vocus in June 2010, the HARO community boasts more than 132,000 registered sources and more than 28,000 reporters (as of the first quarter of 2012). Between the registered HARO sources and pass-along forwards to non-registered users, the HARO currently has nearly 200,000 readers daily.

Any guesses as to which medium those queries and pitches are delivered? You've got it: Email! And not just your standard weekly email. Nope. In fact, it's not even a daily email (like Groupon or Living Social). Instead, HARO sends its subscribers three emails every single day. Yes, you read that correctly! Three emails every single day! On top of that, these emails are nearly all text (see Figure 10.6).

"The HARO's simple and clean mostly text format is a manifestation of function over flare," said Chris Pilbeam of Vocus, which owns the service. It wants to do everything in its power to avoid ending up in spam folders.

HARO is not interested in its emails being pretty, because a good-looking email does not determine success. Instead, a key success metric is a high number of its emails landing in the inbox and being read. Pilbeam said that for HARO to work properly, the sources must receive the emails. Plain text helps the company ensure higher open and read rates.

24) Summary: Need to Interview Moms Who Conduct Business from their Domiciles

Category: General

Email: query-22gm@helpareporter.net

Media Outlet: Anonymous

Deadline: 7:00 PM EST - 14 April

Query:

No sales structures. I need to interview moms and have created their own business that they manage from their home with their children present. Some of the businesses might be: photography, journalist, blogger, florist, seamstress, event planner, wedding cake designer, webpage designer, caterer, concierge, etc. Please do not contact me, if you are with a parent company sales system such as beauty, household, kitchen products, etc.

Thanks for your help.

Requirements:

Must be a mom who conducts business from her domicile with kids at home. No in-home daycare either provided or hired. I need to interview moms who are actively juggling conducting business from their domiciles on their own business while raising their children.

Figure 10.6   *This portion of the HARO (Help A Reporter Out) mostly text email newsletter, shows that the three-times daily email is just a simple, plain text email with just the important links added.*

After a HARO email is delivered to subscribers' inboxes, readers can do a quick scan to see the queries for which they are a good fit. Pilbeam said the simple layout and format is critical for this to happen. Because each email contains 50 to 60 queries and speed is a factor in a company representative's getting the reporter to pick him as a source, simple is best. Dressing the email up with fancy graphics would likely just get in the way of the functionality.

Expectations are important, too. Everyone who subscribes to the HARO emails are expecting them at the three regularly scheduled times each day. Believe it or not, some HARO users even set their alarms so they won't miss the first HARO email, delivered at 5:45 a.m. EST.

As you can tell, text-only emails not only can be effective, but sometimes are more effective than their more graphically-designed counterparts. But let's also look at the opposite end of the spectrum: When an email is nothing more than one, big image.

One Big Image Can Work

"Never send an email that is simply one big image."[3]*—From "Email Marketing Best Practices" by StartUpNation, February 2, 2012*

"Common practice is to wag a warning finger at any commercial email made up mostly (or even entirely) of images."[4]*—Mark Brownlow, November 22, 2007*

Email marketing messages that are made up of mostly images or (gasp!) one big image are often frowned upon in best practice circles for two reasons, both quite valid. One is that emails that are heavy on images are more likely to be flagged as spam. If you use an email service provider, you should get an alert before you send an email telling you whether or not it has too many spam-like characteristics. This service is called a spam filter.

One of the most common content-based spam filters is SpamAssassin, an open source one that generates a score based on various rules. According to Campaign Monitor, an email service provider that uses SpamAssassin, "A score of **more than 5** may cause deliverability issues while scores of greater than 10 frequently develop delivery issues. You should always aim to keep your score under 5 for each campaign you send."[5]

Another reason big images are frowned upon is that most email clients, such as Gmail, block images by default. You can see an example in the email from AAA in Figure 10.7. The message at the top of this Gmail email reads, "Images are not displayed." The subscriber is then given two options:

- **Display images below:** This shows the images for this one email.
- **Always display images from AAA.mail.goaaa.com:** If this option is clicked, all images from this sender (assuming the company uses the same From address) will always appear automatically.

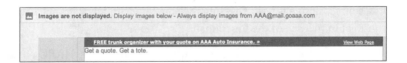

Figure 10.7   *A Gmail user must choose whether images in an email can load.*

For emails with just a handful of images, and none that really impact the overall meaning of the message, this blocking is not a huge issue. However, if your email is one big image, getting your subscribers to understand the contents of the message might be a challenge if they can't see it! Assuming you don't enable images on this email from National Geographic, Figure 10.8 shows what you'll see in your inbox when you open the message.

Now compare that same email with images on (see Figure 10.9), and you get a pretty good sense of what the email is all about.

Figure 10.8   *An email from National Geographic (top half only) with images turned off leaves a lot to the imagination.*

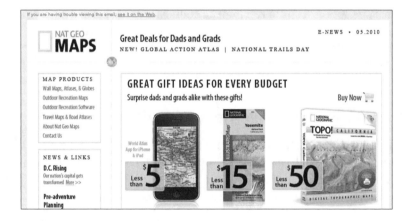

Figure 10.9   *With images turned on, the same National Geographic email becomes a lot more interesting.*

We agree that emails are more likely to get marked as spam if they have a high ratio of images to text. We also agree that with most email clients blocking images by default, "images off" emails like the one from National Geographic in Figure 10.8 are, well, not all that interesting to look at.

However, we don't believe "never send emails with mostly images" is a rule you should follow all the time. In fact, many companies intentionally send emails in this format and are quite successful.

In many cases, the decision to display images from a sender has to do more with trust and value than anything else. Let's step through a real example to explain what we mean. Both DJ and Jason have been Apple fans for years. Between us, we own three iPhones, two iPads, an iPod Shuffle, two MacBook Pros, an iMac, and a MacBook Air. We both frequent the Apple Store, both in person and online.

We've also been subscribers of Apple's email marketing messages for years. We trust the brand. We look forward to seeing Apple's emails. We enjoy reading them. So, when a mostly image email lands in our inbox from Apple, we turn images on without hesitation. Truth be told, we set our respective email accounts to "Always display images" from Apple a long time ago.

The bottom line is this: If someone wants to see your email content, and he trusts you as a sender, he will turn on images for your email. In fact, according to The Relevancy Group, 35 percent of consumers turn on images in their email. The number jumps to 56 percent for 27-to-32-year-olds. Statistics show that the younger the consumer, the more likely he will turn images on for emails.[6]

David Daniels, CEO of The Relevancy Group, not only advocates for using images in email, he goes as far as to recommend adding more images and making them larger to make emails more readable and scannable on mobile devices. Not quite what the email marketing purists would suggest.

Many companies not only send mostly image emails, they do so purposefully.

King Arthur Flour's Image-Heavy Emails

We first introduced King Arthur Flour (or KAF, if you're hip) in Chapter 9, "My Word! You Must Read This Now!" If you recall, this company broke the "never use the word *FREE* or all caps in the Subject line" rule. It's back at rule-breaking, this time sending emails with mostly images, like the one in Figure 10.10.

KAF spends more time on email creative (copy and images) than any other aspect of its email marketing. As you can see from the email in Figure 10.10, it also is not afraid to use mostly images in its messages. "All emails are image heavy and we are okay with that," said Halley Silver, Director of Online Services at King Arthur Flour. "We want people to drool over the screen and click through and buy."

With this goal in mind, KAF also is deliberate about when it sends its image-heavy emails.

"We send them late morning so [subscribers] get them before lunch," Silver reported. "Creatively, the best way to get people to click through is to have a gorgeous shot of something gooey and delicious. A strong graphic works."

KAF takes email marketing pretty seriously. It tests. It tweaks. It experiments. KAF also mixes it up by sending content-heavy emails occasionally. However, the goal of these emails is focused more on content and education. The company often follows up a big promotion with this type of email to keep people interested and engaged.

Figure 10.10   *King Arthur Flour's email is composed of mostly images, sliced up a bit. How good does that Braided Lemon Bread look?*

Making Mostly Image Emails More Readable

One of the biggest arguments against crafting an email with many images, or one big image as shown in the National Geographic example, is that getting a sense of what the message is all about can be tough unless a subscriber enables those images.

Mark Brownlow proposed an interesting workaround to help ensure subscribers will see image-heavy emails. He said, "Anybody wanting to try image-rich emails safely could simply pull out a list of 'people who previously opened at least one email from us' and send this group the image-rich mail. New subscribers and those with no open yet recorded get a 'safe' design with a nice balance of text and images, etc."[7]

In theory, this strategy would work for the most part; however, it assumes that someone who previously opened an email has now enabled all images from that sender. Also, the possibility exists that an open was recorded not due to images being turned on, but because the reader clicked on a link (as discussed in Chapter 9). Either way, this tactic might be worth testing.

You can use two other ways to make image-heavy emails more readable as well as encourage subscribers to enable images. Those include using alt text and a method called "slice and dice."

Alt Text

Alternative tags, also known as "alt tags" or "alt text," are the text associated with an image viewable when images are not available. This tag, which is part of the HTML code of the page, applies to images on web pages as well as in emails. Alt tags are often used in search engine optimization to let search engines know what a particular image is. Search engine bots cannot see an image, only read the code that tells the browser to display it.

When an image is supposed to be loaded on a page (on the web or in an email) but for some reason it doesn't display (maybe the email software prevents images from displaying for safety reasons), the text that populates the alt tag will display where the image should be.

Alt text can be a good way to ensure that your mostly image email is still readable by subscribers who have images turned off by default. If you are using an editor within an email service provider's application, most include an option to include alt text. If you are comfortable editing the HTML of your email marketing messages, you can modify the alt text by changing what's inside the quotes after alt=.

When viewing the HTML in the example from Petco (see Figure 10.11), notice what's in quotes after alt=: "It's Bark Madness! 20% Off Sitewide!" Those two sentences are the alt text and can be modified to show whatever text you want your subscribers to see when images are turned off.

Figure 10.11   *HTML code includes the alt text for this image in an email from Petco.*

Speaking of Petco, most of its emails rely heavily on imagery. The email in Figure 10.12 is one big image that's been sliced into five smaller images and then mashed back together. On the left is part of its email with images turned off; on the right is the same email with images turned on.

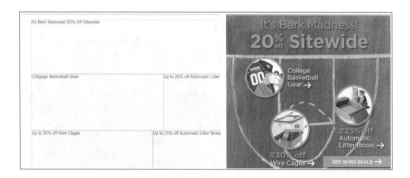

Figure 10.12   *A Petco email with images off (left) and images on (right) uses alt tags to describe what each image is, enticing their subscribers to enable images.*

Petco does a nice job of using the alt text to exactly describe each image. Notice that the alt text for each image is consistent whether or not images are turned on. This allows subscribers to quickly scan the email with images disabled and decide whether turning them on is worth their time.

If you are ready to take it up a notch and really entice subscribers to turn images on, try doing what blogger Chris Penn does in his weekly email newsletter. Remember Penn's in-your-face, quite ugly unsubscribe button that he uses at the top of all of his emails? In case you forgot, we've included it again in Figure 10.13.

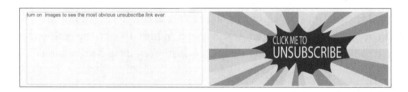

Figure 10.13   *Chris Penn's unsubscribe link with image off (left) and on (right) shows how to use a bit of humor to entice subscribers to enable images.*

The image on the right in Figure 10.13 is what Penn's unsubscribe button looks like with images turned on. See? We told you it was not pretty. On the left is what the image looks like when a subscriber does not enable images in her email client. However, notice that Penn customizes the alt text with a bit of humor: "turn on images to see the most obvious unsubscribe link ever."

Those who enable images are "rewarded" by being able to see the rest of the buttons and pictures Penn includes in his weekly email. For Penn, he's able to get a more accurate open rate number. Win-win.

Another creative way to showcase an email when images are turned off is to do what British company Pizza Express did in the "Celebrating 40 Years of Live Music" email shown in Figure 10.14.[8]

Figure 10.14   *An email from Pizza Express shows a creative way to use images off (see portion on right).*

The screenshot on the left in Figure 10.14 is the Pizza Express email with images turned on. However, if you were to view the same email with images off, you would see the one on the right. Pizza Express has taken quite a creative approach for the "images disabled" version of the email. It has actually styled the images-off email with various background colors to make the picture of musician Jamie Cullum look like the old-school Atari version of him. In fact, the entire images-off email creatively uses styling so not much is lost when images are disabled.

Slice and Dice

In many cases, especially in the B2C world, imagery is essential to an email marketing campaign. As discussed earlier in the King Arthur Flour example, a picture of braided lemon bread, along with step-by-step pictures of it being made, will likely appeal to more subscribers versus a plain-text description.

Even if you come up with the most creative, descriptive, humorous alt text for that one big image, it's still going to appear mostly blank. Also, one image can only have one link. What if your image had multiple places on your website you wanted your subscribers to be taken to? One big image can be limiting.

An alternative is what Molly Niendorf, a member of the Content team at email service provider Emma, calls "slice and dice." Using Niendorf's method, "you're able to slice your large image into more digestible pieces, link those pieces to any number of URLs you desire, and safely send to your audience. [This is] good for you and good for your audience."[9] Ibex Outdoor Clothing, LLC, a merino wool clothing company based in Vermont, employs the "slice and dice" method for most of its emails. You can see an example of this on the left in Figure 10.15. Each grid-like section is a different image slice. Put together—and once images are enabled—they form one big image, as can be seen on the right of Figure 10.15.

Figure 10.15   *The top half of an email from Ibex shows how different the message renders with images off (left) vs. on (right). The bottom half, not shown, includes more text; however, imagery is critical to the Ibex brand.*

Jess Moschetti has been with Ibex for more than five years and is currently its Email Marketing and Website Content Manager. Over that time, Moschetti has seen email marketing become a serious revenue driver for the Ibex direct online business. In fact, about 20 percent of its direct sales can be attributed to the email marketing channel.

With a total list size of nearly 70,000 subscribers—of which 40,000 are active customers—Moschetti spends a lot of time thinking about each and every email.

And, as you can see in Figure 10.15, the top half of many Ibex emails is composed of one big image.

"It's important that we are being true to our brand and our aesthetics," Moschetti said. "We want to hold strong to those factors so that our customers know, recognize, and come to expect our emails to have a certain look." She said they also don't want their emails to be just be about sales but also beautiful imagery and clean design.

One thing to note about the Ibex emails: The company could take advantage of alt text to either add a description of the image or get more creative and style it using HTML. However, this mostly image tactic works for Ibex. According to data from its email service provider (Bronto), it averaged a 20.6 percent open rate, 31.1 percent click-through rate, and 4.7 percent conversion rate.

But what about deliverability issues? After all, it is sending a mostly image email, right? Moschetti told us, in her five years at Ibex, the company has not encountered any deliverability issue that would be attributed to the image-heavy email. Now you know that text-only can work, as can image-only emails. How's that for following the rules? But you need to know about another so-called best practice that affects how beautiful your email is as well. This one might surprise you because it's about inviting people to opt out of your list before they even get to the juicy content.

What If the Unsubscribe Link Is at the Top of the Email?

If consumers want to stop receiving permission emails, they will click the link to unsubscribe most of the time (actually 67 percent, according to ExactTarget[10]). The same ExactTarget report lists a few other actions subscribers take when they are no longer interested in getting emails from a certain organization:

- Delete the emails when they arrive: 17 percent
- Click the "spam" or "junk" button: 8 percent
- Nothing; just ignore the emails: 6 percent
- Set up a filter in an email program: 2 percent

Let's say you received an email from an organization: one you opted-in for, yet no longer want to receive. The content might no longer be relevant, you are receiving too much email, or you just want out for some reason. Let's also assume you are in the 67 percent category of subscribers who click the link to unsubscribe. Where would you look within the body of the email to find the unsubscribe link? The right side? The left side? The preheader? The header? The body? The bottom of the email (the footer)?

If you guessed "the bottom of the email," you would be in the majority. In fact, in the *Unsubscribe Email Strategies Report,*[11] Epsilon found that nearly 99 percent of all marketers put the unsubscribe link at the bottom of their emails. We've been trained to look for this unsubscribe link in the email footer or somewhere near the bottom of the message.

We agree with the 99 percent. The unsubscribe link should be in the bottom of all email marketing messages. If that's where subscribers will first look to opt out, it should definitely be there. However, what would happen if another unsubscribe option were located somewhere else within the email, somewhere a bit more prominent? How would this affect complaints? How would it impact unsubscribes?

We see one issue with putting the unsubscribe link in the footer of emails. Often the unsubscribe is tacked on as an afterthought and blends in with the rest of the message, as shown in Figures 10.16 and 10.17.

Figure 10.16   *This unsubscribe link blends in with the other links in the footer of this email. Can you find it?*

About Us | Archives | Perks | Contact | Jobs | Advertise | Tips
Privacy Policy | User Agreement | Unsubscribe | Editorial Policy

Figure 10.17   *This unsubscribe link is very difficult to find unless you look closely. Notice the smaller, gray font that blends into the background.*

Other times it's buried among legalese or requires users to take multiple steps— clicking a link, going to another web page to log in, unchecking a box—to process the unsubscribe (see Figure 10.18).

This email was sent to   (djwaldow). You can unsubscribe by logging in here, clicking my account and unchecking the email box.

Figure 10.18   *This email unsubscribe requires users to first log in before unsubscribing from their mailings.*

In regard to requiring multiple steps in order to opt out, senders have to be careful. Some language in the United States CAN-SPAM Act makes it illegal to require a recipient to take any steps other than visiting a single Internet web page to unsubscribe. As always, be sure to consult legal counsel for interpretation of the law.

Other websites might have confusing statements on their opt-out page (see Figure 10.19).

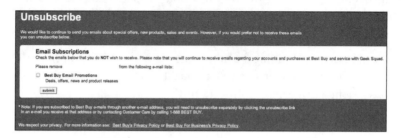

Figure 10.19 *Best Buy's unsubscribe instructions might be confusing to some email recipients.*

"Check the emails below that you do NOT wish to receive." Huh? Also, look at the note at the bottom, under the submit button: "If you are subscribed to Best Buy e-mails through another e-mail address, you will need to unsubscribe separately by clicking the unsubscribe link in an e-mail you receive at that address or by...." We realize Best Buy is trying to cover itself legally by including this statement, but it sure is confusing for the average subscriber.

Others, such as Carnival, give their subscribers a choice to "opt down" (receive fewer emails). After subscribers click the unsubscribe link at the bottom of a Carnival email, they are redirected to the page shown in Figure 10.20.

From this page, subscribers have the ability to "adjust the number of emails [they] receive." They can opt down to one or two emails per month or only receive sales/ promotion messages. Finally, they still have the choice of opting out entirely.

Sometimes a subscriber unsubscribes because that's the only option. What they really want to do is just not get so much email from the sender. This opt-down approach provides that option. It has the potential to decrease both unsubscribes and complaints.

Some marketers are offering a similar option to opting down by allowing their readers to "snooze" their emails.

This snooze feature, provided by email service provider Silverpop, gives subscribers the option to pause all emails from that sender for a specified period of time. As you can see in Figure 10.21, when subscribers click on the unsubscribe link in a J&P Cycles email, they are presented with the option to "snooze me for ... 1 month, 3 months, or 6 months." Of course they are still given the option—via a big button—to unsubscribe, if that's what they really wanted to do.

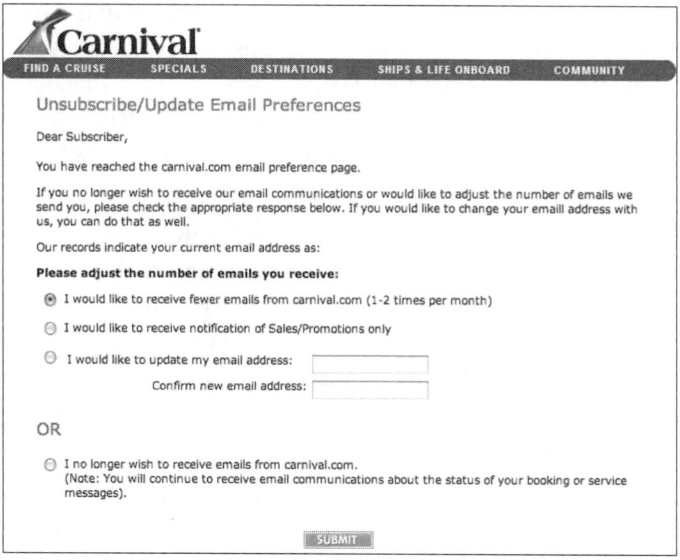

Carnival
FIND A CRUISE
SPECIALS
DESTINATIONS
SHIPS & LIFE ONBOARD
COMMUNITY
Unsubscribe/Update Email Preferences
Dear Subscriber,
You have reached the carnival.com email preference page.
If you no longer wish to receive our email communications or would like to adjust the number of emails we send you, please check the appropriate response below. If you would like to change your emaill address with us, you can do that as well.
Our records indicate your current email address as:
Please adjust the number of emails you receive:
I would like to receive fewer emails from carnival.com (1-2 times per month)
I would like to receive notification of Sales/Promotions only
I would like to update my email address:
Confirm new email address:
OR
I no longer wish to receive emails from carnival.com.
(Note: You will continue to receive email communications about the status of your booking or service messages).
SUBMIT

Figure 10.20 *After clicking the unsubscribe link in a Carnival email, subscribers are redirected to this manage preferences page where they can "opt down" to receive fewer emails.*

Don't unplug us... just hit snooze!
Did you know you can now snooze your subscription to J&P Cycles emails? Select a time frame below and hit snooze to pause your subscription for that length. It's really that simple!
* Email
Snooze me for
1 Month
Snooze
1 Month
3 Months
6 Months
Are you having
omething on our site and would like assistance?
Please visit our customer service center.
No thanks, I just want to unsubscribe
J&P
CYCLES

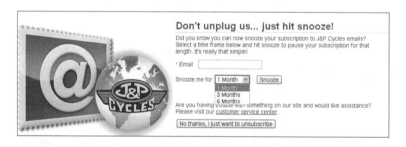

Figure 10.21 *The J&P Cycles email preference center allows subscribers who click on the unsubscribe link to choose to "snooze" their emails for a specified period of time.*

According to Loren McDonald, VP of Industry Relations for Silverpop, retention rates for clients enabling this feature are in the range of 3 to 5 percent. In other words, of those who clicked on the unsubscribe link, 3 to 5 percent chose to stay subscribed by opting for the snooze option.

Several other Silverpop clients have also found success with the snooze feature. Since including it as an option on its manage preference page, Moosejaw has seen 3 percent of customers who click the unsubscribe link opt to put their subscriptions on hiatus. Eoin Comerford, Vice-President of Marketing at Moosejaw, an outdoor apparel retailer, expects this number to reach close to 10 percent over time.[12]

Teletext Holidays reports its snooze number to be 5 percent. In just over a month, 5 percent of those who would have opted out chose to snooze instead. "Not only does this limit the number of customers opting out from receiving our communications but also gives us an opportunity to re-engage with them and capture their new preferences at the point of un-snoozing," said Media Manager Amy Patel.[13]

We can see this working in a variety of industries. For example, let's say you just purchased a new pair of running shoes. You are an active runner so will likely need a new pair in three to six months. This snooze feature allows you to pause all emails from that company until you are ready for that next purchase. It's great for the sender because sending emails to folks who will not read them doesn't make much sense. Also, if the alternative is for you to unsubscribe, the company has been able to retain you. The benefit for the subscribers is that they keep the emails in their inbox more relevant and timely. Win-win.

However, other than the examples from Carnival and J&P Cycles, all others discussed make opting out a challenge. If someone wants to unsubscribe from your email marketing messages, don't make it difficult. Don't create multiple steps. Don't force a login or make it confusing. All of these have the potential to turn a clean break up into an ugly divorce. If a subscriber wants out, let him leave. Good riddance. No hard feelings. It makes more sense to send emails to a list of people who rejoice when they see your emails in their inboxes. Wouldn't it be nice if people set their alarm clocks so they could be one of the first to open your emails (like some people do with the HARO 5:45 a.m. EST email)?

Instead of making opting out a chore, make it easy and obvious. Try flipping this "rule" of the unsubscribe always having to be at the bottom of the email completely on its head. Consider adding an unsubscribe option at the top of the email. Put the control back in the hands of the subscriber.

Another reason to make opting out easy for your subscribers is this: If they really want to opt out, yet have difficulty doing so, they are going to be frustrated. If they're frustrated, they'll be more likely to mark your email as spam, which can impact your overall email deliverability: certainly not worth it. Further, frustrated users who happen to also be plugged in online and active on social media might express that frustration to their social networks. That's the bad kind of viral message: one you don't want out there about your company.

Chapter 5, "The First Impression," previewed the unsubscribe rule breaker method by showing how WhatToExpect.com includes a prominent unsubscribe button in the preheader of its emails (refer to Figure 5.6). Chapter 7, "The Finishing Touches," showed you Chris Penn's far-from-pretty unsubscribe graphic he includes near the top of every email. Plenty more examples exist of both business-to-business (B2B) and business-to-consumer (B2C) companies who include an unsubscribe option at the top of their email. All of these organizations believe strongly in their decision to move it to the top.

We are not suggesting removing the unsubscribe link from the footer. If that's where consumers are trained to look, it should remain there. However, consider adding it to the top, in the preheader or header, as an alternative.

The Most Headache-inducing, Eye-searing Graphic Possible

A few years ago, when blogger and cohost of the Marketing Over Coffee podcast, Chris Penn was spending a lot of time focused on growing his email list, he got tired of reading complaints from his subscribers saying they didn't know how to unsubscribe. So Penn contacted his friend, Paul R.J. Muller of the CaffiNation Podcast, and asked him to create "the most headache inducing, eye searing graphic possible."

Muller answered the challenge and then some (see Figure 10.22).

Figure 10.22   *Chris Penn includes this unsubscribe button at the top of every single email. Hard to miss!*

Penn actually breaks a few rules with his unsubscribe button. First, it would likely fit into the "ugly" category. Unless bright pink, yellow, and blue are your thing, this button is not that pretty. Also, Penn has moved the unsubscribe button to the top of the email—front and center literally. Why would Penn make the unsubscribe button so ugly and obvious? "I wanted it to be really, really obvious," said Penn. His goal was to make it so obvious that if a subscriber missed it, Penn wouldn't feel bad about just outright deleting their email complaining they could not find the opt-out.

Penn has had an unsubscribe button of some kind at the top of his emails since 2010. It was around this time he began sending out his email newsletter on a regular schedule. This increased frequency and volume, Penn thought, would also increase the number of folks who might want off his list.

As it turns out, since adding this big, ugly unsubscribe link at the top of his emails, Penn's unsubscribe rate has held steady at .15 percent or less per email newsletter. Even more impressive is that he has not received a single spam complaint in more than two years. Keep in mind, his list has more than 13,000 subscribers.

Penn's advice on unsubscribes and retention include making it painfully obvious how to get to your preferences center so readers can control their experience with your email. Penn even has a video on his preferences center page that reminds people why they subscribed in the first place, so he has an opportunity to retain those who might be there to opt out.

Setting proper expectations upfront, on your opt-in form and in your welcome email, is important to build trust. However, reminding your subscribers why they signed up in the first place is equally if not more important.

Groupon's Creative Unsubscribe Solution

Groupon also includes a link to unsubscribe at the top of its emails, as shown in Figure 10.23.

Your Daily Salt Lake City Groupon | Go to Groupon.com | Unsubscribe
Be sure to add mail@e.groupon.com to your address book or safe sender list so our emails get to your inbox. Learn how

Figure 10.23 *Groupon includes an Unsubscribe link in the preheader of all of its email marketing messages.*

Although not nearly as in-your-face obvious as Penn's unsubscribe button, the Groupon team makes opting out of its emails easy by placing a prominent link in the preheader of its daily emails. Notice the preheader actually includes a few links: "Go to Groupon.com," "Learn how" (for adding their email address to a subscribers' address book), and "Unsubscribe."

Groupon also includes a standard unsubscribe link at the bottom of its emails just in case subscribers miss it at the top. The messaging reads, "If you prefer not to receive Daily Groupon emails, you can always unsubscribe with one click." Clicking on that link does just that: unsubscribes a user immediately. However, on that same page is the option to manage your email preferences as well as resubscribe for certain Groupon emails. This step is important because it allows subscribers to remove themselves from one list while remaining on others. At the bottom of this page, Groupon provides a link to unsubscribe from all emails from Groupon.

In 2010, Groupon tested a unique approach with its unsubscribe link. If users clicked unsubscribe, they were immediately opted out (one click) but then redirected to a landing page that included a video (see Figure 10.24).

This landing page included a message confirming the user had unsubscribed and saying they were sorry to see them go. In addition, this page had a video embedded on it. When users clicked the "Punish Derrick" button, they were treated to a short video of "Derrick's" co-worker dumping a cup of water on his head after yelling at him for sending all of those Groupon emails. It's a clever and effective tactic. In fact, adding this opt-out link in the preheader resulted in a decrease in spam complaints by 30 percent![14]

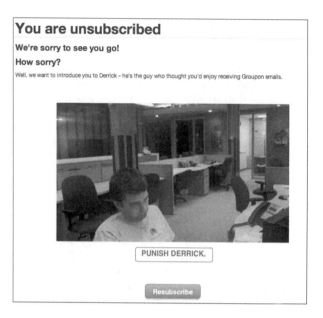

Figure 10.24   *After subscribers opt out from Groupon emails, they have the option to "punish Derrick" as well as resubscribe.*

Test the Rules; Don't Just Break Them Outright

Gary Vaynerchuck is a speaker as well as the founder of WineLibrary.com and Win Library TV. He's full of energy and passion. He also knows how to get an audience to pay attention. That's just what he did in 2011 in Miami when he keynoted the Email Evolution Conference. In his talk about email marketing, he shared something that had many attendees talking for weeks after. He said he had recently hired a team of people whose only job was to pick up the phone and call someone after they had unsubscribed from his weekly email newsletter. Talk about breaking the rules! Although certainly on the innovative end of the spectrum, this tactic is by no means illegal. His team still honored the opt out; however, they found nearly 40 percent of those who had previously unsubscribed ended up re-opting in after the personal phone call.

You don't have to pick up the phone and call (harass?) people who have unsubscribed from your emails, nor do you have to put a big unsubscribe link or button at the top of your emails. Just test some of the rules of email marketing and see what works best for you and your subscribers.

Beauty Is in the Eye of the Subscriber

Some people think an email on either end of the image continuum—mostly images or mostly text—qualifies as ugly. However, the possibility exists for an email with a nice balance of text to images to be unappealing.

We are talking about those emails that are aesthetically repulsive. When you open these messages, your eyes cross and your head spins. Describing exactly that this email looks like can be difficult, but you know it when you see it.

The challenge with truly ugly emails is that they can be very subjective. What makes you say, "That is one ugly email!" might be just the email that someone else opens, clicks, and converts on. You might find emails with 17 different font types and sizes, animated images, and 42 pages long unappealing, yet the person sitting next to you loves it (or at least it doesn't bother him as much as it does you).

We've all heard the phrase, "Beauty is in the eye of the beholder." We'd like to borrow that phrase and modify it slightly for email marketing. Beauty, in this case, is in the eye of the *subscriber*. Each email marketing subscriber, each list, and each segment has the potential to see your message differently. Each has the possibility to react differently depending on the sender, the content, and the offer.

Just like in life, ugly can be quite subjective. Ugly can be confused with bland or boring. However, if the email works for you (the email marketer) or your audience (subscribers), then who cares what it looks like? If your success metric is conversions and your email is consistently converting, whether the email is ugly or pretty doesn't matter.

Ugly Emails That Consistently Perform Well

Take a look at Figure 10.25. This image is from a well-known website, a company you've heard most likely heard of before. It's one of the top 500 websites in the world and top 100 in the United States.[15] In fact, the same image you see in Figure 10.25 is also used on television commercials.

Any idea which website we're referring to? If you guessed Publishers Clearing House (pch.com or "PCH"), you are correct!

When you see that image, using letters in a big font and all caps, one that jumps off the page, what comes to mind? For us, this screams UGLY! If this image was included in an email, some would be less likely to click on it. Some might even mark it as spam or delete it.

Figure 10.25 *Would you call this image from a well-known website pretty or ugly?*

Now, compare Figure 10.25 to an email from PCH. (Figure 10.26 shows the top half of one of its emails.) Did you have the same reaction as we did when you looked at this email? Yuck!

Figure 10.26 *This top half of an "ugly" email from PCH.com is pretty typical of what it sends.*

Let's break down all the components that you could deem ugly:

- **Subject line** (not shown in Figure 10.26): "DJ—Confirmed Contents." We are not even sure what that means.

- **Header:** It has a huge image with lots of things going on: different font size and colors, DJ's first name, and a random person with a bunch of cash at his feet holding a "YOU COULD BECOME A MILLIONAIRE" sign.

- **Copy:** Two more mentions of DJ's name in the first few paragraphs, bold and all caps text, use of the words "InstaPrize" and "SuperPrize," and the number $10,000,000.00 used not once, but twice!

All in all, this email could make your head spin off your shoulders. Remember, too, this is just the top portion of the email. Below the fold is an animated image flashing incessantly at you. Looking through the lens of a "best practices" person, this PCH email would seem ludicrous. All of the above would likely get it blocked by spam filters. Not just that, but it's unlikely anyone in their right mind would click on those links let alone open the email.

As it turns out, lots of folks open these emails; many click on the links, images, and buttons; and several convert (purchase items). In regard to deliverability, you might think the spam filters would flag these PCH emails. Wrong. The typical PCH emails get into the inbox 99.2 percent of the time (as audited by a third party).[16] Compare those numbers to your own email marketing program. Can you claim a 99.2 percent inbox delivery? Our bet is the PCH ones are a bit higher than yours.

If you think that 99.2 percent number is impressive, just wait. Prepare yourself for a few other mind-blowing metrics.

Sal Tripi is the Assistant Vice President of Digital Operations and Compliance for Publishers Clearing House. Since 2002, email has been a critical component of the marketing mix at PCH. It's one channel the company doesn't ever take for granted.

Tripi told us PCH used to have one big prize (remember the Prize Patrol van and the big check?) but have since expanded, thanks to the Internet, to include daily prizes. Email marketing has played an integral role in broadening the reach and growing PCH's online business. "Email has taken what we've done offline and put it on steroids," Tripi said.

PCH has several email lists totaling "in the millions" of subscribers and sends hundreds of millions of emails every year. The majority of its email list is built by way of sweepstakes that people opt into. While they are in the process of entering, PCH uses a pre-checked box (see Figure 10.27) to opt them in for "special contests and offers from pch.com and their partners."

Figure 10.27   *PCH includes a pre-checked opt-in box during the data collection process of its sweepstakes offers.*

Testing is something Tripi and PCH take a lot of pride in. PCH's email team is composed of more than a dozen individuals, eight of them on the creative side. Their entire job is to create new test packages (email campaigns) that beat the control. After the test beats the control, it becomes the new control. Their performance is measured on winning packages.

Other than compliance and other legal regulations, no rules exist in regard to testing. "All of the rules are constantly being updated," Tripi told us. "What works today may not work tomorrow." There is nothing the testing group is not allowed to test. "They can use more images. They can use more text. Everything is testable. Everything is re-testable."

Ugly emails are not the only rule PCH breaks. When subscribers click through on an image or link in their email, they are redirected to a landing page with a similar look and feel. Instead of leading potential buyers nicely through the checkout process, PCH puts obstacles in their way such as checkboxes and popups! In fact, if you close a PCH tab or window, a popup appears asking whether you are sure. "We have found the more we engage the consumers with unique offers, the more they click, the more they purchase."

In February 2010, DJ met Tripi at the Email Evolution Conference. The night before DJ's presentation about "ugly emails," he ran into Tripi and they engaged in a "healthy" debate about the not-so-pretty emails PCH sends. DJ was adamant they were ugly. Tripi did not disagree. That night, DJ learned two valuable lessons:

- As we've said before, beauty is in the eye of the subscriber. What is ugly for some is not ugly for others.
- You are not necessarily your own audience. The average PCH subscriber is female (60 percent), over 40 years old, low to middle income, and lives in a rural area.

So why does PCH use lots of colors, big letters and numbers, and a bunch of flashing stuff in their emails? Simple. The goal of email marketing at PCH has always been to replicate the direct marketing pieces. Its emails intentionally read as if they are a direct mail piece. PCH attempts to speak to its email subscribers about what's most interesting and relevant to them.

Just because the PCH emails are ugly and don't appeal to DJ or Jason does not mean they don't perform.

Now for those mind-blowing metrics: The average open rate across all email marketing programs at Publishers Clearing House is 40 percent, nearly twice as high as the email industry average. Although that number on its own is impressive, it pales in comparison to its click rate. **Of those who open the PCH emails, 87 percent click at least one link. 87 percent!** To be clear, that's not one campaign. It's not their best campaign. It's the average click rate across all PCH email marketing programs.

In addition, 52 percent of its active online members have been engaged with PCH for more than five years. So not only does its approach work in the short term, it's also a great retention tool.

Wow. Ugly works (for PCH).

Why does sending this "less-than-pretty" email work for PCH? It's possible that it works due to the business PCH is in (raffles, sweepstakes, and other free stuff). Although nobody can be certain, the "beauty is in the eye of the subscriber" theory seems to fit. What we think is ugly is likely not as appalling to PCH's subscribers. After all, these are folks who are signing up for PCH sweepstakes offers. This means they've been to PCH's website. They have seen the creative. They have read the copy. Whether or not they find it appealing, they keep coming back. PCH's emails are consistent with the look and feel of its website. The branding is the same. The copy is similar. All of this matters. The user experience is fluid.

Remember: You are not always your own audience.

A Split Test of Ugly Versus Pretty

Marketing Over Coffee (MoC) is a weekly podcast hosted by John Wall, director of marketing at Glance Networks, and Chris Penn. Every week, Wall and Penn record a show in their local coffee shop that covers classic and new marketing. To accompany the podcast, they also send out an occasional email newsletter to their subscribers.

As you can see in Figure 10.28, their email was, well, let's just say it was far from pretty. It was mostly text, had a variety of different font sizes, was long, and was not that aesthetically pleasing.

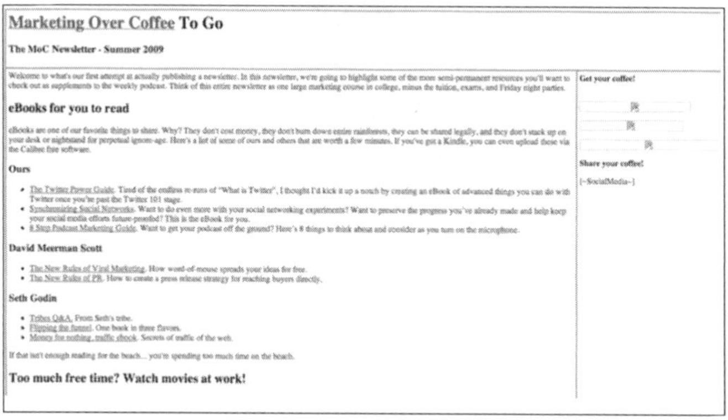

Figure 10.28   *Marketing Over Coffee's email template from August 2009 would likely fall into the "not-so-pretty" category—and this is only the top half!*

However, Wall and Penn were not all that concerned because it was meeting their performance expectations while outperforming industry averages. It was hard to complain with an average open rate of nearly 30 percent and an average click-rate of more than 40 percent. Their subscribers certainly loved what was landing in their inboxes.

Joanna Lawson-Matthew Roberts was a client service manager at Blue Sky Factory (an email service provider) in 2009 and was assigned to the MoC account. When she saw this ugly template, she convinced Wall and Penn to allow her team to design a new template for them. This new template was promised to reflect all the email marketing industry best practices out there. Blue Sky Factory's creative team came up with an industry best practices template, shown in Figure 10.29.

"We don't know about you, but we are confident that this template is a (major) improvement over [old one], said Lawson-Matthew Roberts.[17] She said there were six reasons why the team loved the new template:

- The preheader included snippet text, view in browser, and a mobile version.
- The header included clear branding as well as the MoC logo.
- It had distinct sections, good use of white space, and clear headlines.
- The email width was within the 600–650 range (quite a bit smaller than the previous version).
- It included Forward to a Friend and other social sharing features.
- It had a clean design with clear calls to action.[18]

Figure 10.29   *This Marketing Over Coffee "industry best practices" (pretty) email template was tested against the ugly email from August 2009. (This image is not meant to be read in detail.)*

Take a minute to flip back and forth between Figures 10.28 and 10.29. Don't think too hard; just react. Which email template would you say is prettier and would you rather look at in your inbox? Clearly, the second one, the new and improved template, is the better one.

However, Lawson-Matthew Roberts and the Blue Sky Factory team did not stop with making a new template. They moved forward with testing. After all, even though most people would agree the new template was prettier than the old one, the data would not lie.

They set up a split test; each template was sent to 20 percent of the MoC email list. To keep the test fair, both emails had the same Subject line and content, and were sent at the exact same time. The only thing that was different was the look and feel of the email.

On September 22, 2009, the test began. Twenty percent of the list received the original template while another 20 percent was sent the new template. After two hours, the new template had an 11.6 percent open rate and a 2.3 percent click-through rate. The old template's open and click-through rates were 9.8 percent and 0.9 percent, respectively. Based on this data, the new template was then sent to the remaining 60 percent of the list.

However, after looking at the same metrics the next day, Lawson-Matthew Roberts saw the following metrics:

- **Old (ugly) template:** 25.7 percent open rate and a 4.2 percent click-through rate

- **New (pretty) template:** 27.0 percent open rate and a 4.7 percent click-through rate[19]

Even though the new template certainly outperformed the old template as far as their two key metrics, open and click-through rate, the numbers were not too different. The open rate on the pretty "industry best practices" template were only 1.3 percent higher than the ugly template, while the click-through rate was a mere .5 percent higher.

Although you might be surprised by the results, remember one thing: This is why best practices should be tested against your own subscribers. What works for one audience might not work for another. The same is true for a particular list or segment of your database. Marketing Over Coffee, with the help of its email service provider and its client service manager, was able to effectively prove the "pretty emails perform better than ugly emails" best practice.

Making Assumptions and Challenging Them

The whole ugly versus pretty argument is typically predicated on assumptions. You assume that what you think looks good looks good to everyone. You assume that the prettier email will get more eyeballs, opens, and clicks. You assume that what the industry experts have been saying for years is always and forever true. The truth is just the opposite. Best practices evolve as user adoption increases, trends and tastes in what's appealing ebb and flow, and better technologies and innovations change the game.

What's effective for audiences in terms of what communications appeal to them changes like the fashions of the day. If you don't think so, consider this book title from 1993: "Turn Your Fax Machine Into A Money Machine."[20]

What turns those who blindly follow the best practices, sometimes like lemmings off the cliff, into communications professionals who adjust and adapt with the changes of the audience is taking on a bit of the rebel mentality. Don't assume that because one company or consultant saw an X or Y percent open rate from an email campaign that you will, too, if you follow the same formula.

By challenging the assumptions that all people formulate by following the rules, you often find the rules don't always apply to you or your audience. To prove that point a bit more, the next chapter revisits the concept of growing your list and covers how to do so by breaking those rules.

Endnotes

1. "Why Bother With Plain-Text Emails?" http://kb.mailchimp.com/article/why-bother-with-plain-text-emails

2. White, Chad, AM Inbox. "'Wake-up slap' tactics" 8/23/11. http://www.retailemailblog.com/2011/08/am-inbox-wake-up-slap-tactics.html

3. StartUpNation.com, "Email Marketing Best Practices." February 02, 2012. http://www.startupnation.com/Email-Marketing-Best-Practices/topic/

4. Brownlow, Mark, "Is an image-rich email so bad?" November 22, 2007. http://www.email-marketing-reports.com/iland/2007/11/is-image-rich-email-so-bad.html

5. CampaignMonitor.com (Help & FAQs section), "What does my SpamAssassin score mean? How can I reduce it?" http://help.campaignmonitor.com/topic.aspx?t=104#HTML_IMAGE_ONLY_04

6. "Is an Email Marketing Offer Just Like a TV Commercial?" http://www.clickz.com/clickz/column/2158488/email-marketing-offer-tv-commercial

7. Email Marketing Reports, "How to help ensure your email's images won't be blocked." January 11, 2008. http://www.email-marketing-reports.com/iland/2008/01/how-to-guarantee-your-emails-images.html

8. http://emailfail.posterous.com/pizza-express-have-fun-with-images-off

9. Niendorf, Molly, "Why you shouldn't send one big image—and what you can do instead: Building a slice and dice campaign." June 1, 2011. http://myemma.com/blog/send-big-image

10. Subscribers Fans and Followers, "The Social Break-Up Report #8." 2011. http://www.exacttarget.com/resources/sff8.pdf

11. Epsilon, "Unsubscribe Email Strategies Report." May 2011. http://www.epsilon.com/news-events/press-releases/2011/unsubscribe-email-strategies-report-email-institute-and-multichannel

12. Peterson, Tim, "Moosejaw Mountaineering offers email snooze button." August 1, 2011. http://www.dmnews.com/moosejaw-mountaineering-offers-email-snooze-button/article/208058/

13. Silverpop, Client quotes. http://www.silverpop.com/clients/client-quotes.html

14. White, Chad, AM Inbox. "Third major retailer adds preheader unsubscribe link." April 8, 2010. http://www.retailemailblog. com/2010/04/am-inbox-third-major-retailer-adds.html

15. Retrieved from http://www.alexa.com/siteinfo/pch.com on March 22, 2012.

16. Email Marketing, "How Publishers Clearing House uses "blacklisted" words yet achieves a 99.2% delivery rate." June 1, 2011. http://www. marketingsherpa.com/article.php?ident=31926

17. Blue Sky Factory Blog, Marketing Over Coffee: The Creative Reveal. September 21, 2009. http://www.whatcounts.com/2012/04/anatomy-of-an-ab-test-marketing-over-coffee/. (This is a summary.)

18. Blue Sky Factory Blog, Marketing Over Coffee: The Creative Reveal. September 21, 2009. http://www.whatcounts.com/2012/04/anatomy-of-an-ab-test-marketing-over-coffee/. (This is a summary.)

19. Blue Sky Factory Blog, Marketing Over Coffee: And The Winner Is.... September 28, 2009. http://www.whatcounts.com/2012/04/anatomy-of-an-ab-test-marketing-over-coffee/. (This is a summary.)

20. Hooton, Marcia, How To Turn Your Fax Machine Into A Money Machine. New Wave Consultants, 1993. (http://www.amazon.com/ Turn-Your-Machine-into-Money/dp/0943172071/ref=sr_1_5?s=books &ie=UTF8&qid=1334066144&sr=1-5)

11

The Best Ways to Grow Your List

Part I, "The Secret to Email Marketing: List Growth," addressed the importance of growing your email list. Without a list of email addresses to send to, email marketing becomes quite challenging. However, what we failed to mention (intentionally) in that part of the book is that a few "non-traditional" ways exist to grow your email database.

This chapter focuses on three of them:

- Popups
- Single versus double opt-ins
- Non-permission emails

Yes. You read that list correctly. This chapter covers topics that are often frowned upon by email marketing purists. If you believe permission is black and white, some of the gray areas addressed in this chapter might make you a bit uncomfortable. We anticipate some strong reactions to what we'll be sharing and we're okay with that. The idea is to give you some things to think about and to try.

Sending emails without permission or buying lists is not for everyone. In fact, if executed poorly, they are likely not the best strategies for most email marketers. However, these methods can and do work. We want to nudge you—the email marketer—to push the envelope a bit. We're asking you to do some testing, to see what works best for you and your audience. We're not advocating that your entire email marketing strategy be built around popups, one type of opt-in, or the sending of emails without permission—far from it. Instead, be a bit rebellious.

Know that we're not advocating doing anything wrong, illegal, or unethical. None of these tactics are such. But the email marketing purists have determined them to be less than ethical or optimal in the past without taking into account that not every rule works for every audience. We simply want to show you that some of these so-called "no-no's" according to the industry experts and purists are not only not off-limits but can sometimes prove to be rather effective.

Ready? Let's go.

Spiders, Scorpions, Snakes...and Popups

If you've spent more than five minutes of your life online, you've likely encountered some form of a popup—an ad that appears without warning or a new tab or window that shows up suddenly without any explicit action on your part. In fact, in the early days of the Internet, popups seemed to be everywhere. As soon as you clicked a link, your screen would fill with popups. Every time you closed one, seven more would appear. Often, the only way to actually stop these crazy popups from taking over all the real estate on your screen was to restart your computer. (Hello, Ctrl+Alt+Del!)

In 2012, traditional popups are not nearly as prevalent as they were a decade ago. Anti-popup software, now built into many Internet browsers, including Internet Explorer, Mozilla Firefox, and Google Chrome, have made popups a lot less common. However, marketers have discovered workarounds to popup blockers, new ways to execute interruption marketing. With these workarounds comes somewhat of a resurgence of popups as an effective tactic to grow email marketing lists.

Mark Brownlow, journalist, blogger, and independent publisher of Email Marketing Reports, says popups are like "spiders, scorpions, and snakes": "Email marketers have been reluctant to use 'in your face' website sign-up forms that in any way resemble...popups of the past," he said.[1] Instead of using popups, many best practice folks suggest growing your list by including a form that's embedded directly in a webpage. We don't disagree.

However, not all email address collection forms are created equal. The four most common ones include the following:

- **In-line:** Chapter 2, "How to Grow Your List," covers this form. In-line forms live directly on a web page. They are quite effective in growing your email list.

- **Popup:** This form opens in a new tab or window in an Internet browser. Unless a user manually accepts them, popups are typically blocked by default.

- **Pop-over:** This form hovers within a webpage. They cannot be blocked by most Internet browsers.

- **Lightbox:** This form is similar to the pop-over. It appears on top of the content on the webpage. However, when it shows, the background content becomes semi-transparent, making it easier to see the lightbox.[2]

In-line forms remain the most popular form, but the lightbox form is gaining ground as a way to grow your email marketing list. Email service provider AWeber is one company that allows its clients to create and embed lightbox opt-in forms on various web pages. Additionally, third-party providers such as Popup Domination (popupdomination.com) provide lightbox services.

You'll often see the terms *popup* and *lightbox* used interchangeably. To be clear, a lightbox is a form of popup. However, not all popups are lightboxes. Think of the terms' relationship as similar to the rectangle/square or bourbon/scotch/whisky relationships. Unless otherwise stated, we'll also be using the two words to mean the same thing.

One of the nice parts about most popups and lightboxes is that they can be customized to appear after a specified period of time, on a specific webpage, when a link is clicked, after someone visits a certain number of pages on a site, or upon leaving a certain page. This customization ability allows the marketer to test various approaches to discover which is the most effective way to grow their email lists.

However, regardless of their flexibility, popups are not for every marketer. You might be reading this now and thinking, "I hate popups. I'll never (ever) use them." We don't blame you. We don't care for them too much either. But what if we told you they worked? What if, after including a popup or lightbox, your list doubled or tripled in size? Would that change your opinion? What if we told you that not only would you experience a huge jump in your list size, but also you would have zero complaints? Would you test them?

In the last few years, many email marketers—both in the business-to-business (B2B) and business-to-consumer (B2C) space—have found incredible success by including a popup or lightbox as a means to collect email addresses.

Installing a Lightbox to Increase Opt-Ins

Jeff Ginsberg is the founder and CEO of The eMail Guide—The Search Engine for eMail Marketing (theemailguide.com). Since the site launched in 2009, Ginsberg has included an email opt-in form on the right sidebar of many pages on the site (see Figure 11.1).

Figure 11.1   *Ginsberg includes an email opt-in form on the right sidebar of many of The eMail Guide's web pages.*

This opt-in form was responsible for growing The eMail Guide's email list to more than 1,200 subscribers. His monthly list growth ranged from a low of 30 to a high of 100. Although this growth was not terrible, Ginsberg was confident he could grow his list at a higher rate by making a few changes.

In August of 2011, after hearing lots of chatter and positive comments about popups, Ginsberg decided he would test one out. He chose a third-party service called Popup Domination and customized his lightbox (see Figure 11.2) to appear on all pages ten seconds after someone landed on the site. Additionally, he changed the settings such that the lightbox popup would display once every seven days. In other words, if someone had not been to a page on The eMail Guide for seven or more days, the lightbox would appear.[3]

Ginsberg saw an immediate bump in email subscribers. In the first month, his number nearly quadrupled—from 100 to 388. More than 170 of those opt-ins could be sourced back to the lightbox. The number of additional email addresses collected from the lightbox in September was 219. In the next four months, Ginsberg added almost 700 new subscribers: from the lightbox alone!

Figure 11.2   *In August 2011, Ginsberg launched this lightbox popup on The eMail Guide. It appears after being on the site for ten seconds.*

Ginsberg also added a source field to his web opt-in forms so that he could track where each new email address was coming from. This number might surprise you: 83 percent of all email addresses collected on theemailguide.com came from the lightbox!

Any guesses about how many complaints Ginsberg has received in six months? If you guessed "zero," you would be correct.

Using Lightboxes on Blogs

Even after reading how successful Ginsberg has been with his list growth, you might still be saying, "I don't care. I hate popups. I would never install one on my website or blog." You are certainly not alone. In fact, Chris Penn (whom we introduced in Chapter 3, "Let's Get Technical") doesn't like them either, yet he still has one on his blog (see Figure 11.3).

You know by now that Penn likes to test various email marketing tactics to see what works best for his audience. He sends ugly emails, puts a big (ugly) unsubscribe button at the top of his emails, and includes some humor in his alt text that can be seen with images off. Armed with that information, it should come as no surprise that Penn has also tested popups on his blog to collect more email addresses.

"I personally don't like them much on other sites I visit," said Penn, "but I had to remind myself of the cardinal rule of marketing: I am not my customer."[4]

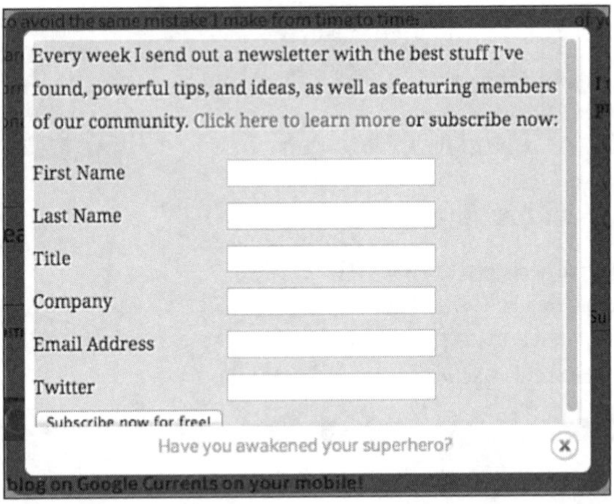

Figure 11.3   *Chris Penn introduced this popup on his blog in November 2010 and, thanks to its enormous success, has had it there ever since.*

Sounds a lot like what we've been saying in this part of the book: Best practices are those that work best for your audience.

Penn is a self-proclaimed data nut. If he is going to test something, he'll almost always use data to not only set up the test, but also to report back on the results. Before installing the popup, he was averaging around 30 new signups per month to his personal email newsletter. From the first day he launched the popup, his subscriber numbers began to increase. At the end of the first month his average shot up from 30 to 133. As of February 2011, it was trending at 250 per month: a 733 percent increase.

"The numbers are incredibly compelling, despite my slight personal dislike for the marketing method; for this blog, the method works incredibly well,"[5] he said. It's hard to argue with a 733 percent increase. Not only that, but Penn's lead conversion ratio—the number of new email subscribers as a percentage of absolute, unique visitors to his website—increased from a pre-popup number of a half percent to more than two percent after the popup was installed.

In case you were wondering, Penn uses a WordPress plugin (a third-party application specifically designed for the blogging platform) called WP Super Popup Pro. It allows for a lot of customization, including the ability to specify how long before the popup appears, showing it once then not again for a certain period of time, and so on.

But will popups work for larger companies and brands? What about those in the business-to-consumer (B2C) space? Can using popups work for them as well? The short answer is yes—but you already knew that as you're well on your way to becoming an email marketing rebel.

Adding Lightboxes on a B2C Site

Chapter 2 introduced Patrick Starzan, Funny or Die's VP of Marketing & Distribution. Starzan shared with us that the company's number one goal of marketing was to drive traffic back to the site. Funny or Die has many methods to reach this goal, email marketing being one of them.

However, it has not been a quick process. From a list point of view, Starzan said things started off quite slowly. The company began adding various opt-in forms on the website, on the homepage as well as other in-site landing pages. It also focused on growing its social media presence at the same time.

It also wanted to stay true to its brand. "[Growing our list] was a slow process. We had never done something this organic, but knew we had to use comedy," said Starzan.

Starzan said the company began seeing popups and lightboxes on many websites, but it didn't love what it saw. Many of the popups were "right in your face." So the company decided to build a lightbox of its own a few years ago, one that fit its needs and was consistent with its brand (see Figure 11.4).

Figure 11.4   *The Funny or Die lightbox is simple and incorporates humor to capture email addresses.*

Before launching the new lightbox, Starzan and his team decided that if they noticed a drop in page views or a huge backlash from their community, they would eliminate the lightbox immediately. They also implemented a critical, customized lightbox setting from day one. For visitors to see the popup, they had to first view three pages on the Funny or Die website.

"We didn't want to ask for something before we gave them something," said Starzan. "If you've gone three pages in, you've gone far enough to [hopefully] like it so we could then ask for something—get your email address."

This approach is one we don't see all that often but fully support. In some ways, slapping a popup on a visitor's monitor immediately is like asking someone for her phone number before you learn her name. Take a few minutes to be sure visitors are interested, then ask for their email address.

Funny or Die also thought long and hard about ways to "not make the popup annoying." It didn't want its popup to be something visitors would rush to close or see and immediately close the page, leaving the site, never to return. To accomplish this goal, it first made sure the lightbox was very large—"two to three times what we'd seen in the marketplace," according to Starzan. In fact, its lightbox fills up nearly half of the entire page.

Next, it chose to make the lightbox very clean with only a touch of copy and one field (for email address). The messaging is simple and clear. The only content before the email address field is:

"JOIN THE funny OR DIE NEWSLETTER. The best of Funny or Die. PLUS EXCLUSIVE CONTENT."

That's it! No hard sell. No social proof highlighting the number of other email subscribers. No detailed explanation of what subscribers would get by opting in.

Finally, Starzan said that keeping the tone consistent with the Funny or Die brand was critical. "We wanted to be very transparent, to be sure people knew that we really just wanted their email to deliver Funny or Die content on a consistent basis."

Notice the text below the email address field. It reads, "We will not use your email for anything sneaky." If someone chooses to not opt in, he has two options—click the "X" in the upper right of the lightbox, or click the NO THANKS, I CAN'T READ button. This button allows people to tell Funny or Die they don't want to opt in, but in a humorous manner.

"Using humor on the popup lets people's guards down in a subtle, nice way," said Starzan.

The lightbox has been an integral part of Funny or Die's email list growth strategy. The company is adding thousands of new email addresses every day and has grown the list to more than one million names in just four years. Nearly 80 percent of all email subscribers can be attributed to its lightbox popup.

On top of that, it has not experienced any negative backlash. "We didn't see any adverse affects of having the popup. To this day, I have not heard anything [negative] about it and we've been doing it for nearly four years," Starzan told us. Additionally, the company's unsubscribe rates are quite low: only 0.2 percent.

Starzan said it's all about meeting the expectations of people. "Once we have their email addresses, we want to make sure why they signed up is what we are delivering, the benefit. Great content and frequency is important to us. [The low unsubscribe rates] tells me two things: growing the list in the right way and delivering the right content is critical."

Park City Mountain Resort Tests a Popup on Its Winter 2010 Website

Another B2C company who has effectively used a popup to grow its list is Park City Mountain Resort (PCMR). Open year-round in Utah, the resort caters to mountain bikers and hikers in the summer, and ski and snowboarders in the winter. Because of this seasonality, PCMR completely overhauls its website twice per year: once for the summer season and again for the winter.

In the later summer/early fall of 2010, as it was gearing up for the switch to its winter website, it decided to test a popup form to collect new email subscribers (see Figure 11.5).

Figure 11.5 *PCMR's email list immediately grew after it added this popup to its summer 2010 website.*

It added a lightbox popup, set via a cookie, to show for first-time visitors. After a user took action—either declining or closing the popup or signing up via the form—PCMR would not display it again.

We love this popup for many reasons. For one thing, the messaging was clear and concise: three paragraphs, each one sentence long. The first told readers what to do (sign up) and introduced the incentive ("you'll be entered to win a pair of Park Passes"). The second included a link to the subscription form ("fill out this form") and reinforced what was required to be entered to win. The third set proper expectations about the prize ("winners picked every Monday...").

Also, the form included three options: a link to fill out the form, a button to close the form, and a button to close the form and not be notified again. People tend to like it when they have a choice.

But more important than how it looked or what the messaging said, the real question is this: Was the popup successful in helping PCMR reach its goal of growing its email list? You bet! PCMR had a 2,200 percent increase in email opt-in signups from July 2010 to August 2010.

"The lightbox popup worked because we did provide an incentive to sign up in terms of winning the drawing and it wasn't just the 'value' of receiving the emails, plus the popup was cookied [sic] to not show once a user opted in or out," said Eric Hoffman, Interactive Marketing Manager at PCMR.

There is no question popups and lightboxes are controversial. Many people, both consumers and marketers, avoid them at all costs. However, if implemented properly, they can have a huge positive impact on email list growth. We talked about the importance of asking for someone's email address in Chapter 2. Popups take asking to a whole new level with their "interruption" nature. Yet if the popup is relevant, timely, and valuable, it can work.

The possibility does exist that popups and lightboxes do cause some potential email subscribers to recoil in disgust, close the window, and abandon the website never to return. In fact, some backlash likely exists; however, the marketers showcased in this chapter have found that the visible pros (huge list growth) outweigh the negatives (potential lost subscribers). So, what they feared might have happened actually turned out to be a nonissue.

A trickier issue exists in knowing whether a single- or double-opt will fly with your audience.

Choosing an Opt-In: Single or Double

In regard to growing your email list, the tactics are endless. As discussed in Part I, making the opt-in obvious and the form easy to fill out are important, as are being creative and using humor, using technology such as QR codes, smartphones, and social media, and even taking the offline channel into account. Or be a bit rebellious as discussed in this chapter and test out a popup or lightbox to add more email addresses to your list.

However, no matter which methods you choose to grow your list, all email marketers must decide whether to allow subscribers to be added to their list through a *single* or *double* opt-in process:

- **Single Opt-In:** A subscriber provides his email address to a company, usually via a web form. As soon as he clicks Submit or Enter, the user is added to the email database. In some instances, a company sends out a thank-you email indicating that he's successfully been added to the list. In other instances, the thank you comes in the form of a welcome email. Either way, no other action is required by the subscriber.

- **Double Opt-In:** A subscriber provides her email address to a company, usually via a web form. However, before she is added to the email database, she must reply to the email or click on a link to confirm her request to opt in. If she doesn't reply or click the link, she is not added to the list. See Figure 11.6 for an example of a confirmation email.

Figure 11.6   *In this confirmation email from Staples, if a user does not click on the button in the image or the link in the preheader, he will not be added to the email list.*

So, much like the question proposed in Chapter 3—to check or not to check—we now ask a similar question: Should you use single opt-in or double opt-in?

Several years ago the case used to be that double opt-in was the gold standard in the email marketing industry. Recently, a switch to single opt-in seems to be occurring. As always, the answer to which opt-in to use depends on who you ask.

Several email service providers strongly suggest or even force a double opt-in method for all of its customers. MailChimp requires its customers to use a double opt-in process when using its signup forms. No way exists to turn off the confirmation email. (However, its customers can create their own single opt-in forms, but MailChimp does not recommend that approach.)[6]

Similarly, AWeber enables double opt-in by default for all subscription methods. It says double opt-in is "the best way to ensure that you have both permission and the audit trail necessary for good message deliverability."[7] It can be turned off, but doing so takes some work. Other providers, although not explicitly stating it, prefer their customers grow their email lists through double opt-in.

But not everyone agrees that double opt-in is the way to go. In fact, Bill McCloskey, founder of Only Influencers (and technical advisor to this book—thanks, Bill!), is not even sure how double opt-ins landed on everyone's list of best practices. McCloskey thinks double opt-in is a terrible idea—assuming you want to grow your list, that is.[8]

We agree with McCloskey and believe this gold standard is outdated and no longer necessary—in most cases. Even though we'll present both sides of the single/double opt-in story, let's be clear where we stand: Single opt-in is the best approach.

Making the Case for Double Opt-In

If you want to ensure a cleaner list—one that has fewer bad email addresses—double opt-in is likely the best route to go. Sending a follow-up (confirmation) email ensures a real human is behind the opt-in. For the email address to be added to the sender's database, a button or link must be clicked to confirm the subscriber truly wants to receive emails.

Confirmation emails also prevent accidental opt-ins or intentionally being subscribed by another person. The messaging in many confirmation emails allows people to easily opt out if they "subscribed in error." Many of these double opt-in emails note that if they ignore the email, they will not be added to the sender's list.

Finally, by sending a confirmation email and requiring someone to click a link or button before she is truly opted in, the sender can validate the email address. Because many Internet Service Providers (ISPs) look at the percentage of invalid email addresses when calculating domain reputation, the more senders can do to minimize this number, the better. Forcing a human to click the confirmation link pretty much ensures the email address is real.

Many people also argue that a double-opted-in list results in more engaged subscribers. In 2011, email service provider MailChimp took a random sample of 30,000 of its users with email list sizes between 500 and 1.5 million who had sent at least ten campaigns. Some sent every day, whereas others sent a few times a month.

For this sample, it found those who used a double opt-in approach had a 72.2 percent increase in unique opens and a 114 percent increase in clicks. Arguing with those numbers is hard. However, remember that the data is only representative of MailChimp's clients and does not necessarily represent a true split test. Although MailChimp's clients can create their own single opt-in forms, MailChimp strongly discourages it and requires "full double opt-in" when using its forms. Still, the MailChimp numbers do not lie and should be taken into consideration if your audience profile is similar to its clients.

"Garbage in, garbage out" is one of the main arguments against a single opt-in strategy. Those opposed to single opt-in worry about bogus email addresses—bots (or your friends, co-workers, family, and so on) automatically signing you up to receive certain emails. We'll address how to control the bot problem shortly, but as far as people signing up other people to receive emails, does that really happen anymore? We don't think so.

Making the Case for Single Opt-In

When DJ was a sales associate at Bronto in 2009, he had a reputation as a talker (not much has changed). This sometimes proved to be a detriment. DJ had a tendency to keep chatting after the sale was closed, giving the new client an opportunity to change her mind. DJ's boss, Matt Williamson, often coached him to "Stop when they say 'yes.'"

How does this relate to a double opt-in method? Asking potential subscribers—people who have just asked to be added to your email list—to open their email and then click a link to confirm their subscription, is similar to talking after the sale is over. They've already said "yes." They've raised their virtual hands (or clicked the "Sign me up!" button) and asked to be added to your list and start receiving emails from you. However, you've now said, "Are you sure? Are you really, really sure?" You've required them to take an extra step in the process. Stop when they say "yes!"

Consider this fact: Only 76.5 percent of all commercial email reaches the inbox.[9] Those email marketers who send double-opt in messages run the risk of a portion of those emails never being delivered. On average, nearly one quarter of folks who want to receive email from an organization might never have that chance because the message does not reach their inbox. Before you say, *"But wait! Using that same logic, one quarter of welcome emails will never reach the inbox!"* remember that with a single opt-in approach, you already have permission to email those subscribers. If the welcome email doesn't reach them for some reason, they are still opted in and will still (likely) receive other emails from you. The possibility exists that the first email was temporarily blocked or just went unnoticed by the new subscribers.

However, if potential subscribers do not receive the confirmation email—an email that's usually sent just once—they will never be added to your list. All of that time, effort, and money that went into earning those new subscribers will be lost. They'll never get any email from you, ever.

Let's not forget the cost of sending an additional (confirmation) email. If you are using an email provider that charges by total emails sent, as the majority do, this extra email will cost money. If you follow the advice given in Chapter 3 about sending a welcome email, you now have not one but two additional emails for every new subscriber added to your database. Depending on the number of new monthly subscribers, this (unnecessary) expense could add up quickly.

Finally, even email that lands in inboxes is not guaranteed to be opened, let alone read. With the average open rates for all email marketing messages hovering somewhere near 20 percent, a confirmation email getting lost within an already cluttered inbox is quite possible. To be fair, by setting proper expectations, like Tom Martin does (with humor) in Figure 11.7, your confirmation email is more likely to get opened and clicked. However, this often is not the case.

Figure 11.7   *Tom Martin uses humor to remind subscribers to check their inbox for his confirmation email.*

In a 2009 white paper, email service provider iContact said that "around 40 percent of subscribers that initially opt in fail to ever confirm their subscription. This means, that out of every 100 new subscribers, you would never be able to reach 40 of them. Losing 40 percent of your newsletter subscriptions over the long run could have a large negative impact on your sales."[10]

Even if you think the iContact number of 40 percent might be on the high side, arguing with the 76.5 percent inbox delivery rate from Return Path (as mentioned in the Introduction) is hard. Would you be willing to lose 23.5 percent of potential subscribers?

Using a single opt-in approach ensures an easy process for your subscribers as well as a larger email list for you. Win-win, right? You are not asking your potential subscribers if they are really sure. You are not asking them to jump through hoops or take extra steps to confirm they really want to receive email from you (after they just opted in). They put their email address in a form on your website, and bam! They're on your list. Assuming the email address was properly typed, nearly every single person who asks to be added to your email list will be. You win. They win. Everyone is happy.

Sure, a chance exists that some email addresses will be typed incorrectly, either accidentally or intentionally; however, plenty of companies provide services to ensure an email address is valid before adding it to your database. Some tactics, such as requiring a potential subscriber to enter his email address twice, often cuts down on human errors. Other services, such as including a CAPTCHA (where a subscriber must perform a simple task such as typing the letters seen below the form), prevent non-humans (bots) for signing up to email lists with a malicious intent. Additionally, many email service providers will do a check for validity on all new email addresses before they enter their system.

But remember! The rules only apply to you and your audience. Where there're success stories for double opt-in practices, there are also success stories for single opt-in practices.

Village Voice Media Moves from Double to Single Opt-In: Sees Significant List Growth

Village Voice Media (VVM) is a media company based in Phoenix, Arizona. It owns more than 14 publications across the United States and uses email marketing as a means to keep in touch with its subscribers. Prior to 2010, it required all new subscribers to confirm their email address (double opt-in) before being added to the company's email lists. The main reason it went this route was to help mitigate some of its deliverability issues from the past. As mentioned earlier, a double opt-in process can lead to a cleaner list.

But when Ron Hauwert was hired in early 2010 as the "Email Czar" for VVM, he immediately shook things up. He submitted a proposal to the management team with the goal of growing its email program. According to Hauwert, 50 percent of VVM's potential new subscribers were lost in this process. In other words, they never clicked on the confirmation email. Fifty percent!

On Hauwert's recommendations, VVM moved from an in-house, homegrown email platform with double opt-in to an email service provider (ExactTarget) with a single opt-in. The results were quite dramatic.

VVM made a few other tweaks to the signup process, including only requiring an email address; however, just factoring in the move from double to single opt-in, its monthly list growth doubled.

Among the reasons you would use a double opt-in over a single one include making doubly certain the people you will send your emails to have absolutely taken not just one, but two steps to confirm they want your communications. This falls in line with the spirit of the CAN-SPAM Act and is a pure opt-in approach to email marketing.

However, while not as prevalent as it used to be, there still is a chance that someone can intentionally sign someone else up for an email list. For companies who sell adult-related services or products such as cigarettes, liquor, gambling, or other forms of adult entertainment, this can be an issue. For this reason, we believe these types of sites are an exception to the "always use single opt-in approach" and instead are better suited for double opt-in. For legal reasons, it's always better to be (double) covered. Additionally, religious organizations are probably better off employing a double opt-in strategy. The general rule of thumb is that if your organization sells or promotes products and services that can be controversial, double opt-in is a safer bet.

However, going overboard on the opting in is another best practice, or rule, we're here to help you rebel against. Now let's look at why you would actually send emails to people who haven't opted in first.

Sending Emails Without Permission

In 1999, the best-selling book, *Permission Marketing*, written by marketing guru Seth Godin, preached a new way of doing marketing. Instead of interrupting potential customers, permission marketing focuses on creating trust and building brand awareness to develop long-term relationships with prospects. This, according to Godin, is accomplished only by communicating with people who have expressed an interest in your company, product, or service.

Even though Godin discussed email marketing in his book, he was really talking about marketing as a whole. However, the conversation was not lost on email marketers. You won't find a more hotly debated topic in the email marketing industry than permission.

In regard to permission in the email world, most people fall on either extreme of the continuum. On one side are the companies, vendors, and email marketing consultants who believe wholeheartedly that no one should ever send an email without explicit, opt-in permission. One the other side are those who believe it can work—for some marketers, in some industries—if executed properly.

In the United States, sending unsolicited, non-permission-based email is not illegal. However, in the European Union, Australia, and Canada, it is. For the purposes of this section, we're going to focus on U.S. law.

Several U.S.-based email service providers (ESPs) have chosen to make their permission marketing policies a lot stricter than the baseline requirements outlined in the CAN-SPAM Act of 2003 (and its 2008 updates). For example, in Bronto's Permission Marketing Promise, it "expressly forbids any of our clients to send unsolicited bulk email, commonly known as 'spam', through our email marketing product." Its definition of spam is "email sent to a group of recipients who have not explicitly requested to receive it."[11]

ESP CampaignMonitor states that "spam is any email you send to someone who hasn't given you their direct permission to contact them on the topic of the email."[12] Again, notice the use of the phrase *direct permission*. However, it seems to soften a bit in regard to explicit versus implicit permission. Its policy states that its customers can email subscribers through its system if someone has made a purchase from that sender within the past two years. Although the company still advocates for including an opt-in checkbox as part of the purchase process, this form of implied permission is still permissible under its policy.

Bronto also incorporates its permission standards for every new customer email list imported into its application, reminding users of its policy (as shown in Figure 11.8). Notice how they've bolded the phrase "explicit and deliberate permission." Its permission marketing policy is reiterated below that text and users have to manually check a box stating they agree to the Terms of Service. Finally, Bronto requires a brief description of the "source and methods used to collect" these email addresses. In regards to permission, Bronto is quite clear on its policies.

Yet, what exactly qualifies as an explicit permission email opt-in depends a lot on who you ask. We define it as a person who knowingly and willingly asks to be added to your email list.

Based on this definition, a non-explicit permission email would fall into the following categories (note that this list is not exhaustive):

- Adding someone to your list through a pre-checked opt-in box on a web form
- Adding someone to your list after he's made a purchase (but not opted in)
- Adding someone to a different list within your database

- Using an email change of address (ECOA) service that updates inactive or "bad" email addresses to ones that are valid
- Using an email append service that matches an email address against other data, most often first and last name and mailing address

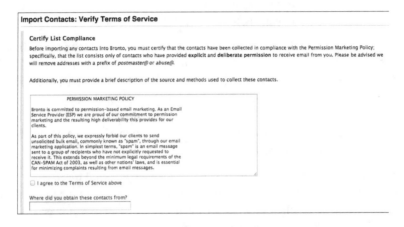

Figure 11.8 *Before importing email addresses into Bronto's application, customers are required to agree to its permission marketing policy.*

MailChimp breaks down various scenarios of how it defines an email list it allows customers to send through its application. As it says, "MailChimp is a tool for sending email newsletters and permission marketing."[13] Some of the "it's not okay to send to this list" scenarios include the following:

- Purchased lists
- Lists obtained from a tradeshow host
- Email addresses collected from business cards

One could debate the various levels of permission here, but suffice it to say that none are explicit. None of the preceding involve someone knowingly and willingly asking to be added to your email list.

However, in the United States, explicit permission is not required by law. Ken Magill, author of MagillReport.com, confirms this:

"No, explicit permission is not necessary. Marketers who don't get explicit permission are playing a dangerous game, but, no, it's simply not required. A marketer who doesn't get explicit permission but sends relevant, segmented, compelling email to customers based on past interactions and exercises good list hygiene ...probably won't have any trouble."[14]

Magill says that Internet Service Providers (ISPs) ultimately decide which emails get delivered regardless of permission policies. If you think about it, do ISPs really know whether a subscriber gave explicit permission to opt in to your list? Nope. How could they?

In a 2012 survey, ESP BlueHornet asked a series of questions to a mix of 1,033 consumers about their views of email marketing.[15] This group all lived in the United States and was between 18 and 40 years of age. Also, 79 percent were employed and 77 percent had an income more than $35,000.

One of the questions asked was, "Is it OK for companies to send promotional emails if you made a purchase, but didn't sign up to receive emails?"

An overwhelming 75.8 percent of respondents said no, it was not okay.

We are dedicating a section of this chapter to asking you rethink this "rule" of email marketing. We are in no way telling you to run your entire email marketing strategy by a non-permission model. Far from it. However, we are suggesting to test non-permission email marketing tactics along the way. They are not illegal (in the United States) and many companies have been successful sending non-explicit permission emails.

Sending an "Opt-Out" Email

In the summer of 2010, media company KSL.com changed ESPs. At the same time this Salt Lake City, Utah, company made this switch, it decided to add an additional email campaign to the mix: a "group deals" email similar to Groupon and Living Social. KSL.com sent an email to its entire subscriber list of more than one million people informing them of this change. The copy of the email was quite short and included the following:

Also as of July 2010, all KSL.com accounts will be subscribed to our new group deals email. We are excited to offer all of our users these exclusive great deals. If you do not wish to receive our new deals just click this link to Unsubscribe. If you would like to receive them you do not need to do anything, but will have the opportunity to unsubscribe at anytime.

Did KSL have permission to send this email to its subscribers? Yes, definitely. The email was sent to everyone who had opted in to receive email from KSL.com. In fact, Daniel Coburn, Director of Operations and Support for Deseret Digital (who runs KSL.com's email marketing program and oversaw this campaign) confirmed that everyone on the list had previously signed up for an account at KSL.com and had checked the "allow us to send you emails" option. In other words, they had opted in.

"Instead of assuming everyone on a sizeable list would want to receive the emails we decided it was best to say, 'Hey you are already on our list, and we are going to start using it, are you sure this is what you signed up for?'" said Coburn.[16]

When these subscribers originally opted in to the KSL.com email list, they gave their consent, but this is where it gets tricky. They did not give explicit permission for KSL.com to send group deal emails. However, during the initial opt-in process, asking permission to opt in for group deal emails would have been impossible because KSL.com didn't have a group deal email program. It had not even been conceived at that point.

When the idea for group deal emails was born, the KSL.com team had two options. It could have sent an email to its entire list, similar to the one mentioned earlier, instead including a big button or link to opt in. The downside to this option would have meant risking a substantially smaller group deals email list.

KSL.com chose the alternative. It sent an "opt-out" email. If subscribers did nothing, then they were going to start receiving the group deal emails. KSL.com did make it clear in this email that subscribers could unsubscribe from this new list immediately or anytime going forward.

Hauwert, the "Email Czar" for VVM, also sent an opt-out email. While he was going through the transition from double to single opt-in, he noticed almost 100,000 email addresses from the past twelve months from people who had opted in but never clicked the confirmation email. He decided to send a "reclamation" email (as seen in Figure 11.9) to those people who had never finished the subscription process.

Figure 11.9 *VVM sent a series of "reclamation" emails to people who had opted in yet never clicked the confirmation link.*

The messaging included: "If you'd rather not receive another email from the Miami New Times [one of VVM's publications], please click here to unsubscribe, and we'll never speak of this again..."

The results:

- 36 percent bounced
- 1 percent unsubscribed
- 0.2 percent marked the message as spam
- 63 percent did not opt out

Although the high percentage of bounced email addresses could have been problematic, they were delivered using different IP addresses and sending domains so as not to negatively impact overall deliverability and sender reputation. The most recent email addresses were attempted first; the oldest were sent last. All said and done, the low unsubscribe rate and the 63 percent that was "reclaimed" (did not opt out) was well worth it for VVM.

However, another way to "reclaim" customers as email subscribers is by using something called an eAppend.

Using an eAppend

Another way to grow your list is to match email addresses from a third party with contact information in your customer database such as name, phone number, address, and so on. This process, known in the industry as an *email append*, or *eAppend*, can be an effective way to build your list. Using it is often frowned upon by many best practice practitioners because it tends to be on the outer edges of permission.

In the past, many eAppend providers sent opt-out emails. In other words, people receiving the eAppend email had to click a button or link indicating they did not want to receive email. However, several eAppend providers are now moving to an opt-in model.

Here is how a typical opt-in eAppend works:

1. You send the eAppend company your customer data file.

2. It matches the customer data against its database and sends an email to that list asking for permission on your behalf.

3. You are sent a file of email addresses who have opted in and agreed to receive email from you.

4. You send the eAppend company some money.

Does this method work? It can, if executed correctly and with some patience.

Bill Kaplan, CEO of FreshAddress (a Boston company that provides eAppend services), suggests that eAppends often provide better open rates and revenue compared to an existing house list. "The logic behind it is that at times, house lists can be tired," he said. "They are used to hearing from you weekly or monthly, and might not be excited. But when you reconnect with a former customer and start to tell your story again, all of a sudden it's fresh. They are excited to hear your story."[17]

So what happens when a company uses eAppend and sends an email to someone who recognizes right away she never opted in to the company's email communications? It happened to Karen Talavera. She is the Founder and President at Synchronicity Marketing, an agency that provides digital and email marketing strategy, training, coaching, and consulting. Talavera has been in the email marketing industry for more than a decade, on the email service provider side and now running her own firm. Suffice it to say she knows a thing or two about the email space.

A few years back Talavera received an email from Macy's (see Figure 11.10). We think it's a pretty nice-looking email with a clear call to action. Then again, beauty is in the eye of the subscriber. Whether or not you like the email, it does have one issue with it. Talavera never subscribed to the Macy's email list. Not via a webform on its website, not over the phone, not through a postcard permission request, not in the store with a sales associate, not through a smartphone app or a QR code (which didn't even exist then!). Instead, at one point in the past, she had purchased some items from a Macy's brick-and-mortar store.

As it turns out, Talavera was sent this email through an eAppend. Macy's opted her into its email list because she had "shopped our store." According to Talavera, Macy's did not get her permission before sending this email. Notice the company still does provide a way for her to opt out; however, it's not nearly as clear and obvious as KSL.com did in its email.

So what did Talavera do? Remember, she is not your average email consumer. She opened the email and liked what she saw. Talavera told us she was impressed with what she called a "compelling, contextually relevant" offer (20 percent off her first order of $100 or more at macys.com). Notice this offer was only valid on the Macy's website, not in a physical store.

Talavera told us the offer was "on target" because it recognized her as someone who had purchased in one of Macy's stores. She felt it was not only relevant to the communication channel (email driving online versus offline shopping) but was also exclusive to the channel. In other words, this was not an offer Macy's would have included offline as well. It was meant to drive offline shoppers to buy online at macys.com. Finally, it had a deadline date.

Figure 11.10   *Karen Talavera received this email from Macy's—a company she never explicitly gave permission to email her.*

At the end of the day, Talavera was not offended by this eAppend. She cannot recall whether or not this email led her to purchase something from Macy's; however, she certainly did not opt out or report the email as spam.

Although using an eAppend is certainly skirting the comfort level of many email marketers who advocate for a total opt-in approach, it's far from the most controversial of all email marketing practices that we argue are not always wrong to consider. That status is reserved for buying email lists.

Buying an Email List

When is it okay to buy an email list? Never! End of story. End of section. End of chapter.

In fact, that's exactly what DJ said in a 2010 blog post.[18] It was the shortest blog post he had ever written. The title of the post read, "When Is It Okay to Buy an Email List?" The body of the post said, "Never." And that's exactly what DJ thought at the time.

The post generated quite a bit of buzz: 207 shares, 43 comments, 112 Facebook shares, and several tweets. What was interesting is that of those who left a comment, many actually were in favor of buying email lists. This gave us reason to pause, to reconsider our "all or nothing" approach to list buying.

Before we continue with this section, let's make something very, very, very clear. Neither DJ nor Jason personally advocate for buying lists of email addresses as a long-term strategy to grow your database. Although it might be effective in the short run, if executed improperly (which many list buys often are), buying email lists can have some serious, long-term, negative impacts.

But throughout the comments from various marketers in various organizations, there was a general theme—a common thread if you will. It was, "It depends." Like most things in life, business, and the world of email marketing, every story has two sides.

To be clear, buying and renting a list is not the same thing. Buying an email list requires an exchange of email addresses—the list seller gives the list buyer email addresses in exchange for money. With list rentals, email addresses do not change hands. For example, if Company A wants to rent Company B's email list, Company A would pay Company B for the right to have its message sent to Company B's list. Company A never sees the email addresses on Company B's list.

However, while several email services providers do not allow their clients to rent or buy email lists and send through their application, neither renting nor buying an email list is illegal in the United States. Nothing in the CAN-SPAM Act mentions either tactic.

"[It] drives me utterly bonkers when people start spouting off about how buying lists is illegal. It's not,"[19] tweeted Laura Atkins, founding partner of the anti-spam consultancy and software firm Word to the Wise. "If you are otherwise violating CAN-SPAM it's an increased penalty, but harvesting/buying/making up addresses is not illegal."[20]

So if it's not against the law (in the United States) why do many people have such a strong, negative association with buying email lists?

Take the website caniuseapurchasedemaillist.com, for example. When you navigate to that URL, you land on a page that says, "**No**," with the "I'm watching you" scene from *Meet the Parents*.

It's pretty clear where the folks from MailChimp stand.[21]

Jim Ducharme, formerly of The eMail Guide, even went as far as creating a make-believe group: the Email Marketers Association for Puppy Protection (EMAPP). He invited all ESPs and responsible email marketers to join and help educate the public that buying email lists is wrong. He suggested that "every time you buy an email list a puppy dies."[22]

We're certainly not for the mistreatment of animals, but remember that these puritanical attitudes are centered around the notion that email marketing is **best** when it is done in a completely opt-in fashion. If an audience does not ask to hear from you, your emails may not be wanted. But as we've shown throughout this book, not every rule is true all the time. With the right list (audience), the right message, and the right timing on your send, you can be more successful with open rates and conversions than with a completely opt-in audience.

Know, however, that most every email service provider includes some mention of purchasing email lists being against their policy, but it's not illegal. The far majority of email marketing practitioners are adamantly opposed to buying lists, but it's not illegal. The authors of this book (us!) do not outright advocate for list buying, but it's not illegal.

So why bother talking about it? As stated earlier, we don't believe in absolutes— black and white. Always do this. Never do that. If a list broker approaches you with a "permission" list of hundreds of thousands or millions of email addresses for very cheap, run. If you use a reputable list service, yet the campaign is poorly executed, you'll likely see a spike in complaints and the number of bad (undeliverable) email addresses will be high, both of which negatively impact your sender reputation and deliverability.

However, times occur when email list buying can and does work, most often in the business to business (B2B) space with small list sizes (no more than a few thousand), buying a very targeted list, and buying one that's sent over a long period of time.

Craig Rosenberg is the Vice President of Sales and Marketing at Focus, a Software as a Service–based content marketing platform and network of more than one million contributors that makes it possible for brands to easily create, publish, and distribute content at scale.

He believes that list buying can work, yet tends to perform best for B2B marketers. Companies who buy a list, send one email, and "hope it works out" are often not those that are most successful.

"Relevancy rules," says Rosenberg. "To be successful in B2B, you have to reach out to people who have not heard of you. Those people are less likely to call your email spam if it's relevant."

Rosenberg also stresses it's a long-term process that requires multiple touch points—phone, email, direct mail, and so on—and patience. Remember that B2C and B2B are very different in regards to buying lists. "If you 'cold email' someone to buy immediately, that typically does not work," said Rosenberg. "Instead, the cold email is to get them to raise their hand and ask for more information. Relevant educational material converts, not a one-time offer for 20 percent off."

Several companies are in the list brokerage business. One of them, NetProspex, has a database of B2B contacts of more than 25 million. It uses a proprietary verification technology that ensures the email address is deliverable and the email sent complies with CAN-SPAM regulations. Purchasing a list of relevant, targeted business contacts, including their email addresses, is simple using NetProspex (see Figure 11.11).

Figure 11.11 *Purchasing a list of targeted business contacts using NetPropex is easy.*

However, it's not the buying of an email list that's difficult. Far from it. It's as simple as selecting your criteria, searching, adding the search results to your cart, and purchasing. If you are willing to spend the money, buying a list is not too hard. Instead, what you do with that (hopefully) very targeted list can make all the difference in the world.

At this point you might be saying, "Great. So I understand that buying lists *can* work (in theory), but does it? Show me some case studies of it being successful!" That's a fair request.

As we ventured out to find an individual or company that had purchased email lists, something very interesting happened: Everyone went silent. Nobody wanted to talk about it. It's odd. We know it happens (as evidenced by companies such as NetProspex being in business), yet getting anyone to share their stories with us was a challenge. It could be because marketers have tried it and had a bad outcome. It could also be because the email marketing purists have preached "permission permission permission" for years and therefore many are skeptical to this list growth tactic. However, we believe that list buying does work, for some companies. The problem is that the email marketing purists out there have made list buying a dirty phrase, and nobody wants to admit they do it.

We were able to find one company (who requested anonymity, of course) to share some compelling data with us. Not only did list buying help it grow its list, but the list also positively impacted the top line!

Company A,[23] a small chain of restaurants with three locations, purchased a bridal list for catering offers. The total list size was only 422 contacts and was sent over an extended six-month period of time.

The price of the list was $1,000 and it generated $16,470 in revenue. Not too shabby of a return on its investment, huh?

But before you run off and buy a list, let's break down what Company A did with this list buy to help generate such an ROI. Notice the size of the list: 422 targeted email addresses. They didn't purchase a list of hundreds or thousands.

Also, Company A did not send a one-time email and hope for stellar results. As Rosenberg mentioned, using a purchased email list is a long-term process. This list was sent a series of emails over a six-month period.

But can this sort of list buying work on a much larger scale? How about a list purchase of 48 million from a well-known multi-billion dollar company?

You read that correctly: A company purchased a list of 48 million email addresses!

In September 2011, as part of the Borders bankruptcy settlement, Barnes & Noble purchased all of Borders intellectual property for $13.9 million. A significant portion of this purchase price included Borders 48-million-customer database.[24]

As you can imagine, the email marketing "best practice" folks out there were up in arms. Emails, blog posts, and articles were being penned at a frantic pace, most of them criticizing Barnes & Noble for not only buying the Borders email list, but also the manner in which they communicated it to the 48 million (former) Borders customers.

Here is how it all went down: Quite logically, Barnes & Noble chose email as the medium to tell Borders customers about its recent customer database acquisition. That email, sent on October 1, 2011, to past Borders customers, announced this news and then some.

The sender (From name) was "Barnes & Noble" yet interestingly, the From address was borders@e.borders.com. In other words, although the email was "from" Barnes & Noble, it was really being sent through Borders. The Subject line of this email read, "Important Information Regarding Your Borders Account."

The email, written by the Barnes & Noble CEO, William Lynch, informed Borders customers about "changes to their account." Specifically, the email mentioned that Barnes & Noble had acquired some of the Borders assets including its entire customer list. The email alerted former Borders customers that they had until October 15, 2011 to opt out of having customer data moved to Barnes & Noble. The company provided in the email a unique link to visit in order to process the opt-out.

The actual language in that section of the email read:

> "It's important for you to understand however **you have the absolute right to opt-out of having your customer data transferred to Barnes & Noble. If you would like to opt-out, we will ensure all your data we receive from Borders is disposed of in a secure and confidential manner. Please visit** www.bn.com/borders **before October 15, 2011 to do so.**"

Arthur Sweetser, former CMO and COO for email service provider e-Dialog and current CMO of 89 Degrees, thought the Barnes & Nobles list acquisition was brilliant. He offered this suggestion about purchasing lists of competitors that had gone out of business. "If you can convert 20 percent over to your brand and the price is right, I'd say you should consider yourself a BRILLIANT marketer!"[25]

We asked Barnes & Noble to comment on the Borders list purchase, the decision to send this opt-out email, and the results of the campaign. However, it declined to comment. We told you nobody wants to discuss list buying! (For the record, this wasn't your typical list purchase, but rather an asset purchase. No one else could buy Border's list. But it does offer some similarities that help us illustrate our points.)

Although knowing the exact outcome of this email is difficult, whether it lead to a high number of complaints (potentially causing deliverability issues for Barnes & Noble) or whether it was much ado about nothing for the Borders customers who received it, this much we do know: Barnes & Noble is still sending email to its customers on a regular basis. DJ averages about five emails a week from Barnes & Noble.

Coming Full Circle

There are recurring themes in this book we know you're seeing. One is that the rules espoused by the industry experts over the years, like never using pop-ups or buying lists, aren't exactly rules but suggestions based on either experience or, more likely, opinion. Another is that you have to determine which rules you are going to follow by taking these suggestions and testing them with your audience, in your industry, and around your product. Test with the attitude you want to prove the suggestion right, then test to try and prove the suggestion wrong. That's the only way you'll ever know what truly works with your customers.

In a sense, we've come full circle with this chapter. Part I of *The Rebel's Guide to Email Marketing* focuses on how to build your list. Part II helps you understand the anatomy of an email. Part III dives into all these so-called rules and how you can be a better email marketer if you sometimes break them. Now this chapter circles back to growing your list and talks about how some of the rules involved in list building are also worth testing, perhaps even breaking, to drive more subscribers, reach, and even revenue.

However, you have another part of the book to go, and it's an important one, too. Email marketing doesn't exist in a vacuum, and the online world in the last 10 years has been overtaken with an exciting new method of interacting with your customers. Nothing has shaken up business communication quite like social media. And while many digital marketers think oil and water when they look at email, traditionally a one-way mechanism of communications for companies, and social media, more of a conversation-based or two-way method of communicating. We don't. In fact, we think they go together and compliment each other rather nicely. So let's dive in to Part IV and see how these two channels work together like Batman and Robin.

Endnotes

1. Email Marketing Reports, "Double your sign-up rate? Practical advice for popover forms," December 20, 2011. http://www.email-marketing-reports.com/iland/2011/12/popovers.html

2. AWeber FAQs, Adapted from "How Do I Create or Edit A Pop Up Web Form?" http://www.aweber.com/faq/questions/225/How+Do+I+Create+or+Edit+A+Pop+Up+Web+Form%3F

3. Ginsberg, Jeff, "Using a Lightbox to Grow Your Opt-In Email Marketing List," February 12, 2012. http://www.theemailguide.com/our-world/feature/using-a-lightbox-to-grow-your-opt-in-email-marketing-list-by-jeff-ginsberg-dad_ftw/

4. Penn, Christopher S., "Do welcome popups work?" February 3, 2011. http://www.christopherspenn.com/2011/02/do-welcome-popups-work/

5. Penn, Christopher S., "Do welcome popups work?" February 3, 2011. http://www.christopherspenn.com/2011/02/do-welcome-popups-work/

6. MailChimp Support, "Can I shut off the e-mail that asks people for confirmation that they want to join my list?" http://kb.mailchimp.com/article/can-i-shut-off-the-e-mail-that-asks-people-for-confirmation-that-they-want-/

7. AWeber FAQ, "Can I Disable Confirmed Opt-In?" http://www.aweber.com/faq/questions/66/Can+I+Disable+Confirmed+Opt-In%3F

8. McCloskey, Bill, "Are You Really, Really Sure?" February 12, 2009. http://www.clickz.com/clickz/column/1700534/are-you-really-really-sure

9. Return Path, "The Global Email Deliverability Benchmark Report, 2H 2011." http://www.returnpath.net/downloads/reports/returnpath_globaldeliverability2h11.pdf

10. iContact, "The Pros & Cons of Double Opt-In 2009." http://www.icontact.com/static/pdf/Email_Marketing_Best_Practices_iContact.pdf

11. Bronto's Permission Marketing Promise, http://bronto.com/permission-marketing-promise

12. CampaignMonitor, "What you need to know about permission." http://www.campaignmonitor.com/resources/entry/558/about-permission/

13. "Is my list okay to use in MailChimp?" Updated 01/27/2012. http://kb.mailchimp.com/article/is-my-list-okay-to-use-in-mailchimp

14. Magill, Ken, "Permission Debate is Settled; Please Stop Yapping About it." http://www.magillreport.com/permission-debate-is-settled/

15. Bluehornet Report, "Consumer Views of Email Marketing" http://www.bluehornet.com/assets/Report_Consumer-Views-of-Email-Marketing.pdf

16. Waldow, DJ, "Assumptions And Opt-Out: A Deadly Combination." July 13, 2010. http://www.mediapost.com/publications/article/131860 (see comment from Daniel Coburn).

17. Bannan, Karen J., "Establishing an effective email append strategy." October 20, 2011. http://www.btobonline.com/article/20111020/EMAIL06/310209999/establishing-an-effective-email-append-strategy

18. Waldow, DJ, "When Is It Okay To Buy An Email List?" July 6, 2010. http://blog.blueskyfactory.com/best-practice/when-is-it-okay-to-buy-an-email-list/

19. Tweet from Laura Atkins (@wise_laura) on February 8, 2012. https://twitter.com/#!/wise_laura/status/167377428375810048

20. Tweet from Laura Atkins (@wise_laura) on February 8, 2012. https://twitter.com/#!/wise_laura/status/167376110907170816

21. MailChimp owns the domain, caniuseapurchasedemaillist.com.

22. Ducharme, Jim, "Every time you buy an email list a puppy dies." July 6, 2010. http://www.theemailguide.com/email-marketing/every-time-you-buy-an-email-list-a-puppy-dies/

23. The client asked to remain anonymous.

24. Brown, Nick, "Borders, B&N get court's OK on $14 million IP sale." September 26, 2011. http://www.reuters.com/article/2011/09/26/us-borders-idUSTRE78P5US20110926

25. Fresh Address, "Partner Insights: Barnes & Noble's Acquisition of Borders's Email List." http://biz.freshaddress.com/November2011_PartnerInsights.aspx

12

How Email and Social Media Go Together

Social media is—and has been—one of the most talked about topics over the past few years. However, somehow we've managed to go a full eleven chapters with only a few mentions of social media. That should not surprise you as this book is about email marketing. What does email marketing have to do with social media? A lot. Over the next few chapters, we show you how email marketing and social media go together like Batman and Robin.

However, before we bring Gotham City into the mix, let's first review why everyone—and we mean everyone—can't stop gushing about social media. If you're not talking about Facebook, Twitter, LinkedIn, Google+, Pinterest, Instagram, foursquare, or [insert latest-and-greatest-social-media-site here], you are probably in the minority. Social media is popping up everywhere, including in traditional media such as billboards, magazines, storefront windows, radio, direct mail, and even television. You know when mainstream media talks about social media, it must be hot.

It seems like every day on CNN, ESPN, and every other major American television network there is some talk of a celebrity or athlete and his use of social media. CNN talk show host Anderson Cooper goes to every commercial break saying things like, "Find us on Facebook and circle us on Google+. I'll also be tweeting."

Speaking of Twitter, while 10 percent of Americans ages 12 and older use this social network, 89 percent of them are familiar with it. Before you say, "only 10 percent," imagine if 10 percent of Americans ages 12 and older used your product or service. Not bad, right? And 89 percent awareness of Twitter? Incredible. This statistic as well as some of the other findings from The Social Habit 2012[1] might surprise you (they did us):

- 56 percent of Americans ages 12 and older have a profile on one or more social networking sites.
- 54 percent of Americans ages 12 and older have a profile page on Facebook. Compare this to 13 percent on LinkedIn, and 8 percent on Google+.
- 22 percent of all Americans (not just users) check social networks several times a day.
- One-third of regular social networking users follow brands.

The report includes a ton of other compelling data around Americans' "social habit." Suffice it to say that social media is on-fire hot. Everyone is talking about it, doing it, and even sharing that they are talking about and doing it. Unless the "Big 4"—Facebook, Twitter, LinkedIn, and Google+—somehow disappear, we don't see social media going anywhere anytime soon.

Okay. So are we all on the same page about social media? Good. It's time to introduce our superheroes.

Batman and Robin

At this point, you might be thinking: "Great. I get that social media is all the rage these days. But how does it relate to this book? What does social media have to do with email marketing? And remind me why we are talking about superheroes?" We're glad you asked.

Let's start by discussing the dynamic duo, Batman and Robin.

Batman: The Caped Crusader. The Dark Knight. The superhero of all superheroes, Batman has been around since the early days of comic books. In fact, according to Wikipedia, Batman was "born" (first published) in May 1939 in Detective Comics.[2] He has proven that, when called upon, he's more than capable of saving the city. He's the old workhorse. He gets the job done, no questions asked.

Robin: Boy Wonder. According to Lee Daniels, author of *Batman: The Complete History* (Chronicle Books, 2004), Robin was conceived to attract a younger reader base, eventually doubling the sales of the Batman related comic books.[3] Although in time he became a superhero himself, Robin started out as a sidekick to Batman. He can save the city on his own but always seems to do better when Batman is by his side.

Email marketing is like Batman. It's been around since the early days of the Internet. It has a proven ROI ($40.56 per dollar invested according to the Direct Marketers Association). It gets the job done and then some. It can operate on its own, with no help from other channels. Social media is like Robin. It's new. It's fresh. It's "for the kids" (though social media users are beginning to skew to an older demographic). It also can work effectively on its own, but is still the up and comer. However, when their forces are joined, email marketing and social media make for a quite the dynamic duo.

We believe very strongly in the integration of email marketing and social media. It has tremendous potential to grow both your email list and social network following, to extend the reach of your email campaigns (more opens, clicks, and conversions), and to identify your key influencers.

Email: The Digital Glue of Social Media

Before we get into the specifics, you must understand that email is central to all of social media. It's the core. In fact, as Greg Cangialosi, founder of email service provider Blue Sky Factory, said in 2008, "email is the 'digital glue' of the new media landscape, and a medium that is not to be overlooked."[4] Email marketing holds it all together. We like it.

If you are one of the 56 percent of Americans ages 12 and older who have a profile on one or more social networking sites, think back to when you first signed up for an account. If you created a Facebook or Twitter account a while ago, quite possibly you will not remember the account set-up process. Take a minute (now) to log out of Twitter and Facebook and try to create a new account for each social network.

If you don't want to put this book down, go to Twitter and Facebook, log out, and try to create an account, you can just look at Figure 12.1 to see what we mean.

As you can see, both Facebook (on the left) and Twitter (on the right) require an email address as part of the sign-up process. It's not optional. Email, the digital glue, is central to social media.

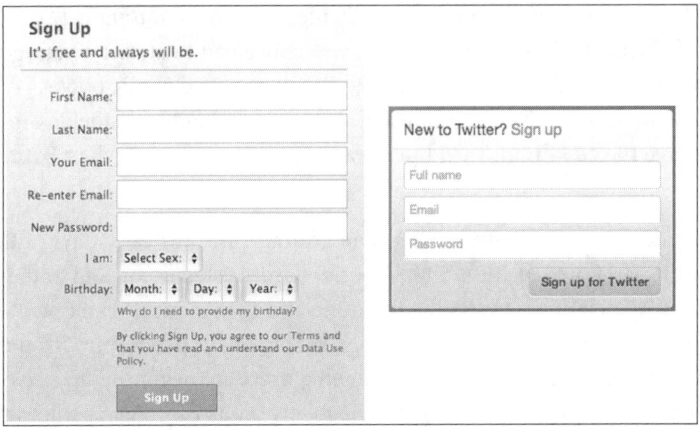

Sign Up
It's free and always will be.

First Name:
Last Name:
Your Email:
Re-enter Email:
New Password:
I am: Select Sex:
Birthday: Month: Day: Year:
Why do I need to provide my birthday?

By clicking Sign Up, you agree to our Terms and that you have read and understand our Data Use Policy.

Sign Up

New to Twitter? Sign up

Full name

Email

Password

Sign up for Twitter

Figure 12.1   *Users must have an email address to sign up for a Facebook (left) or Twitter (right) account.*

This email requirement is not just limited to Facebook and Twitter. LinkedIn requires an email address to create an account. For those still interested in joining MySpace, you'll need to provide an email address. The entire backbone of Google+ is built around having a Google account—which requires an email address.

In addition to the registration process, most social networking sites require an email address to sign in. See Figure 12.2 showing both the Facebook and LinkedIn login boxes.

Email   Password
                                    Log In
☑ Keep me logged in   Forgot your password?

Email address:
Password: Forgot password?
Sign In or Join LinkedIn

Figure 12.2   *Users must also use their email address to sign in to Facebook (top) or LinkedIn (bottom).*

Other social networks, such as Twitter, give users the option to log in using a username or email address. Still others, such as Pinterest (see Figure 12.3), provide an alternative to logging in using an email address.

Figure 12.3 *Users of Pinterest have the option to log in with Facebook, Twitter, or an email address.*

Instead of requiring an email address, it lets you link your profile with other more popular sites, such as Twitter or Facebook. This is often referred to as a "social sign in." Now, don't get too excited! You still need an email address to create a Facebook or Twitter account in the first place, so we're not contradicting ourselves. However, notice that the default login option still includes "Email Address." This covers the folks who either don't have a Facebook or Twitter account, are not clear about what it means to "Login with Facebook" or "Login with Twitter," or choose not to link their profiles.

For those still wondering about MySpace, its default login also requires an email address.

But wait! There's more proof of the digital glue concept!

Most, if not all, social networking sites send member updates and alerts through (you guessed it) email. New LinkedIn "requests to connect" are emailed. There is an option to have Twitter direct message (DM) or mentions (@s) emailed. When there is new activity on your Facebook account, users are emailed. Google+ allows people to email you from a link on your profile.

The bottom line is this: Email is at the core of nearly all social networking sites. Social media relies heavily on email to allow members to communicate with each other as well as to send alerts when an account has new activity. Most of these social media sites also depend on email marketing to keep their membership in the loop on company news, updates, events, policy changes, new features, and the like.

That's exactly what Facebook did in 2011 when it tested a new feature. In somewhat ironic fashion, the email (shown in Figure 12.4) alerted Facebook members about a function that would "reduce the amount of email" the site sent.

Figure 12.4   *Facebook sent an email alerting members about a feature that would reduce the amount of email received from the site.*

Email is certainly the digital glue of social media, but how do the two channels play together to create an unstoppable force, much like the dynamic duo of Batman and Robin?

Social Connecting vs. Social Sharing vs. Social Promoting

When most people discuss the integration of email marketing and social media, they are usually talking about one of three things:

- **Social connecting**—Asking email subscribers to connect (follow) you on social networking sites
- **Social sharing**—Asking email subscribers to share email content on social networking sites
- **Social promoting**—Using social media sites to promote email

Social Connecting

More marketers are beginning to incorporate social connecting icons in their emails. These Twitter/Facebook/Google+/YouTube buttons invite the subscriber to follow the sender on Twitter, like him on Facebook, circle him on Google+, or subscribe to his YouTube channel. The goal is to use email to power a company's social media channels: increasing followers, likes, circles, or subscribers. Figures 12.5 and 12.6 show two examples of social connecting.

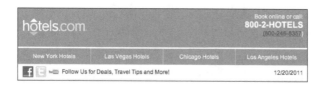

Figure 12.5   *This email from hotels.com includes social connecting icons and a reason to follow the site.*

Notice in Figure 12.5, hotels.com not only includes the Facebook, Twitter, and YouTube icons, it also adds some copy giving subscribers a reason to connect with it: *Follow Us for Deals, Travel Tips and More!* Remember the whole "What's in It for Me?" discussion in Chapter 2, "How to Grow Your List"? The same concept applies here when using email to grow your social following. Providing readers a reason to follow, like, or otherwise connect is critical.

Figure 12.6   *McCormick creatively adds a social connecting option in its email header.*

McCormick takes a slightly different approach with its social connecting option. In the header of one of its emails (see Figure 12.6), it includes a banner with the McCormick logo next to a Find us on Facebook button. We did a bit more digging to see why McCormick was only promoting Facebook in its emails and noticed that it's the one social channel the company is really focusing on. It promotes Facebook heavily on its website and, with nearly 300,000 likes on its Facebook page, seems to be doing quite fine there. Interestingly, as of the writing of this book, McCormick did not have a presence on Twitter.

So why is this so important? Why are email marketers spending valuable resources on social connecting icons?

Remember that every prospect and every customer is different. Just because you create content in many places—email, blog, offline, social media, and so on—does not mean your audience is consuming it everywhere. By providing another platform for them to connect with you, you're able to communicate and interact with your community in different ways.

Additionally, it's quite possible email is not the best channel for some people in your community. Clearly we are big fans of email marketing; however, we're not naive enough to think it's the only (or even always the best) way to connect with your audience. By including these social connecting icons in your emails, you are allowing your audience to interact via the channel of their liking.

Each channel at your disposal to engage your audience—be it Facebook, Twitter, blogging, email, and so on—has slightly different technical and audience needs and expectations. A tweet doesn't necessarily work on LinkedIn considering Twitter's somewhat unique language. A Facebook post might not jive with the expectations of your email list.

What this means is that your email marketing messages might (and sometimes should) be vastly different than that which you post on social channels. For instance, you can leverage social connecting to ask questions, conduct polls, and share links to interesting content, then use your email marketing messages to peel back the curtain a bit and show them a bit more of your company or brand. By connecting to your community in other places, you can carve out special purposes for your email marketing content versus your social media content.

Social Sharing

Although social sharing options are certainly not as prevalent as social connecting icons, more marketers are starting to include them within their email marketing messages. Social sharing, sometimes referred to as "Share With Your Network" (SWYN), happens when an email contains buttons or links to share the entire email or a specific content block within the email with a subscriber's social network.

The Sony email shown in Figure 12.7 is pretty typical of how most email marketers are leveraging SWYN in email. Notice how Sony includes the phrase "SHARE this email" immediately preceding the email, Facebook, and Twitter icons. Clicking on the Facebook or Twitter icon will open a new browser window or tab. Assuming a subscriber is already logged into Facebook or Twitter, the dialog box is pre-populated, most often with some text and a shortened URL of the web version of the email. This makes for easy sharing on the part of the subscriber.

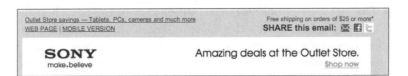

Figure 12.7   *Sony includes social sharing options in the preheader of this email.*

Notice that Sony does break one "mini" rule in Figure 12.7. The social sharing icons are in the preheader instead of further down in the email. As you'll recall from Chapter 7, "The Finishing Touches," most often sharing buttons are near the bottom of the email closer to or in the footer. This does not mean it's where they should be placed within an email, just where they appear most often.

Another example of including social sharing icons is the "MarketingProfs Today" email shown in Figure 12.8. MarketingProfs, an online publisher, includes Twitter, Facebook, and LinkedIn icons at the bottom right of each article in its daily email newsletter.

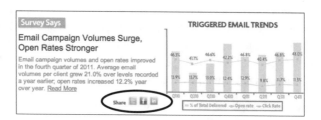

Figure 12.8   *The MarketingProfs email uses social sharing options to let readers share individual articles.*

The advantage of this approach is that instead of subscribers being forced to share the entire email, they can share only those blocks of content, such as specific articles, that they believe their social networks would be most interested in reading. The potential downside to this method is that the email tends to be filled with social sharing icons that might distract from the rest of the email.

And, yes, the screenshot we choose for Figure 12.8 was intentional! Look at the article headline and the supporting graph: "Email Campaign Volumes Surge, Open Rates Stronger." Who said email was dead?

Another alternative is to combine social sharing with social connecting as DAZ 3D, a company that provides 3D animation software does, as shown in Figure 12.9.

Figure 12.9   *DAZ 3D combines social sharing with social connecting in some of its email campaigns.*

Although the messaging next to each icon clearly states what happens if a person clicks ("Share This on Facebook" or "Share This on Twitter" or "Subscribe to Our Channel"), the risk in this approach is that it might be confusing for subscribers.

It was not all that clear to us either! The only indication whether the icon was for sharing or connecting was the word "share" versus "subscribe."

Smart marketers include SWYN icons in their emails for many reasons. One is that social sharing has the potential to extend the reach of a normal email marketing message. The more subscribers who share, the more potential exists for more opens, clicks, and conversions. Remember the short URL that gets created after clicking the Share on Twitter button? Most email service providers are able to track which specific email subscriber shared the email or block of content as well as how many times the unique link was clicked (representing an email open). Additionally, many providers can track how many of those socially shared emails that were opened were also clicked. Both of these metrics can increase the overall open and click rates on each email campaign deployed.

This sharing effect can quickly be amplified depending on the size and reach of each subscriber's social network. For example, let's say one of your subscribers shares your email with his Twitter followers, which happen to number at 10,000. If 1 percent of those followers clicks on the short URL, you now have an additional 100 views (opens) of that email—and all with minimal effort on your part.

The key to this, of course, is not only making your email content share-worthy, but also making it easy to share. We'll talk a lot more about this in Chapter 13, "The Power of Pairs."

Social sharing also provides some interesting data on key influencers. Most email service providers capture data and provide metrics on exactly which of your email subscribers are sharing as well as how often they are sharing. Some will even track the number of opens, clicks, and conversions each social share results in. With this information at your fingertips, you can identify those "key influencers" or at least folks who deem your email content share-worthy. If appropriate, you can then send dedicated email campaigns to your biggest supporters.

Finally, SWYN can help grow your email list. The more an email is shared across various social networks, the more opportunity non-subscribers have to learn about you, your company, or your brand. This can result in a portion of those folks signing up to your email list. Some email service providers even provide built-in features to change the creative on the shared email to include an opt-in. We'll discuss more about the benefits and successes of SWYN in Chapter 13.

Social Promoting

The third way to integrate email marketing with social media is to use social media to promote email. This can mean sending out a tweet or updating your Facebook page with a link to your email sign-up form. It can also entail posting a link to one of your social networking sites alerting your community about your recent email marketing campaign. The first tactic has the potential to grow your list whereas the second can be used to increase the number of eyeballs on your email campaigns. We'll discuss this in much more detail—including examples of companies who are finding great success with each of these approaches—in the next chapter.

As we move into Chapter 13, keep in mind we'll be talking less about breaking the rules of email marketing and more about using different methods to integrate email and social. If you think social media is in its infancy, the integration of email marketing and social media is even more recent. Because of this, many of the established "best practices" and "rules" of email marketing have not yet been created. People are trying new and different approaches to combine Batman (email marketing) and Robin (social media), each with various levels of success. These folks are paving the way for this new method of integrating the two channels. They are, as social business expert and *The Now Revolution* (Wiley, 2011) coauthor Amber Naslund would call "the wayfarers."[5]

Our hope is that in another decade or so, we'll be talking about breaking the "rules" of Batman (email marketing) and Robin (social media).

Endnotes

1. The Edison Research/Arbitron Internet and Multimedia Study 2012. "The Social Habit 2012."

2. Wikipedia, http://en.wikipedia.org/wiki/Batman

3. Daniels, Les (2004). *Batman: The Complete History*. Chronicle Books, p. 37.

4. Cangialosi, Greg, "Email Marketing's Role in New Media: Podcamp Boston Presentation," July 20, 2008. http://www.thetrendjunkie. com/2008/07/20/email-marketings-role-in-new-media-podcamp-boston-presentation/

5. Naslund, Amber, "Attention, Wayfarers: Win A Free Pass to BlogWorld LA," October 10, 2011. http://www.brasstackthinking. com/2011/10/attention-wayfarers-win-a-free-pass-to-blogworld-la/

13

The Power of Pairs

Imagine you are being held captive by the Joker. Suddenly, out of nowhere, Robin appears. You are saved! But wait, Robin is having trouble. He can't seem to rescue you on his own. Enter Batman, who swoops down and lands next to Robin. There is once again hope. Together, the Dynamic Duo is able to get you free from the Joker and save your life. You are forever indebted.

Batman and Robin. Email marketing and social media.

Although the rest of this chapter will not be as superhero-ish as that first paragraph was, keep in mind the Batman and Robin metaphor we introduced in Chapter 12, "How Email and Social Media Go Together." Email marketing, like Batman, has a proven track record ($40.56 return per dollar invested). It can get the job done on its own with no help from other channels. Social media, like Robin, gets more attention for its flashy newness. It can also perform well on its own. However, when joined together (integrated), email marketing and social media can be an unstoppable force.

In regards to integrating email and social, think about the power of pairs—specifically, using email marketing to power social media and social media to power email marketing.

When it comes to using email marketing and social media together, it's less about being rebellious and breaking the rules and more about making the rules. Although recommended tactics certainly exist for effectively integrating email and social, it's just too early in the game to have any established best practices. Different kinds of companies have leveraged the two channels for an overall positive impact on their marketing efforts.

Social Connecting

In Chapter 12, we introduced the concept of social connecting—asking email subscribers to connect (follow) you on social networking sites. We shared a few examples of what it looks like within the body of an email marketing message.

There are many reasons why a company would want to increase its social media following. From a pure numbers game, more followers means more eyeballs. More eyeballs means more potential conversions—sales, webinar registrations, and so on.

Now let's take a look at how several organizations are using social connecting to increase their followers on social media sites such as Twitter and Facebook and—more importantly—how that's positively impacting revenue.

Using Email Marketing to Grow Your Social Following

As with most things in marketing, if you want someone to take action, you make the desired action obvious and easy to take, and you tell them what's in it for them if they take that action. These steps are an integral part of growing your email list. They also hold true for using email marketing to grow your social following.

We often chuckle when we see social media icons slapped on the bottom of a television ad, billboard, on the back cover of a magazine, or on the bottom of marketing collateral. The problem is, as marketers, we assume people not only know what those icons mean, but more importantly what they are supposed to do when they see them.

Every time we see a tiny Twitter icon on a television commercial, our instinct is to click it. But without the context of why we should go through the trouble of opening up a computer and going to see what this brand is doing on Twitter, the call-to-action is quite ineffective. Sure, it could be argued there is value in the "brand impression"; however, tying that back to a specific campaign is quite a challenge. This same "What am I supposed to do?" confusion occurs when marketers put

Twitter, Facebook, and Google+ icons in their email marketing messages, assuming all readers know what they mean and what happens when they click.

Take this email from travel website Expedia (see Figure 13.1). Can you find the Facebook icon?

Figure 13.1 *If you squint, you can see the Facebook icon in the upper-right side of this Expedia email.*

If you look very closely, you'll notice the Facebook icon in the upper right of the header of this Expedia email. It's there, trust us. However, it's unclear what happens if you click on it. Considering it's located directly after the Feedback link, it's possible the "f" stands for feedback. Assuming you do recognize the "f" icon to be associated with Facebook, do you know what happens when you click it? Will you be taken to Expedia's Facebook page? Maybe you'll be sharing this email on Facebook? Maybe something else entirely will happen.

Sure, we're being a bit overdramatic, for illustration purposes. The point is that without a clear description, a clear call to action, or a clear "What's in it for me?" type message next to the "f" image, Expedia just reduced the likelihood of an email reader clicking the Facebook icon and liking its page.

On the far other end of the spectrum is this email from content marketing and website software company Copyblogger (see Figure 13.2).

Figure 13.2 *This Copyblogger email is dedicated to getting its email subscribers to like it on Facebook.*

The entire email, from the Subject line ("Do You Like Copyblogger?") to the three calls to action in the email—the "Give Us a Like on Facebook" button, the Copyblogger Facebook page link, and the "Click Here" link—all encourage readers to like the Copyblogger Facebook page. Additionally, the messaging within the body of the email focuses on why readers should like Copyblogger on Facebook. The site even uses "what's in it for you" language!

Take a minute to compare the Expedia email to the Copyblogger one. Based on the email alone, which Facebook page would you be more apt to "like?" We thought so.

Although the two examples we've provided are using email marketing messages to grow Facebook likes, the same type of email campaign can work for other social networks such as Twitter, LinkedIn, Google+, and Pinterest. In fact, Copyblogger has sent a similar dedicated email campaign to encourage its community to follow it on Twitter. The messaging also told readers why they should take action: "We deliver a lot of daily advice here on Copyblogger. And yet, in the fast-moving world of online marketing, web publishing, and social media, there's a lot to know." Copyblogger also posted this same content to its blog to be sure it covered as many community members as possible for the largest impact.

While the previous example from Copyblogger is wonderful in theory, can email marketing really be used to grow a company's social presence? Nope. Just kidding! Of course it can; otherwise this would be a pretty short chapter.

Using Email Marketing to Grow Facebook Likes and Revenue

Until 2011, Bella Soleil didn't do much with social media. The Italian pottery, glass, and craft items online retailer generally drove its sales through search engine optimization, pay-per-click advertising, and customer retention through email marketing. Bella Soleil founder and president Elaine Robbins uses her background in computer engineering to ensure that the company is tracking and measuring all of its digital marketing efforts to ensure it's getting the biggest bang for its buck. She also knows her customers can be a little quirky.

"A lot of our customers are an older generation," Robbins said. "They sometimes won't click the links in our emails, but will see the email, go to Google and search our name. But because of the timing of the visit, we're confident the visit came as a result of our email communications."

But this age factor was also one of a few factors that made Bella Soleil slow to adopt social media as part of its customer communications strategies, until its email provider, Constant Contact, approached the company with its then-new social media product in the fall of 2011. Bella Soleil then emailed its customers, inviting them to "like" the brand on Facebook. If they did, Bella Soleil would provide that customer with a coupon. Within an hour of the email distribution, Bella had collected 75 likes. It eventually got more than 130 from the promotion.

While those numbers don't sound like much to many companies or brands on Facebook, remember that we're talking about an older and wealthier demographic (they buy imported Italian pottery), and one the company knows is not exactly tech savvy. Now, before you say, "So what? That's only 130 people from a promotion!" keep this in mind: Several of those 130 people downloaded the coupon (made available only to Facebook fans), cashed it in while purchasing something new on the Bella Soleil website, and spent money the company could track. How much? Try more than $10,000 on for size!

Certainly, several factors were at play here, but integrating social media with email means that one can fuel the other. Ideally, you want to lure your social media network to subscribe to your newsletter or promotions list and have those on your list connect with you on social channels. Making exclusive offers to one audience to join the other works.

Winder Farms, a company that delivers fresh produce to customers' homes in the Utah and Nevada areas, was stuck on 9,500 likes on its Facebook page for a few months. Winder's marketing specialist, Austin Whitaker, was frustrated that the company just could not seem to "get over the hump" and surpass 10,000 likes, an internal goal. He took matters into his own hands one afternoon and began crafting an email campaign that would push the number of likes over the edge.

To cross into the 10,000 "likes" category, Whitaker turned to Winder's email marketing list. "I wanted to offer a pretty good incentive for customers to like us and I really wanted to play up the number 10,000," Whitaker told us. "The 10,000 pennies idea just came to me. It was a good dollar value ($100) for free groceries, but also sounded like more and played off the 10,000 theme I wanted to go with."

Whitaker created the email campaign and chose "Win 10,000 Pennies from Winder Farms" as the Subject line for the email, shown in Figure 13.3.

Whitaker was pleasantly surprised by the results. Normally, when he sends an email to the entire Winder Farms customer base, the open rate is somewhere between 24 and 27 percent. This email had a 29 percent open rate. However, what really got Whitaker and the Winder team excited was the fact that 870 customers clicked on the Facebook link.

The email, deployed at 2:45 p.m. on March 6, 2012, single-handedly pushed Winder Farms to its 10,000 goal by the end of the day. Over the next few days, the likes continued to trickle in: 124 on March 7, 30 on March 8, and 14 on March 9. "By the end of the week," said Whitaker, "we had gained around 700 new likes on our Facebook page, putting us around the 10,200 range." What's even more impressive was that of the 870 readers who clicked the Facebook link in the email, about 80 percent of them liked Winder Farms' Facebook page. In addition to the new likes, Winder Farms received quite a few posts on its wall: mostly testimonials about how much people love the milk, food, and service.

Figure 13.3   *Winder Farms sent an email campaign dedicated to growing its Facebook likes by incentivizing subscribers with a chance to win 10,000 pennies.*

Winder Farms was able to grow its Facebook likes by nearly 700 with one email and a 10,000 penny ($100) incentive. Even after factoring in the cost to send an extra email to its entire customer list as well as the $50–$60 cost due to its margins (according to Whitaker), this is still not a bad price to pay for an increased Facebook following and several customer testimonials: comments that can be used in other marketing collateral.

Like Winder Farms, BabySteals.com also sent an email to its subscribers that was dedicated to its Facebook fans. However, this email (as shown in Figure 13.4), was not an attempt to reach a milestone, nor did it provide readers an incentive to like BabySteals.com on Facebook. Instead, it was a simple announcement and a thanks to the company's 200,000 fans.

As you can see, BabySteals.com provided a link inviting those email subscribers who were not fans to "join the festivities and share a pic of your babe on our wall."

Figure 13.4 *BabySteals.com sent an email to its customers celebrating its goal of reaching 200,000 Facebook fans.*

Angie Fairbanks, social media manager at Steal Network, the parent company of BabySteals.com, told us this email campaign resulted in unique open and click-through rates that were 25 and 33 percent higher, respectively, than the average BabySteals.com email. The same day this email was sent, BabySteals.com saw its Facebook likes increase by 1,958. Additionally, fan page views went up by 376 percent and its unique fan page views went up by 628 percent. It experienced a seven-day spike in interaction on its page, mostly attributed to fans sharing a photo of their babies on BabySteals.com's Facebook page, as they were encouraged to do.

"We love interacting with customers and try to make our Facebook page a personal place where not only can they interact with us as a brand, but they connect with other moms for support and fun," said Fairbanks. "Moms love sharing how cute their little ones are (and we, of course, love seeing them), so this follow up requesting them to share a photo was a fun way to introduce new moms to our page while also engaging current fans."

We asked Fairbanks to share with us why integrating email marketing and social media is so important for BabySteals.com. Here's what she had to say:

> "In so many ways, social media interaction is the core of our business and email marketing helps support that. While we constantly engage with our fans on Facebook and other platforms, we can't assume our customers are already fans or even that current fans are engaging with our brand regularly. Email is an additional way to bring them back to

our community. The way we have been successful at merging email and social media is by being authentic and newsworthy. We only send emails like this sparingly, and when we do, we make sure it's worth their time and relevant to them."

Let's look at a different industry example. Tahoe Mountain Sports (TMS), which sells clothing and gear for the rugged outdoors, leverages email marketing and social media marketing to help stretch the company's modest budget for marketing. Owner Dave Polivy uses email marketing to promote TMS's Facebook page.

"We've woven social media icons into our email welcome series, including several touch points along the way to entice our subscribers to connect with us on our social channels," Polivy told us. Instead of just slapping those social icons within each email, including order confirmations, TMS includes some copy about why people should connect with it. Here is the call to action for its Facebook icon: *"Contests, Events, News and More. 'Like Us' today!"*

TMS sweetens the deal for email subscribers who like its Facebook page by providing $10 off their first order. To get the coupon, fans have to first like the page, which is hidden behind a Fangate.[1] TMS gets about 15 new Facebook likes per email send to a 3,000 subscriber list.

In case you are thinking "Only 15 per day? That's nothing!" keep in mind that TMS is a relatively small company. "While our numbers are not hugely impressive," said Polivy, "for a small company, campaigns like this make huge differences!" In fact, TMS generated about $1,700 from each marketing email that heavily promoted the Facebook incentive. Polivy told us this number was well above revenue generated from a traditional marketing message about sales or new arrivals.

However, social media can also help to put your email newsletter content in front of more people. This, in turn, means each email can generate a higher ROI.

Social Sharing

Using email marketing to encourage subscribers to connect with your company or brand on your social networks is important, but the real power of email and social integration is with social sharing. Giving your readers the ability to share your email campaigns with their network is an easy way to get more eyeballs on your content. More of those means more clicks on links, buttons, and images. More clicks leads to more conversions: webinar signups, purchases, and the like. Finally, the more people who view your email newsletter, the better the chance your email list will grow. Sounds easy, right?

In many ways it is easy. In fact, adding social sharing or Share With Your Network (SWYN) functionality to your email marketing campaigns is simple to do. If you use an email service provider to help send your emails, chances are quite high they offer a built-in SWYN capability that incorporates a drag-and-drop or WYSIWYG (What You See Is What You Get) editor. For those with more resources to write and design emails, providers often supply the code to make social sharing possible. This allows marketers to create their own look and feel for SWYN calls to action, as DAZ 3D does in many of its email campaigns (see Figure 13.5).

Figure 13.5 *DAZ 3D designs its own SWYN buttons using code supplied by its email service provider, Bronto.*

Including SWYN functionality in your email campaigns might be (relatively) easy, but getting subscribers to share your emails is the tricky part. We don't believe it has to be that hard. However, for some reason not many companies are finding success with SWYN. Part of this has to do with social media being in its infancy. Couple that with email marketing and social media integration being very new, and we're not seeing many folks getting it right consistently.

A few key steps can make SWYN more successful. To make your emails more shareable:

- Ensure the SWYN feature is visible and obvious in the email.
- Make it clear what happens when the sharing icon, button, or link is clicked.
- Provide a strong call to action to click to share.
- Make sure emails are easy to share.

Shareability really starts with the first bullet point. We equate this step of "make it visible and obvious" to what we discussed earlier about growing your list. If your readers want to share your emails yet can't quickly locate the share button, they are never going to do it. You've lost them. Instead, if you want to encourage sharing, don't hide the functionality. Make it clear, obvious, and easy. Although most SWYN icons are located at the bottom of the email, placing them there is not always the best way to get a reader's attention. For example, can you spot the social sharing icons in Figure 13.6?

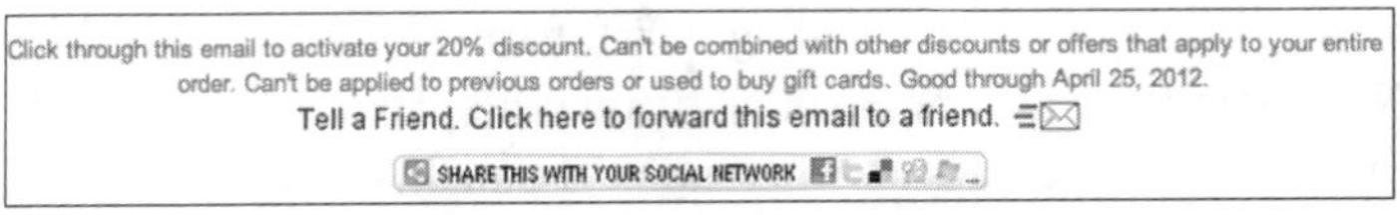

Click through this email to activate your 20% discount. Can't be combined with other discounts or offers that apply to your entire order. Can't be applied to previous orders or used to buy gift cards. Good through April 25, 2012.
Tell a Friend. Click here to forward this email to a friend. ≡⊠

⊠ SHARE THIS WITH YOUR SOCIAL NETWORK

Figure 13.6   *These social sharing icons are hidden at the bottom of this email. Sharing is difficult if readers can't easily find a way to do it.*

Instead of being located close to the "20% discount" offer (something more likely to be shared), the SWYN icons are at the very bottom of the email. Although the icons are visible (barely), they are far from obvious.

Let's be clear, though. SWYN icons can still work at the bottom of an email. The social sharing options from email service provider WhatCounts's welcome email, in Figure 13.7, are located just above the footer.

Figure 13.7   *Although WhatCounts puts its social sharing icons near the bottom of its welcome email, the messaging is clear and the icons are obvious.*

The difference between the email in Figure 13.6 and the one in Figure 13.7 is that the WhatCounts SWYN icons are large, clear, and quite obvious. In addition, the messaging tells readers what to do: "SHARE THE GAMECHANGER" (the name of its weekly email campaign series).

This messaging is the second aspect to making the SWYN options effective: Be clear about what happens when a reader clicks one of the icons. Most often, you can accomplish this by including language as simple as "share this," "share with your network," "post to Facebook," or "Share," followed by the name of your newsletter.

If you want to get a bit more creative, you can implement something similar to what social media marketing evangelist Laura Roeder does in her weekly "The Dash" emails (see Figure 13.8).

Instead of just including the Twitter icons, Roeder adds the recognizable symbol for Twitter (the bird) with a big button call to action that reads, "TWEET ABOUT THE DASH." She told us that this image accounted for 5 percent of her total clicks in a recent email campaign. That's not an earth-shattering number, but it's better than nothing!

Figure 13.8   *Laura Roeder includes a "TWEET ABOUT THE DASH" button at the top of her emails.*

Notice also that her social sharing button is located at the very top of the email, below the header and before the main call to action (a link to "Creating Fame" in this case). Those who are opposed to putting SWYN icons at the top of an email argue that sharing something you haven't read yet doesn't make sense. This isn't a bad point, but it's certainly worth testing.

What's even more unique about Roeder's Twitter call to action button at the top of her emails is that, when clicked, it automatically populates a subscriber's Twitter update with the following phrase: "RT reading this week's Dash - free social media advice from @lkr http://GetTheDash.com." The URL at the end of the tweet sends those who click it to a landing page where they can opt in to Roeder's email newsletter. Roeder uses email to share with social to grow her email list. Smart, right?

The third aspect of effective SWYN use is if you want more people to share your email, be sure you include a strong call to action (an incentive) and a reason for them to share. Digital marketing executive Chris Penn does a nice job with this in his weekly email newsletter as shown in Figure 13.9. In Penn's "stuff you did" section of his email newsletter, he recognizes a weekly winner: the person who shared the previous week's newsletter the most through his or her social media channels. Penn's call to action to encourage social sharing reads, "Want to have a chance to be seen here in front of over 13,000 subscribers? Share this issue." Just below that are five social media icons for easy sharing.

The final area we see many marketers fall short in regards to SWYN is making emails easy to share. Penn does a nice job of ensuring his email easy to share, as shown in Figure 13.9. So does MarketingProfs, as discussed in Chapter 12, with its daily email newsletter that includes social sharing icons after every article. This method enables subscribers to share just those articles they feel are most relevant to their social network.

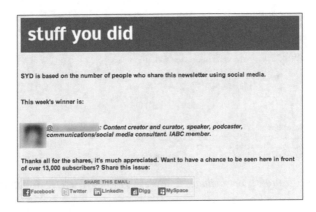

Figure 13.9   *Chris Penn dedicates a section of his weekly email newsletter to show-case the person who socially shared the previous week's email the most.*

SmartBrief, an online media company, takes this same article-sharing approach and adds a unique spin. The daily SmartBrief email (see Figure 13.10) includes LinkedIn, Facebook, Twitter, Google+, and email icons immediately following each article or blog post, similar to the MarketingProfs approach.

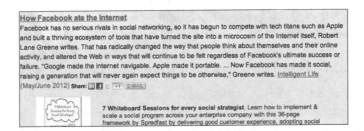

Figure 13.10   *The SmartBrief emails include social sharing options after each block of content so subscribers can share a particular article as opposed to the entire email.*

Like with most SWYN functionality, when a reader clicks on one of the icons, the social network he chose is pre-populated with the article name and a link. However, instead of that link redirecting to a web version of the email or to the full article, SmartBrief sends users to a page that looks like the one illustrated in Figure 13.11.

On the left side of this landing page is a short summary of the SmartBrief article from the email that was shared. Below it are actually more social sharing icons, so readers who land here can also share with their network. In addition, a sentence explains where the news summary appeared (in this case, the 4/18/2012 email newsletter), and a link is available to view the full issue/email. Finally, there is a link at the very bottom to view the original article.

Figure 13.11 *When a person's follower clicks on the short link shared from SmartBrief, he lands on a page similar to this one.*

On the right side of this landing page is an email opt-in form! We love it. SmartBrief combines what MarketingProfs does by allowing its subscribers to share a specific article within its newsletter with what Roeder does with her "TWEET ABOUT THE DASH" button by giving readers a chance to opt-in to its email marketing program. This is a very smart strategy.

Joe Webster, director of marketing at SmartBrief, said the company changed the landing page to this new layout in mid-April 2012. The goal was to strip out the ancillary stuff and just focus on the article and the email signup. SmartBrief wanted to remove the clutter to make it easy to sign up for its emails. "One of our core objectives is to continually grow our subscriber base," said Webster.

The reason the left side of the landing page (see Figure 13.11) includes a link to the full article is because SmartBrief wants to continue driving people to the publisher. "We could have just asked them to sign up to get the content from SmartBrief, but we didn't want to go that route. By including a link to the full article, it helps legitimize our brand promise," Webster told us. That brand promise is the SmartBrief tagline, "We read everything. You get what matters." Its goal is to save busy professionals time. "There is not only value in the content," said Webster, "but also value that we found it, summarized it, and added to our newsletter."

Show Me the Money: How One Online Retailer Netted $250,000 Using SWYN

J. Hilburn, an online custom-tailored luxury menswear company, had traditionally relied on word-of-mouth referrals to acquire new customers. The only problem was it had no way to track and manage these offline recommendations or to amplify their effect. It needed a way to "reward its advocates, increase the brand's social presence, and gain insight into its customers' social behaviors."

So, in September 2011, J. Hilburn, with the help of Extole (a leading consumer-to-consumer social marketing platform), launched a social referral program. It was promoted through its website, via email marketing, and through J. Hilburn's personal style advisors. The offer was simple: The referrer would receive a $50 store credit for each person he referred (who made a purchase). The person referred also received a $50 credit towards his $100 purchase after he created a J. Hilburn account and provided his email address!

After an email subscriber clicked through to the landing page (see Figure 13.12), customers could refer their friends via Facebook, Twitter, email, and a personal URL.

Figure 13.12 *J. Hilburn's "REFER YOUR FRIENDS AND EARN REWARDS" campaign makes sharing this incentive with readers' social networks quite easy.*

Notice how clear the social sharing icons are. Although hard to see in the black-and-white image in Figure 13.12, the Email, Facebook, Twitter, and Personal URL icons all pop off the page. Additionally, the call to action is clearly spelled out: both at the top ("REFER YOUR FRIENDS AND EARN REWARDS") as well as in the "SHARING IS EASY" box on the right side. As a bonus, J. Hilburn even includes a social connecting icon and reason to like the company on Facebook in the lower-right side of the page.

The results of this program, after just 45 days, were quite stunning. J. Hilburn identified more than 1,000 brand advocates, each who shared the program with an average of 12 friends. In just a month a half, there were more than 10,000 social shares across Facebook, Twitter, and email. With an average order value of more than $315, these referrals drove 600 new transactions and $250,000 in new sales.

When the program ended in November 2011, this campaign was shared nearly 13,000 times—and email represented nearly 70 percent of those social shares.

"Email IS social media," says Nicholas Einstein, Vice President of Professional Services at Extole (who helped J. Hilburn with this campaign). "It's the social channel that consumers are most comfortable converting through. Consumers today share stories, opinions, and reviews through Facebook, Twitter, Pinterest, and others, but often ultimately convert through campaigns sent to their inbox. Social marketers who are able to effectively integrate email into their social sharing programs [as J. Hilburn has done] can leverage the unique strengths of each channel, and more efficiently drive core business objectives."

Social Promoting

Although using email marketing to power your social media efforts can be extremely effective, so can the other way around—using social media to power email marketing.

One of the most common ways this is executed is by sharing an email campaign with your followers on one or several of your social media networks, as Scott Hardigree does on occasion on Facebook (see Figure 13.13).

Figure 13.13 *Scott Hardigree shares his email campaign on Facebook. Clicking on the link sends people to a web version of the email.*

Many email service providers provide an easy way to share an email message with your social network at the same time you deploy a campaign. That's exactly what Hardigree does when he sends his emails through MailChimp. Another email service provider, Infusionsoft, also makes social sharing part of the email sending process. After providing your social network login credentials, which links your account, sharing your email requires only a simple click on a checkbox. Figure 13.14 shows how this looks in Infusionsoft and MailChimp. Both of these providers also enable senders to edit what the message looks like after it's shared.

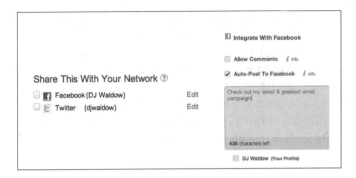

Figure 13.14   *Email service providers Infusionsoft (on the left) and MailChimp (on the right) make sharing email campaigns on your social networks during the sending process easy.*

Even if you are not sending your emails through a third party or if your provider does not have this feature built in, sharing a web version of your email campaign to social networks is still possible. It's just a more manual process. Simply put, you would have to click the web version of the email and then copy and paste that URL into a social networking site like Facebook or Twitter to share.

Social promoting is similar in many ways to social sharing. The main difference is that with social promoting you, the sender, are sharing with your social network. Although social promoting can be effective as a cross-channel message—remember, not everyone who follows you on social media sites are subscribed to your emails—the social amplification effect is much broader when your email subscribers share your content (social sharing).

The second, and likely more impactful, method for using social media to power email marketing is using social media to grow your email list. You can do this in a couple ways.

One way is that you can use social media to post links that redirect back to your email opt-in form on your website. Athletics Alberta (as shown in Figure 13.15) does this on occasion.

If you have a large following on Twitter, this tactic has the potential to really grow your list. Also, if you send folks who click to a unique email opt-in landing page, you can measure exactly how effective your tweets are in growing your list. Not only can you track clicks, you can also see total email opt-ins. Just like that you have a conversion rate. Who said it was hard to measure the ROI of social media?

Another approach is to embed an email opt-in form directly on your Facebook page, as we showed in Chapter 2, "How to Grow Your List," with Park City

Mountain Resort. This method will likely require some technical know-how; however, many email service providers include step-by-step instructions for using their application. Some will even build it for you for a fee.

Figure 13.15 *Athletics Alberta sends tweets with links to its email opt-in form as a way to grow its list.*

Using Social Media to Grow Your Email List and Make Money

Remember (from earlier in this chapter) Tahoe Mountain Sports, the small company with a small marketing budget? It not only used email marketing to power its social connections, it also used social media to grow its list. In 2012, Polivy's team coordinated a free sticker campaign giveaway campaign. After an impressive first day—1,583 visits to the sticker page, a day that "surprised the heck" out of Polivy and his team—TMS decided that if a user wanted a sticker, she had to either "like" TMS on Facebook or sign up for its email list.

As a result of this campaign, TMS saw as many as 280 new likes in a single day. Although the email opt-in numbers were not quite as high, it still saw an average daily list growth of 15 new email addresses—not too bad for the cost of a free sticker.

Graham Knuttel also uses social media to grow his email list. However, instead of a one-time campaign, his efforts are ongoing. Knuttel, a well-known and accomplished Irish sculptor and painter, hired Niall Newman of Boomclick to build a Facebook page to help drive online sales.

His Facebook page includes an embedded email opt-in form (see Figure 13.16).

Notice the incentive for his Facebook fans to provide their email address: A free, monthly sweepstakes drawing to win some of Knuttel's artwork. He even adds a secondary "bonus" to sign up—subscribers will receive "lots of other benefits" for being on the VIP list, including free screen savers and exclusive coupons.

Figure 13.16   *Graham Knuttel includes an email opt-in form on his Facebook page to grow his email marketing list.*

Knuttel encourages email signups by including Facebook "reminder" posts like this one made on April 2, 2012:

> My monthly sweepstake draw will take place TODAY and I will be selecting 2 WINNERS!! One winner will come from my main list and the other winner will be selected directly from my NEW SUBSCRIBERS! If you still have not joined my V.I.P list, now is the time!! Go to my FREE sweepstake tab at the top of the page now!! Thank you

In this Facebook status update, Knuttel clearly states that both winners will be selected from his email newsletter: one from the main list, the other from new subscribers. He follows that by alerting readers where they can go to opt in. Nicely done!

According to Newman, about 80 percent of Knuttel's email list growth can be attributed to social media outlets. Besides Facebook, Knuttel also promotes his email newsletter on Twitter and LinkedIn. All of these efforts combined generated at least 30 to 40 new subscribers within an hour of his posts.[2]

Knuttel then uses his email newsletter to announce the winners, adding extra incentive and urgency to open the email by telling subscribers they need to claim their prize within a set period of time.

"When people sign up for our newsletter through the sweepstakes," says Newman, "we kick off an automated welcome series. One of these emails includes a 65 percent discount that expires in seven days."

He also posts across social media networks that winners have been announced in the email newsletter, further driving opens. "We create a sense of urgency and build anticipation around the email newsletter," says Newman. "We try to make them emotionally attached."

Many subscribers eagerly await the next email newsletter. Some of them post on Knuttel's Facebook wall messages such as, "When is the newsletter coming out?" Newman believes this is why Knuttel's email newsletter open rates and click throughs—consistently 60 to 70 percent and 40 percent respectively—are higher than the industry average.

After the newsletter is sent, there is chatter on the Facebook page about the contents of the email, such as 'Oh. I didn't win. Next time!' This provides social proof and validates the value of the email.

Newman calls Knuttle's Facebook fans "warm leads," who create buzz and ultimately drive new email subscriptions. The best part? Knuttel is grossing €10,000 in sales directly from each mailing.[3]

A Truly Integrated Email Marketing and Social Media Campaign

All of the case studies we've discussed so far showcase companies that are doing it right—combining email marketing and social media to create a powerful force—and seeing some pretty great results. However, if you are ready to take it to the next level, check out the snow globe cookie decorating contest King Arthur Flour (KAF) ran at the end of 2011.

In November, KAF asked its community—on its website, catalog, in its retail store, on Facebook, on its Baking Circle, on Google+, and of course via email—to decorate a snow globe cookie. You can see a copy of the top half of the email announcing the contest in Figure 13.17. (Note: The actual email was an animated image that rotated through four screenshots, ending with this one. Animated screenshots don't seem to render well in print.)

Notice that this email asked readers to post a picture of their snow globe cookie on the KAF Facebook page: a great use of email marketing to drive engagement on social media.

Over the next several weeks, KAF collected submissions and posted them all to an album on its Facebook page. It chose a small panel of judges, selected winners, and then announced them on its homepage and other social media channels as well as via a "Happy Holidays" Christmas email. The contest culminated in a blog post detailing the voting process and sharing the winners.[4]

Figure 13.17   *King Arthur Flour used multiple channels to announce its snow globe cookie decorating contest, including email. This is the top half of the email.*

The results were that KAF

- Received 186 total entries: Many community members, including entire classrooms of children, baked for this contest.

- Crowdsourced and repurposed content: KAF was able to reuse some of the crowdsourced content (that voluntarily contributed by its audience) for its annual email holiday card, an email that generated one of its highest open rates ever for a full-list mailing.

- Sold 3,000 snow globe cookie cutters: The KAF team projected it would sell about 900 of the cutters. It blew away its projections by selling 3,000!

- Generated tons of conversation across all social media channels: Isolating how many new Facebook "likes," Google+ circles, and email subscribers were generated as a result of this campaign was quite challenging.

On top of these incredible results, KAF gave all the entrants each a surprise $20 gift card just to thank them for their time and for being such dedicated bakers and fans. Certainly this was not something KAF had to do. It didn't mention the gift cards in the original rules of the contest; however, the company understands the power of community and keeping its fans engaged and coming back for more.

Two *Is* Better Than One

Not only do email marketing (Batman) and social media (Robin) prove that there truly is power in pairs, but the two ways we've outlined for them to do so, give that power a double dose of goodness. You can ramp up your social networks by promoting them through your email communications. You can also bring your weakly tied audience members on social networks closer to the fold with your company by persuading them to subscribe to your email offerings. Using the two in collaboration with one another fortifies both sides and makes your total digital marketing effort stronger.

We've made a bit of a transition away from breaking the rules because social media is so new that few rules really exist to break. In the next few years we might be revisiting the social media topic to add more entries to our list of rules to break.

But that's in the future—which is precisely what we want to talk about now. What should you watch and be prepared for in the coming years as email marketing and overall digital marketing (including social media) matures?

Endnotes

1. Prior to March 2012, Facebook business pages could use Fangates that forced new fans to "like" a Facebook page before seeing other content on the wall.

2. "Knuttel Print's monthly email newsletter has been generating €10,000 in sales every issue." http://www.newsweaver.com/Knuttel-Prints

3. "Knuttel Print's monthly email newsletter has been generating €10,000 in sales every issue." http://www.newsweaver.com/Knuttel-Prints

4. Hammel, PJ, "Fantasy on ice(ing): Our first Snow Globe Cookie Contest." December 24, 2011. http://www.kingarthurflour.com/blog/2011/12/24/fantasy-on-iceing-our-first-snow-globe-cookie-contest/

What's Next?

What's next? Where do you go from here?

If you've made it this far, or if you just skipped ahead to this section, you know that email is not dead. It's alive and thriving. It's starting to get integrated with other channels such as social media. If you put in the time, effort, and sometimes money into your email marketing efforts, you can attain the $40.56 ROI the Direct Marketers Association reports is out there. Getting it is not simple or easy, but it is possible.

The past 13 chapters have detailed the current state of email marketing and drilled home the importance of building your email list. You've learned the anatomy of a typical email marketing message, and how to be a bit rebellious and break some of the "rules," those best practices many of the purists say are non-negotiable. You've been introduced to some of the ways email marketing and social media can work together.

What the book has covered up to this point is the state of email marketing today, in the year 2012. It's kind of like we are the President of the United States who just presented the State of the Union, only instead of television as the medium, we chose this book. Now it's time to discuss what's next: the future of the email marketing industry.

This is the fun part in many ways. We get to pull out our crystal ball and predict what the email marketing world will look like in the next 5, 10, or 30 years. Our predictions will be written in stone, or rather, ink if you are reading this in a book, or pixels if you are reading this in an electronic format. Whatever we say over the next several pages cannot be modified (until we release an updated version, of course). In fact, it's kind of like clicking Send on an email—we can't take it back! If we're right, they'll call us geniuses. If we're wrong, they'll point fingers and laugh. Well, maybe not, but at least they'll tell us we were wrong.

Let's do this.

The Current State of Email Marketing

It's funny—for all of this talk about a marketing channel that is alive and thriving, email has not fundamentally changed since its early days. Sure, it has evolved and grown up a bit. For example, there didn't use to be a way to include images and other graphics in an email. You couldn't always send an email out to hundreds of thousands of people in a matter of minutes with one click of a button. Up until a decade or so ago, there was no such thing as an email service provider. Email delivery companies such as Return Path and Pivotal Veracity did not exist. There was no need for companies such as Litmus to provide inbox previews of what your emails look like in different email clients. None of these companies existed because none of them were necessary. Email had not yet become an integral channel for marketers.

So yes, we have seen changes in the email marketing industry; however, the act of creating and sending an email has stayed much the same over the past 10 to 20 years.

Think about it. To send an email you must

- Have a list of email addresses
- Have a message (text, HTML, images, and so on)
- Have an email client (or vendor) to send from

That's pretty much it.

If you want to get a bit more fancy, you can

- Personalize emails based on subscriber demographics: name, city, ZIP code, and so on
- Include forward to a friend or social sharing functionality
- Track and measure subscriber activity, such as opens, clicks, and conversions

- Split test your emails by Subject line, From name, content, time of day, and day of week
- Work with an email service provider and a company that specializes in email deliverability
- Use dynamic content features so that each email you send is specific to each subscriber

These are all features and functionality that already exist. Most email service providers offer all the preceding and more. So what lies ahead for email marketing?

Email Marketing Predictions

It's time to look into that crystal ball and predict what the future of email marketing will look like. In order to get a more well-rounded, broader prediction, we asked some of the sharpest minds in the email marketing space to share their thoughts on where email marketing is headed. These five individuals have been in the email marketing industry, collectively, for more than 50 years. Three of them founded their own companies, one is the spokesperson at his organization, and one is the head of research at an email service provider. Finally, all five contributed to this book in some way, shape, or form.

We asked them the following question: What does the future hold for the email marketing world? Not next year or the year after, but how do you see email marketing evolving over the next decade?

First up: Bill McCloskey, the founder at Only Influencers, a professional, invitation-only, private networking group for all digital marketers (and technical editor of this book). Here is what McCloskey had to say:

It has been my good fortune to be involved in one way or another in the growth of the email marketing industry for over a decade. I've been a writer, organizer of email trade shows, an email technology provider, and now overseer of the largest community of email marketing professionals in the world (onlyinfluencers.com). Without a doubt it is the most passionate group of people I have ever met.

The future of email marketing is strong because the passion and dedication of the people in the email marketing industry is second to none and, unlike other industries, the openness of email marketers to help each other, to share information, and to enjoy each other's company is unheard of in any other industry I've ever been involved in. The future of email marketing? One look at the people involved gives you your answer: the future is innovative, strong, exciting, and one of the best career moves you could make.

Earlier in the book, we referred to McCloskey as the "godfather of email marketing." It has nothing to do with his age, merely his experience. McCloskey has been involved with email marketing since its early days. We could not agree more with his assessment of the people in the industry, especially their passion and willingness to share information.

Also, as McCloskey said, the future is exciting. If you are reading this now and thinking about making a career change, look no further than email marketing. Although it might not look the same in 20 years, we're confident in saying that it's here to stay.

Next up is Mark Brownlow, journalist, blogger, and independent publisher of Email Marketing Reports. When it comes to email marketing, Brownlow is one of the brightest minds in Austria and the world. We first introduced you to Brownlow way back in the Introduction, referencing his EmailIsNotDead.com site. Here is what Brownlow had to say:

Changes to any online marketing landscape are hard to predict, but we can certainly expect attention to grow scarcer and available sources of information and offers to become more diverse and fragmented. The last decade online taught us to expect the unexpected, live with change, and embrace new opportunities.

Those who succeed most at email marketing in the coming ten years need a philosophy and habits that reflect this unpredictable dynamism. Specifically:

1. *Understand the true meaning of value to your subscribers: Value (in all its facets) demands and retains attention.*

2. *Be prepared to tweak things in response to inevitable changes in the email environment, user needs, and user behavior.*

3. *Keep the fundamental elements of good email marketing practice (like welcome messages and list hygiene) in mind while embracing new tools and tactics.*

4. *Aim for uniqueness through your email content or personality, and build subscriber trust (which will grow in importance).*

5. *Use common sense and keep a sense of perspective, especially when evaluating the latest tools and trends.*

6. *Exploit the data your tools and services make available to increase the value and timeliness of messages.*

Having said that, there should still be a place for basic email marketing efforts. Of course, all the clever tools and tactics coming our way can and will improve results. But a transparent sign-up process means subscribers have self-selected themselves as interested in your content/offers. Remain focused on delivering value, and a "simplistic" approach to email marketing can continue to deliver success well into the future.

Brownlow's suggestions echo much of what was discussed in this book. Specifically:

- "Be prepared to tweak things" (#2) is analogous to testing. What worked today might not work tomorrow. What is successful for one audience, say "best practices," might not be the most successful for your audience. Test!

- "Keep the fundamental elements of good email marketing practice" (#3) is similar to our discussion early on about the secret to email marketing: growing your list! Being effective at email marketing without a list of addresses to send to becomes quite challenging.

- Finally, to reiterate Brownlow's last point, email marketing is all about delivering value to your subscribers. Sometimes, we think that means breaking the rules and being a bit rebellious.

Next we hear from Andrew Kordek, cofounder and chief strategist at Trendline Interactive, an email-centric marketing agency. Kordek is a big believer in breaking the rules of email marketing. Even his email signature infers some rule breaking: "We know best practices, but we don't always follow them. When everyone follows best practice, you've merely redefined mediocrity." Here is what Kordek thinks about where email marketing is headed in the next ten years:

Email marketing will evolve over the next decade in three ways. First and foremost, the inbox as we know it will become a centralized communication hub whereby we will be able to communicate with brands and individuals via a hub with integrated social and email capabilities. Long gone are the days where you will need separate apps to communicate on Facebook, Twitter, email, and other social networks that will spawn. The experience will be mirrored on mobile devices and the hub will be unified across all devices.

Second, email will come alive or have the appearance of being "alive" in this hub. Dynamically driven campaigns will become the norm where the creative, messages, and appearances will update in real time. Emails will come when the subscriber wants them and there will be no such thing as the deployment of a batched "campaign."

Lastly, this communication hub will all be driven by subscriber behavior across all channels in the world. Someone's behavior in the store, action in the car, or even the television shows they watch will drive communications between brands and their subscriber. Hyper-personalization will replace batch and blast as the norm, and digital and marketing privacy will be non-existent to the end user.

Kordek's view of the inbox as a "centralized communication hub" is spot on. We are already starting to see the early phases of this with services such as Rapportive, a plugin for Gmail that displays the most recent Facebook posts, Twitter updates, and other social media comments on the right side of your Gmail inbox. With a few clicks of the mouse, you can easily connect with your email contacts on their social networks.

We also agree with Kordek's second point about more one-to-one communications. We're already starting to see fewer "batch and blast" campaigns—emails that are sent to the entire list without any consideration for segmentation or dynamic, personalized content.

Finally, Kordek's thoughts on email content being driven by "subscriber behavior across all channels in the world" is somewhat Big Brother-ish, but is certainly getting closer to reality. With the advancements of social advertising, which is hyper-targeted based on your own profile information provided to sites such as Facebook or Google+, email customization is soon to follow. In 2012, it still takes more opt-in from consumers to trigger emails based on in-store behavior, though sometimes swiping a credit card is all it takes. Soon, with location-based services and even augmented reality applications used by store employees or security cameras, that customization could come to the inbox.

Chad White, Research Director at Responsys, a global provider of on-demand marketing solutions, and founder of the Retail Email Blog, weighs in next with three predictions for the future of email marketing:

1. **Rich responsive content.** *In the future, emails will look much more like the mobile apps and microsites of today, with subscribers able to browse content, watch videos, and complete transactions without leaving an email. Enabled by much faster cellular, Wi-Fi, and broadband networks, this content will also adapt to a wide range of screen sizes, paring itself down to only the key functionality when viewed on a smartphone but allowing for expanded messaging when viewed on a tablet, desktop monitor, or TV.*

2. **The unified inbox.** *Driven by Google's integration of Gmail, Google+, Google Talk, and other platforms on the market-dominant Android OS, inboxes will become a mix of email, social updates, push notifications, voicemail, and SMS. Users will have lots of control over how messages are displayed in the inbox, which ones generate alerts, and how many from a particular sender will be kept at a time. This ability to auto-delete messages—particularly commercial ones—has significantly alleviated inbox overload.*

3. **Privacy reform.** *Facebook going public was the catalyst for an eventual Consumer Privacy Bill of Rights and several "Do Not Track" laws that returned many personal information ownership rights to consumers and severely limited data-sharing between companies. For marketers, these changes will lead to near-universal adoption of preference centers, as well as profile editors that allow consumers to view and edit all the personal information collected by a brand, regardless of the channel of origin. Despite the high level of brand transparency and consumer control, segmented and triggered emails will make up the majority of commercial emails sent and generate the vast majority of email revenue.*

We really love White's take on email marketing becoming more like mobile apps and microsites. The ability to engage with an email is something that seems to be a huge void currently, which translates into great opportunity. The user experience of an email will, hopefully, evolve as technology continues to change.

White's vision of a "unified inbox" is similar to what Kordek calls a "centralized communication" hub, one that we also see as being a huge, yet natural, next step for email marketing. If and when that happens, the integration between email marketing and social media will also evolve into a more seamless process.

Finally, White's view of the importance of privacy is certainly something all marketers, not just those in charge of email, must be cognizant of. Several years ago, it seemed as though most consumers didn't really care (or just were not aware) of privacy issues on the Internet. That pendulum appears to be swinging back to the other side now, or at least to the center.

Loren McDonald, Vice President of Industry Relations at email service provider Silverpop and one of the most prolific writers and speakers about email marketing, also weighed in:

In 2022, email will remain an extremely vital channel of communications for both consumers and business users, and email marketing will retain its title of "King of Marketing ROI."

For recipients of email marketing messages, the changes they see in ten years are likely to be evolutionary rather than earth-shattering. Inbox overload will diminish as marketers become smarter users of the channel. Consumers will switch their preferences to SMS, mobile apps, and social channels for most non-commercial messages. Additionally, Web mail providers and third-party applications will finally develop inbox management tools that increase email productivity and prioritization.

For email marketers, the biggest change will be the increased use of "smart" technology and more sophisticated practices that deliver a true one-to-one experience for recipients. Underpinning this evolution will be a fundamental transformation of email programs to those that are mostly based on individual recipient behaviors and automated programs and messages.

Broadcast, or "batch and blast," messages won't disappear completely. They will still play a role in branding and broad awareness but will likely comprise less than one-fourth of the volume of average to sophisticated marketers' email programs.

Static, one-off messages, or even series such as a welcome series sent to all new sub-scribers, will be replaced by multi-track messaging programs that deliver messages in real time to individual recipients based on their multi-channel behavior, demograph-ics, and preferences. A minority of very sophisticated email marketers are deploying this approach today, but it will become the norm by 2022.

Generating enough new and compelling content has become one of the marketer's biggest challenges in 2012, but most companies already have plenty of content. They just haven't organized it or been able to leverage it effectively. As such, a new automation category—or, in some cases, functionality—will emerge that takes con-tent from blogs, communities, social channels, and the marketing department and throughout the enterprise and deploy it dynamically in one-to-one emails.

While a much-discussed topic in 2012, "social CRM" is too narrow of a concept, because it ignores mobile and local behaviors as well as traditional online and offline actions. By 2022, marketers will be deploying automated, behavior-based email and multi-channel programs based on a recipient's influence and engagement, along with user-generated content across social, mobile, and local channels that are then ratio-nalized with purchase behavior, demographics, interest, and lifetime value.

Deliverability will be a non-issue for most senders, because ISPs/Web email providers will have refined their algorithms, and email marketers will be delivering more rel-evant email and learning to play by the ISP rules. Deliverability will remain a chal-lenge only for marketers who don't respect the channel and ignore generally accepted best practices.

Designing for mobile will also be a long-forgotten challenge. In ten years, reading and engaging email on mobile devices—whether smartphones, full-sized and mini tablets, and touch-screen netbooks—will be the norm. Marketers will deploy emails in a "mobile first" approach, which optimizes emails for the dominant mobile operat-ing systems, likely still iOS and Android plus perhaps one more.

Emails will also finally become more "Web-like" with the use of HTML5, enabling inline video and forms and greater use of dynamic emails, which will employ a sig-nificant percentage of real-time content.

Looking back at the differences in email from 2002 to 2012, I see very few revolu-tionary changes. The next ten years will likely be similar, with the biggest evolution occurring when the majority of email marketers finally adopt the sophisticated tech-nologies and practices that are, in fact, available today in 2012.

We're certainly glad McDonald believes email will continue to be thriving ten years from now. Of course, we agree. We also like how he predicts email will become more one-to-one, similar to what Kordek suggested. We're already starting to see very sophisticated email marketers take advantage of multi-channel data, using technology to deliver very timely, targeted, and personalized messaging.

McDonald digs a bit deeper into this concept of true multi-channel marketing in his prediction of the evolving social CRM. We talked a lot about the how email marketing and social media go together, and McDonald takes this even further by layering in mobile and local and even hinting at the impact of influence: a hot topic in the social media world in 2012.

We also agree with McDonald's take about deliverability and "designing for mobile" becoming less of an issue. We're already seeing email marketers become smarter in both of these areas and this trend will only continue.

Finally, McDonald's last point is an important one and a good one to conclude on: Ten years from now, email marketing will not fundamentally change. The technology and tools exist now; however, the sophisticated email marketer just needs to catch up a bit. It will happen, but it will take some time.

One thing none of the five mentioned (though McDonald touched on it) was the integration between blogs and email marketing. Blogging, like email, is not dead. Many people consume blog posts through some type of blog feed reader. Although many readers exist, Google Reader is one of the more popular ones. Feed readers take the RSS (Really Simple Syndication) feed produced by most all blogging platforms and enable users to read new posts without visiting the blog at all. The updates come to you rather than your having to visit them. Feed readers also make it easy to share blog posts on social networks and through—you guessed it—email.

Several email service providers offer RSS-to-email functionality, yet many marketers are not taking advantage of the tool. This feature allows email marketers to pull fresh blog post content into an email newsletter for easy sharing. We see this feature continuing to become more important for email marketers going forward as the various online channels continue to converge.

The future of email marketing looks bright. Email is here to stay, yet will certainly evolve in the coming years in regards to more personalized content, a more unified inbox, and more of an integrated, multi-channel approach. However, the changes will not be dramatic and sweeping, but instead gradual and steady. That being said, if folks like you continue to push the limits and break the rules, who knows what lies ahead?

Now go forth—and conquer!

15

Go Forth and Conquer

So what about your future? Are you going to fire up that next email newsletter and do it the same way you've always done it? Are you going to follow all the rules you were taught once upon a time about email marketing? Don't use ALL CAPS in headlines! Don't use one big image! Don't buy your list!

You certainly don't want all the email marketing experts in the world shaking their finger at you, do you? Or do you not care what they think, as long as your email marketing delivers the opens, clicks, conversions, or sales you want?

When you think about your goals for your email marketing, whether you look at them on an individual, email-by-email basis or holistically, do you really consider what anyone outside your organization (well, other than your customers) thinks about whether you're doing it right? If so, we suggest reassessing whose opinion is important.

It doesn't matter what the experts say. It doesn't matter what DJ and Jason say, either. What matters is whether your emails are being delivered, opened, and read, and whether they motivate your audience to do what it is you want them to do. Period. If anything, *The Rebel's Guide to Email Marketing* is about knowing that the only rules you should ever follow are the ones that apply to you. And the only way you'll ever know which ones do and which ones don't is to test and measure. Your audience, industry, company, and product are all unique. The way your competition does email marketing might not work for you. The way *Funny or Die* does it might not, either.

No business book, especially one about digital marketing—email, social media, search engine optimization, website design, mobile marketing, and the like—can do the work for you. There is no easy button here. It is now time for you to do the work to make email marketing work for you.

Fortunately, you now have the guide book to do just that.

What You Know

You know that email is not dead. Whether you're like Emily, our dozen-inbox-visits-before-lunch example from the book's Introduction, or a brand marketer that knows mastering email marketing can help put your company's messages in front of more people, more often, you use email. In fact, you know that 94 percent of people use email.[1]

You know that the most important component of email marketing is being able to grow your list. If you don't have a list to send to, there's really no point in having an email marketing program. So we've shown you how to build and grow your list. You know that you need to make it easy for website visitors to sign up; that you should be creative, perhaps even humorous, in asking people to sign up; that you can use technology or social media to promote registrations; that you should tell people what's in it for them when signing up; and that you can also grow your list offline.

You know the technical stuff necessary to be a smart email marketer, too. You've read about the pre-checked box on registration forms, the sign-up process, sending welcome emails, and making a good first impression to your subscribers. You also know and understand the anatomy of an email, from the Subject line all the way down to the footer, what each component does, and how it fits into the average email newsletter or template.

You know about the importance of the "first impression" material in the Subject line, From address, preheader, and header. You understand the table of contents, calls to action, and the various buttons, links, and images you'll need to consider for your email marketing. You also learned about the makeup of your emails including adding the finishing touches of social sharing and connect features, the footer, and the all-important unsubscribe feature.

The book went through the various "rules" that we now argue are not rules, but suggestions, and ones that might or might not work for you and your email marketing efforts. In fact, you saw examples of companies executing the exact opposite of many of these rules and doing just fine, thank you very much.

You now know:

- Words some "experts" have told you to avoid aren't always problematic
- Using ALL CAPS in a Subject line actually does work in some cases
- Using the word *free* doesn't necessarily throw up spam filters and make your email less likely to be delivered to the inbox
- For Subject lines, short isn't always good and long isn't always bad
- The perfect email only happens when you've tested every aspect until you know what works for your audience

You've learned that beauty is in the eye of the beholder when it comes to email design as well. Whether you send mostly text or mix in images and graphics, compose letters as opposed to newsletters, use or refrain from using one big image, slice and dice your email design, or put the unsubscribe button in the footer or elsewhere, some audiences will respond to the counterintuitive way of thinking.

You've even learned that some of the popular no-nos of email marketing (using pop-ups and single opt-ins and even sending emails to addresses of people who haven't yet opted in to your list) aren't always no-nos. In fact, they might be the absolutely right thing to do, depending upon your situation.

You've also gone to school about how email and social media go together like Batman and Robin, providing the Gotham City of your marketing with double-barrel, caped-crusader protection.

Finally, you've looked with us into the future of email marketing. What trends and changes do you need to be ready for? You have them in this book.

The only thing that's left to do is take all your newfound knowledge and put it to work for your business.

What Now?

You don't think we're going to leave you with that, do you? Love ya, Nike, but we're going to be a bit more specific than, "Just do it." What you need now is an actionable to-do list to follow after you put this book down, or it might wind up being one of those books that was really awesome to read, but never really made it past the drawing board in helping you beyond a good pep talk.

The challenge for us in giving you one is making sure that you have these items to do no matter where your company is along the continuum of email marketing maturity.

Four Steps to Email Marketing Success

So, without further ado, here is your four-step guide to take *The Rebel's Guide to Email Marketing* and put it in practice now.

1. Grow Your List

First things first. Go to your website now. If a potential customer wants to be added to your email list, how would they do so? Do you make it easy or is it a challenge to find the opt-in form? Do you give folks a reason to subscribe or do you just slap up a form with a submit button on it?

Next, actually go through the opt-in process for your company's website. Enter your email address and any other information that's required. What happens next? Are new subscribers sent to a landing page thanking them for opting in and telling them what to expect next? Do you receive a welcome email immediately?

Finally, think outside the box a little bit. We've discussed many ways to grow your list. Pick three to five of them today and make it your goal to test them out for a few months. Keep the ones that perform the best, ditch the others, and add three to five more into the mix for the following 30 days. Remember: Growing an email list is not a one-and-done type of thing. Thanks to list churn, fatigue, and inactive subscribers, it has to be an ongoing process.

2. Plan Your Content

What are you going to include in your email campaigns that is going to have your subscribers say, "Holy cow! This is awesome. I can't wait for the next email to land in my inbox"? What is going to be so compelling in your emails that folks are going to set their alarms to read it first thing in the morning (like some Help a Reporter Out [HARO] readers do)?

Be ready to pivot. The content you include in your email campaigns today is bound to get stale over time. Just like your business, you always need to be looking ahead. When your subscribers become disinterested in the content of your email campaigns, reeling them back in is a challenge. Don't think about the content that you would like to see, unless you represent your average customer. Focus on content that matters to your audience.

3. Determine Success Metrics

Determining what constitutes success is one area where many email marketers fall off the cliff. Why are you engaging in email marketing? What is your goal? If it's to get people to open your emails, start building trust so that when they see the From name, they open without hesitation. If you want people to read your emails, see step #2: provide them content that will "wow." However, if you want subscribers to take some type of action on your emails, ensure that the call to action is clear, obvious, and in-their-faces.

Remember: Your success metric is not necessarily the same as the metric for the person or company down the street. Just as with best practices, what matters most to you is not always what matters to others.

Make sure your success metrics are clearly outlined before jumping into email marketing. If you are already actively sending emails to your list, step back and think about how you are going to measure whether it's working. Our bet is you're so busy sending email, you've forgotten why you are doing it. Take that step today. Write down your goals and track towards them.

4. Send, Test, Analyze, Adjust, Repeat

Finally, don't get complacent. Email marketing, at both the macro and micro levels, is evolving. As we talked about throughout this book, the key is testing what works best for your audience. Is it possible that the best practices of email marketing truly are best for your audience? Sure. But the only way you'll know this to be true is if you send, test, analyze, adjust, and repeat. We hate to break the news to you, but this process never goes away.

Are you finding that your list is not growing at a fast enough pace? Try popups. Are people not opening your emails as much as they used to? Test using all caps or longer Subject lines. Are your spam complaints on the rise? Consider moving the unsubscribe button to the top.

Go ahead, be a rebel and break some rules—as long as you are testing to ensure they work best for your audience.

And Now, It's Your Turn

So you have the knowledge to be an Email Marketing Rebel. You have a to-do list to take that knowledge and put it into action that can start improving your email marketing efforts right now. Before you put the book down, though, go back to the earlier four-step list and put step 1 on your calendar for tomorrow. Set an alert or reminder so a bell goes off to remind you about the calendar item. Then do the same for the next day for step 2, or even next week if you need some time to get through step 1, and so on. Incorporating the to-do list into your actual, daily, get-things-done process will help you follow through. So get that calendar out and add away!

We'll leave you with one last bit of inspiration, which was also much of what drove us to write this book. You're always going to have experts telling you how or why to do this, when or where to do that. Taking advice isn't a bad thing. Following your experienced predecessors isn't bad, either.

But you are not incapable of developing your own best practices for your email marketing, or even your digital marketing, social media, advertising, or any other area of your communications. You have everything it takes to read and react to your audience, the market, competitors, and more.

Instead of following the conventional thinking or trying to push the easy button and doing what the thought leaders and experts say, do what a rebel would do— think for yourself.

"There's a rebel lying deep in my soul. Anytime anybody tells me the trend is such and such, I go the opposite direction. I hate the idea of trends. I hate imitation; I have a reverence for individuality." —Clint Eastwood[2]

Don't be an imitator. Be an innovator.

And wear the title of Rebel proudly.

Endnotes

1. Pew Internet & American Life Project. "Generations 2012," http://www.pewinternet.org

2. Rand, Yardena. *Wild Open Spaces*. Maverick Spirit Press, 2005.

Your Prize

GO TO ar.gy/prize TO CLAIM YOUR PRIZE!

Index

E

M

Q

R

S

Biz-Tech Series

Straightforward Strategies and Tactics for Business Today

The **Que Biz-Tech series** is designed for the legions of small-medium business owners, executives and marketers out there trying to come to grips with emerging technologies that can make or break their business. These books help the reader know what's important, what isn't, and pro vide deep inside know-how for entering the brave new world of business technology, covering topics such as social media, web marketing, mobile marketing, search engine marketing and blogging.

- Straightforward strategies and tactics for companies who are either using or will be using a new technology/product or way of thinking/doing business.

- Written by well-known industry experts in their respective fields — and designed to be an open platform for the author to teach a topic in the way he or she believes the audience will learn best.

- Covers new technologies that companies must embrace to remain competitive in the marketplace and shows them how to maximize those technologies for profit.

Visit **quepublishing.com/biztech** to learn more.

ALWAYS LEARNING   PEARSON

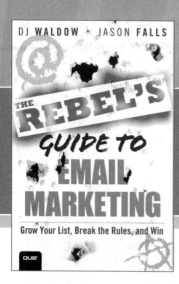

DJ WALDOW · JASON FALLS

THE REBEL'S GUIDE TO EMAIL MARKETING

Grow Your List, Break the Rules, and Win

Safari
Books Online

FREE
Online Edition

Your purchase of *The Rebel's Guide to Email Marketing* includes access to a free online edition for 45 days through the **Safari Books Online** subscription service. Nearly every Que book is available online through **Safari Books Online**, along with thousands of books and videos from publishers such as Addison-Wesley Professional, Cisco Press, Exam Cram, IBM Press, O'Reilly Media, Prentice Hall, and Sams, and VMware Press.

Safari Books Online is a digital library providing searchable, on-demand access to thousands of technology, digital media, and professional development books and videos from leading publishers. With one monthly or yearly subscription price, you get unlimited access to learning tools and information on topics including mobile app and software development, tips and tricks on using your favorite gadgets, networking, project management, graphic design, and much more.

Activate your FREE Online Edition at
informit.com/safarifree

STEP 1:   Enter the coupon code: YJQSUWA.

STEP 2:   New Safari users, complete the brief registration form.
Safari subscribers, just log in.

If you have difficulty registering on Safari or accessing the online edition,
please e-mail customer-service@safaribooksonline.com